To the Victor, the Potatoes!

Historical Materialism Book Series

The Historical Materialism Book Series is a major publishing initiative of the radical left. The capitalist crisis of the twenty-first century has been met by a resurgence of interest in critical Marxist theory. At the same time, the publishing institutions committed to Marxism have contracted markedly since the high point of the 1970s. The Historical Materialism Book Series is dedicated to addressing this situation by making available important works of Marxist theory. The aim of the series is to publish important theoretical contributions as the basis for vigorous intellectual debate and exchange on the left.

The peer-reviewed series publishes original monographs, translated texts, and reprints of classics across the bounds of academic disciplinary agendas and across the divisions of the left. The series is particularly concerned to encourage the internationalization of Marxist debate and aims to translate significant studies from beyond the English-speaking world.

For a full list of titles in the Historical Materialism Book Series available in paperback from Haymarket Books, visit:
https://www.haymarketbooks.org/series_collections/1-historical-materialism

To the Victor, the Potatoes!

Literary Form and Social Process in the Beginnings of the Brazilian Novel

Roberto Schwarz

Edited and translated, with an introduction, by
Ronald W. Sousa

Haymarket Books
Chicago, IL

First published in 2019 by Brill Academic Publishers, The Netherlands
© 2019 Koninklijke Brill NV, Leiden, The Netherlands

Published in paperback in 2020 by
Haymarket Books
P.O. Box 180165
Chicago, IL 60618
773-583-7884
www.haymarketbooks.org

ISBN: 978-1-64259-344-0

Distributed to the trade in the US through Consortium Book Sales and Distribution (www.cbsd.com) and internationally through Ingram Publisher Services International (www.ingramcontent.com).

This book was published with the generous support of Lannan Foundation and Wallace Action Fund.

Special discounts are available for bulk purchases by organizations and institutions. Please call 773-583-7884 or email info@haymarketbooks.org for more information.

Cover design by Jamie Kerry and Ragina Johnson.
Cover photo by Gabriele Basilico, MoMa collection, Museum of Modern Art, New York. Image edited by Carmela Gross, Carolina Caliento and Gustavo Motta, from the work of Antonio Dias: *The Invented Country (God-Will-Give-Days) [O País Inventado (Dias-de-Deus-Dará)]*, 1976. The authorizations to use this image were kindly granted by Antonio Dias' inheritors and by the Gabriele Basilico Archive.

Printed in the United States.

10 9 8 7 6 5 4 3 2 1

Library of Congress Cataloging-in-Publication data is available.

Contents

Reading the Truth of Falseness: An Introduction VII
  Ronald W. Sousa
Acknowledgements XXI
A BBC Interview with Roberto Schwarz, on the Subject of Machado de Assis XXII

1 **Misplaced Ideas** 1

2 **The Importation of the Novel and Its Contradictions in Alencar** 16

3 **Paternalism and Its Rationalisation in Machado de Assis' Early Novels** 48
  1   General Considerations   48
  2   *A Mão e a Luva*   56
  3   *Helena*   70
  4   *Iaiá Garcia*   93

Bibliography   149
Index   153

Reading the Truth of Falseness: An Introduction

> ... study [the ideas] in their functioning, of which falseness is a true part.

∴

These few initial pages come to introduce the reader to an English version of Brazilian cultural critic Roberto Schwarz's groundbreaking 1977 book *Ao vencedor as batatas* ('To the Victor, the Potatoes' in my translation), a study principally of the early novels of the prominent Brazilian novelist Machado de Assis (1839–1908). I have a long history with the little book, which this project continues. I recall quite well the first time I heard of Roberto Schwarz and *Ao vencedor*. It was sometime in the 1970s when one day my friend and colleague Russell Hamilton handed me a copy he had recently received from a colleague in Brazil, saying he thought it was something I'd be particularly interested in reading. Russell was right – as usual. Initially I planned to do a quick page-through to get an idea of the contents and then set it aside for further exploration at a more propitious time. But I found it very dense – too dense to be treated that way – and I also found it rhetorically unlike Brazilian literary/cultural criticism of the time and therefore intriguing. I ended up spending several days with it and went back shortly thereafter to re-read sections. It soon became, through excerpts that I gave to students, a part of some of my classes – whenever, that is, this poor Portuguese scholar was given the opportunity to wander westward.

So what did I see in that initial encounter? First of all, a – to me – new, innovative and powerful explanatory discourse in Portuguese, one that worked somewhat like some German or French critical approaches of the time but, even so, not enough like them to say that the author was simply using terminology and processes developed in, say, German literary criticism, to work on a Brazilian problematic. In fact, one of the book's first analytical steps involved proclaiming Brazilian cultural problematics to be radically sui generis and pointedly setting out to create a critical discourse appropriate to the task of dealing with it. In any case, the book did a couple of things that only a few Brazilian critics of Brazilian culture had done before, and, even so, those predecessors – among them Schwarz's own mentor, Antonio Candido – were not as dense, did not create so detailed an analytical terminology and did not engage in textual 'explication' to the degree that this book wished to – that explicatory dimension being, I supposed, a reflexion of the sway that Anglo-American new criticism then held in Brazil. A curious mixture. Still in all, there was more to it than just those considerations. In fact, a lot more.

Now I'm not going to review here in any systematic way the book's content-and-argument base. That is for you the reader to do. But, as you are likely unfamiliar with Brazilian history and culture, you will, I suspect, benefit from some introductory orientation tailored to what appears in the ensuing pages, an orientation that will, in order to fashion some overall coherence, lead me some small way into sectors of Roberto's argument. Before going that far, though, a scattering of even more basic considerations.

In Roberto's words: 'the purpose of this study is to follow the formation of a thematic and formal complex that would be both observed and coherent' (p. 78). The 'thematic and formal complex' he refers to is one he sees as the foundation for the novels of the aforementioned Machado de Assis, which he reads – very persuasively – as explorations of aspects of the superstructural problematic that a developing Brazil was undergoing in Machado's time, explorations relevant for understanding subsequent developments as well. (To be clear, Roberto is careful to remind us on occasion that his specific focus involves a dimension he has chosen to explore for reasons of importance and not necessarily somehow 'the' way to approach the problematic – or the novels.) Let us begin with aspects of his statement.

To begin with, the reader must know some basic information: that Joaquim Maria Machado de Assis is still today, out of all the great writers Brazil has produced over the past one-hundred-and-fifty-or-so years, well-nigh-universally considered the predominant figure – and was even more so considered at the time when *Ao vencedor* was written. The so-called 'warlock of Cosme Velho' wrote short stories, chronicles, poetry, literary criticism, and novels. His reputation derives more from that last category than any other – and it is the sole focus of *Ao vencedor*. Criticism has generally divided Machado's novel production into two distinct phases, the earlier comprising the first four novels as regards publication date and the later involving the final five out of the total of nine. The first phase comprises *Resurreição* (English title: *Resurrection*; date of the book publication of the Portuguese original: 1872), *A mão e a luva* (*The Hand and the Glove*, 1874), *Helena* (*Helena*, 1876) and *Iaiá Garcia* (*Iaiá Garcia*, 1878). The so-called 'second', or 'mature', phase comprises *Memórias póstumas de Brás Cubas* (*The Posthumous Memoirs of Brás Cubas*, also translated into English as *Epitaph of a Small Winner*, 1881), *Quincas Borba* (*Philosopher or Dog?* 1891), *Dom Casmurro* (*Dom Casmurro*, 1899), *Esaú e Jacó* (*Esau and Jacob*, 1904) and *Memorial de Aires* (*Counselor Ayres' Memorial*, 1908). (By the way, the title of the book you are reading, *Ao vencedor as batatas*, is a famous phrase that appears in the second-phase novel *Quincas Borba*.) As to the centrality of Machado's novels to Portuguese-language literary study, I recall quite vividly being told early on – and in no uncertain terms – that to do what I wanted to do professionally, I had to be thoroughly familiar with the novels of Machado de Assis.

Roberto accepts the early-versus-mature evaluation and the accompanying periodisation and dedicates this title to study of the four 'first phase' novels. What is more, he makes it clear here that this is the first part of a set, the second volume to be dedicated to continuing the same project directed to Machado's last five novels. That follow-up volume appeared in 1990 under the title *Um mestre na periferia do capitalismo: Machado de Assis* [A Master on the Periphery of Capitalism: Machado de Assis]. That work takes a somewhat different methodological tack from this volume. (Too it appeared briefly on the Brazilian best-seller list, a remarkable achievement for a book of literary criticism.)

Now another point: you will have noticed that I have usually been referring to the novelist simply as 'Machado.' Put in a simplified – and illustrative – way, it is common Brazilian practice to refer to culturally recognised/recognisable figures by a single name, or at least one reduced to a couple of words. I shall forego review of the messy rules about the available choices of shortened forms in given cases, the contexts in which those forms are likely to be used or not, and so on. In referring to the subject of Roberto's critical acumen as, simply, 'Machado' I then merely echo near-universal practice (which, incidentally, thereby bestows upon 'Machado' a matrilineal identifier). There is even a consecrated adjectival form, 'machadiano' (or 'machadeano'), that means 'pertaining to or akin to Machado de Assis and/or his work'; I anglicise it to 'Machadian' and use it in translating. My usage replicates Roberto's practice in the Portuguese original of this book. By the same token I shall usually be referring to *him* – as I just have – simply as 'Roberto.' In this context it would seem unnecessarily repetitive to say 'Roberto Schwarz' every time and to say just 'Schwarz' would be either inappropriately formal or outright dismissive, according to how one reads the tone. As I translate I shall briefly gloss several other names that appear in shortened form and ask the reader to bear in mind, as she or he reads, the cultural practice involved. (One of several things I shall be asking you to bear in mind as you read.)

Now another dimension that must be understood: it is to deal with the first four novels to the ends that he sets for himself that Roberto fashions the innovative critical discourse I refer to above, and he sets it out in relative abstraction in the first chapter, which is in effect a separable essay-meditation on critical method in general and in particular as an introduction to his ensuing chapters (in truth, all of the book's chapters are potentially separable pieces in their own right). That first chapter is subsequently treated as just such a stand-alone piece by other critics as well as by Roberto himself. He names that first chapter 'Idéias fora do lugar,' conventionally translated into English as 'misplaced ideas', a translation I find particularly unsatisfactory (more about that issue shortly). That chapter has appeared partially or totally summarised in various publications – and has subsequently been translated in toto – and used as the basis for critical projects of various sorts. It is used also as the title of a book-length edition of selected essays by Roberto translated into English. I shall return to consideration of the phrase in a moment.

Roberto further develops in a second chapter the concepts introduced in the first. In that second chapter he deals with one of Machado's predecessors in novel-writing in Brazil, simultaneously setting forth basic historical information and analysis regarding Brazilian culture and cultural problematics (and in its last pages producing what I consider one of the most brilliant exercises in literary reading in the Portuguese language). That chapter too has been separately translated, though it has not produced widely-used critical concepts parallel to 'misplaced ideas'. In any case, the two initial chapters have become go-to statements about the dynamics of dependent cultures as well as sources of critical terminology and exemplars of analysis not only for Brazilian culture but as well for work of a similar sort about other cultures.

It is no great exaggeration to say that Roberto's international prominence owes much to those two chapters – logically enough since they, especially the first, lend themselves to wider application than to Brazilian culture/literature alone and too because the rest of this book, superb though it is, presumes some knowledge of Machado de Assis, hardly a household name in the English-speaking world, and his work.

Now back to the phrase 'misplaced ideas' – by way of introducing the reader to some dimensions of the cultural problematic involved. The consecrated English translation, which, while it constitutes a nice phrase touching generally on the right area, utterly misses much of what the Portuguese signals. In colloquial English something that has been 'misplaced' is being regarded as likely not irretrievably lost; it was probably left in the glove compartment of the car or the pocket of the shirt I wore yesterday. It is likely to turn up tomorrow, and everything will be fine. What is more, the whole matter doesn't sound urgent. If it were, 'misplace' wouldn't be the word of choice. By contrast, what Roberto wishes to signal with 'idéias fora do lugar' – which I have always wanted to translate with the admittedly awkward phrases 'out-of-place ideas' or 'ideas out of place' (to, I confess, near universal rejection by colleagues) – is something very important indeed: in Roberto's coining and critical use with respect to Brazil, it gestures toward a sui generis hybrid Brazilian culture constructed precisely around the 'out-of-placeness' of some basic societal 'ideas' and serves as a key to explanation of much of the public language, cultural history, cultural production (e.g., Machado de Assis novels), and even subject formation produced as a part of that hybridity. And it certainly does not hold out the hope that the 'ideas', in the sense meant in Roberto's analysis, will ever find a 'proper place' – much less ever 'go home', as it were – and leave some 'Brazil' to itself. Indeed, Roberto is clear on this score, pointing out that 'it helps little to insist on their [i.e., the ideas'] obvious falseness. It is better to study them in their functioning, of which it – namely the falseness – is a true part' (p. 11). (I have somewhat butchered the phraseology of that passage to create an epigraph to these pages of mine.)

By setting out the exemplary cases of Brazilian naming practices and the tragic history of 'idéias fora do lugar,' I once again give the reader notice that some care should be taken in reading, especially in reading passages where those matters, or situations analogous to them, present themselves. In the specific case of 'idéias fora do lugar' my solution in this volume is the adoption of a half measure: rather than insist on my preferred translation and thereby clutter up with inconsistent terminology the canon-in-creation about Roberto's work, I use the inherited 'misplaced ideas' but urge the reader to remember what it actually means and the actual import of that meaning, rather than be led astray.

While the reader will certainly see this for him- or herself in its general outlines, one of the central motives in Roberto's analysis of Machado is that of nationality. The specific deployment of that element is not so clear, however. It is roughly as follows: *Ao vencedor* in effect sees countries as having 'a literature' and that literature as having a history both within the general national history and in itself, the two really being one and the same seen in different perspectives. According to that logic, literature thus is, consciously or not on the part of practitioners, a field of reflective national-ist (which is to be kept separate from 'nationalistic') endeavour, among other things, of course. In the case of culturally dependent countries like the Brazil of Machado's time and before (later too) it was (and has been) an endeavour to have a literature that bespeaks coherently, in some way or other, the country's specificity. (Thus a step, perhaps a slightly sideways one, in our civilisational movement from categorical transcendence as anchor, to rational transcendence, to various forms of analysis as functional anchor in the place-and-absence of transcendence – in Machado, according to Roberto's reading, analysis in establishment of a specifically Brazilian national-cultural authenticity.) In cases when a country/region/city, etcetera, is dependent on other parts of the world for models and categories available for use in self-reflection, that self-reflection all-but-necessarily includes a correlative quest for a liberation of sorts from that dependency.

Roberto's reading here of the first four instalments in Machado's 'project' with a focus on that set of issues ultimately identifies a kind of 'aesthetic' project on Machado's part of developing a literary discourse (sensu lato) cogently expressive of the ideological complexities present in urban Brazil of the late nineteenth and early twentieth century. 'Urban' because Machado spent his entire life in Rio de Janeiro, which was then the national capital and the cosmopolitan centre of the country, and too his novels were all set in Rio and initially published there. In Roberto's reading, Rio becomes for Machado a synecdoche for Brazil. In that respect, he writes:

> Throughout the course of its social reproduction, Brazil tirelessly affirms and reaffirms European ideas, always in inappropriate ways. It is in the light of that fact that they will be both material and problem for literature. A writer may not be aware of that fact, nor does he need to be in order to use the ideas. But he will achieve a deep, attuned resonance only if he feels, registers and develops – or avoids – the displacement and the dissonance.
> p. 13

And there lurks in the mix the implicit corollary that Machado's prominence as a writer derives in some significant part from his handling of this 'nationalist' strand and his ability to capture 'Brazilness' through this handling it.

There are several other corollaries attached to this 'nationalist' focus. An obvious one is to be seen in the fact that Machado's novels clearly presume a Brazilian readership – a Rio one, of course – roughly contemporary to their writing. At the time, novels were almost always first published in serial form in newspapers or magazines, therefore functioning first as part of daily local discourse rather than as the free-standing 'art objects' they would become when published in book form and circulated outside the site of their initial serial production – not to mention when they are canonised, multiply reedited, and translated into other languages, as is the case with all nine of Machado's novels. The books, then, not surprisingly contain a large number of references and cultural presumptions that will bypass partially if not completely the English-language reader (indeed even, albeit to a lesser extent, the present-day Brazilian reader), though, I believe impressionistically, this is truer of Machado's later novels than of the earlier ones. As I will detail later, I add notes explanatory of a few of those 'lost allusions', though the more pervasive but less concrete ones are not easily dealt with short of composing an essay for the purpose, so I – yet again – urge careful and reflective reading. By the way, *Ao vencedor* itself clearly does something similar, addressing as it obviously does a contemporary Brazilian readership – i.e., it should be borne in mind that the 'we' and 'us' and 'our,' etcetera, of Roberto's text do not bespeak a distanced, perhaps scholarly, identification of his textual voice as Brazilian for anyone who might be reading; it instead refers to the Brazilianness that writer and originally-intended reader share as countrymen. We are, then, something like onlookers to a conversation among Brazilians about an important chapter in the history of the development of 'Brazilness'. What we make of that opportunity for our own benefit is, to no inconsiderable extent, up to us.

Now to the question of the analytical terminology and analytical discourse that Roberto uses to carry out his task. As is obvious right from the start of the first introductory chapter, the book's basic framework is constructed around and within a loosely Marxist concept of history and with Marxist and Marxian analytical terminology: 'constitutive contradiction', 'ideology', 'commodity form', 'ruling class', and other terms used pretty much as in their function in traditional Marxist cultural critique. I, for one, continually hear Lukács the analyst – though not Lukács politically – and, to a lesser extent, Adorno. Other figures to be sure – as Roberto's notes and bibliography evidence. Many of the terms and concepts are, though, heavily nuanced in the light of the specific social structure being dealt with. (As an obvious example: it is hard to speak at any length of 'class conflict' in the basic Marxist sense with regard to a society that does not have more than one social grouping at least moderately conscious of itself as a 'class.') So, as you will see, adaptations, usually implicit ones, are made. One thing that will fascinate, then, will be the specific details of those adaptations. (To my mind, that issue alone recommends a critical reading of this book.) The terminology created or adapted in the process is quite tight and specific in the Portuguese, though much less so in my attempt to render it in English (more detail about that later ...).

As is obvious, this adoption of continental literary-critical terminology – which brings with it a very European sense of the nature and social operativity of the nineteenth-century novel – can be, and has been, seen as contradictory in the context of a work like this one, especially as it overtly argues for the radical non-European specificity of its object of study. I for one have always seen this as a quasi-paradox, since Roberto's elaboration makes it clear, without saying it in so many words, that features of the European novel as form include an implicit procedural imperative to create a logically consistent narrative discourse as regards the society in question, be it German or French – or Brazilian.

The other major strand of generalised Marxist analytics that appears is a rendition of a somewhat later development, namely the Marxist version of '60s and '70s dependency theory, which was being actively worked on internationally at the time of the writing of *Ao vencedor*. The terminology and argumentative base of such authors as the American Immanuel Wallerstein and, I think, the Chilean Osvaldo Sunkel find echo in *Ao vencedor*. They are used to promote consideration of what Wallerstein dubbed 'the world system' and to argue for the depth of the permeation of national dynamics by relationships with hegemonic sites – in the case of Machado's Brazil, with Europe – and especially for the role of technological development and technology transfer in that context.

At root, in Roberto's formulation, the aforementioned Brazilian cultural hybridity derives from the centuries-long slavocratic regime and slave-based economy – which at one point he calls simply the 'primary' form of social alienation in the time he is dealing with (p. 4) – initiated and maintained in Brazil by the Portuguese colonial regime. (From the sixteenth into the nineteenth centuries an estimated three-to-four million Africans were transported to Brazil as slaves; in the 2010 census something approaching half of Brazilians identified themselves as partially or principally Africa-descended). At the same time, starting in the second half of the eighteenth century the country notoriously began to take on the trappings – the 'ideas' – of the European Enlightenment and use them, formally and seriously, to address its current state, direct discussion of societal goals, engage in social planning, inform official culture, and so on, a process that accelerated with the move of the Portuguese royal court to Rio de Janeiro in 1808 (it returned to Portugal in 1821). In that socio-cultural environment was created a practice of continually eliding or avoiding the obvious categorical contradiction lying at the heart of the 'national task', which process boiled down to finding ways to deal with the legacy of a superstructure grounded in considerable part in political liberalism with its emphasis on free markets and the autonomy of the individual on the one hand and, on the other, the legal and thriving presence of slavery and the rigidly hierarchical society necessarily correlated with it – a highly constrained labour market and labour force and vertical social-power relationships – as the principal base of the economy. (Brazil, which became independent from Portugal in 1822, abolished the slave trade in 1850, proclaimed in 1871 that anyone born in the country from that time on was a free person, and finally abolished slavery completely in 1888, the last Western country to do so.) From the root contradiction instantiated by slavery, Roberto argues, literally dozens of reactions and counter-reactions, attempted accommodations, and other strategies arise over time, some at first blush apparently quite removed from the root cause. Hence the importance and complexity of the term 'ideas out of place' (or, 'misplaced ideas').

Roberto's analytical endeavour is structured specifically around a basic opposition between what he calls 'liberalism' and what he calls 'favour.' The former will be clear, referring as it does to the generalised model of socio-economic structures and observed practices that, in very broad terms, come (according to Wallerstein, almost accidentally) at the beginning of modernity in Europe: exchange value, commodification, individualism, wage labour, class society, and so on. It is the latter that will require some unpacking, though in advancing his argument Roberto gradually fleshes it out pretty well. So just a few words here: 'favour' is, obviously, not coordinate with liberalism, being an anthropological label describing a discrete social practice, namely the power to choose to patronise someone for no necessary reason and the reciprocal loyalty and service that, implicitly, the patronised is obliged to show the patron who has chosen to favour him. In this context 'favour' works not only in that narrow sense but also as a kind of label for a wide set of practises, of which it is one, that provide for and effectuate such functions as the justification for, and maintenance of, hierarchical society, the nature and working of social mobility in such a society, the performance of labour within it, and so on. What unites the two is that, like 'liberalism,' 'favour' here suggests a type of social organisation, which can profitably be counterposed to 'liberalism.' Much of Roberto's reading of Machado's early novels finds its ground in some aspect or other of that enabling opposition.

Now there is something in – or, really, not in – Roberto's approach that is likely to strike today's reader as worrying – though it would not have struck us that way in the 1970s. It is his reference to 'an ideology' or to 'ideologies' – at one point he simply says, in reference to Brazilian 'importation' of the novel form from Europe, 'to adopt the novel was to accept the way it dealt with ideologies' (p. 16). The image, often repeated, suggests that 'an ideology' is just there, somewhere, confected in the form that it somehow has when it is abstracted from a cultural source through *ideologiekritik* analysis (I mean that term a bit more generally than Frankfurt School usage, but all the English alternatives carry extraneous baggage). There is no sense in which the specific picture of 'ideology X' is in that instance created by the analysis, that, then, 'ideologies' are performed – in writing, in critical operations, in perception, etcetera – and are not somehow existent as pre-formed parcels. To which people in the 1970s and 1980s, following the lead of such writers as Hans-Robert Jauss and Wolfgang Iser, would add, as regards literary studies, that these kinds of issues require some modicum of grounding in a theory of reception. It would be easy, from the vantage point of today, to ask of *Ao vencedor* more than it ever intended to contribute – or needed to. Everything is the product of its moment, and while, in the 1970s, we would probably have understood the problem I point to here, we would likely not have considered it important: *Ao vencedor* shows what it shows about the subject matter it addresses and does so in ways that met – indeed, advanced – the times. (Remember my own initial reaction to it). Now in the sequel one can see Roberto modifying his critical outlook in ways that leave room for what one could call a more 'performative' view of ideology. The reader interested in such matters is invited, after finishing this book, to read that sequel: the aforementioned *A Master on the Periphery of Capitalism: Machado de Assis*. The extended journey will be well worth it.

Now, some of the features and implications of what follows.
- First the source: the base text for this translation is *Ao vencedor as batatas* of 2000, put out by Livraria Duas Cidades. I have also had a few occasions to consult the first edition, *Ao vencedor as batatas: Forma literária e processo social nos inícios do romance brasileiro*, put out by the same publisher in 1977.

  And, as I have already mentioned, I have had recourse to the previously-published translations into English of the first two chapters. I have also had infrequent recourse to a published translation of each of the four novels being analysed, though my translation of those passages from the novels reproduced in Roberto's text may or may not replicate that in the corresponding published translation, since my goals involve getting out of the passage what I judge Roberto wants and also maintaining his tight analytical terminology, of which I shall speak momentarily.
- The Portuguese original contains a good many notes – to the novels, to period documents and prior scholarly work as well as to critical sources. What is more, as I have explained above, I have felt the need to add a few clarificatory notes of my own, including some about Brazilian society, always within square brackets (in the body of this book, anything appearing within square brackets is an addition of mine, and conversely everything – save the bibliography – that is an addition of mine is in square brackets). I engage in that task in anticipation that the reader will need to know that, for example, 'Alencar' refers to the prolific mid-nineteenth-century Brazilian novelist José Martiniano de Alencar (1829–77), who would be totally familiar to a likely Brazilian reader. The collection of notes in this volume will, then, be longer than in the original, and note numbers will not correspond between original and translation.

  The Portuguese original does not include a bibliography, wisely opting instead, given its intended audience, for a sometimes-informal bibliography

in the notes. I have added a bibliography as I went along in the translation process, though even here the sometimes-informality of the original shows through.
- Some few of the bibliographical items in Roberto's notes refer to light items, principally from the Brazilian popular press of Machado's time but also from other sources. As I cannot imagine that any English-culture reader will have an interest in such an item – or access to it – I have left them in the corresponding notes but not included them in the bibliography.
- Almost all of Roberto's bibliographical notes refer to works written in, or previously translated to, Portuguese and presumably consulted by him in that language, with the exception of a few critical sources that he consults and cites in German or French. I have kept all of them in those languages and in a highly schematic but, I think, clear and consistent format roughly parallel to Roberto's, but in the bibliography to this book I have glossed titles – just titles – in English as another half-measure, attempting to create a version that will serve readers who have the requisite language(s) while not abandoning those who do not. In so doing, I recreate Roberto's bibliographical style – again in the name of consistency, as is the case with my grudging adoption of the term 'misplaced ideas'. I also adapt that style to fit the needs of the final bibliography rather than use today's standard style, thus saving the reader the task of shuffling over what would sometimes be incompatible formats between notes and bibliography. I believe that the result, while not standard, is a readable and at the same time researchable rendering of Roberto's work with as little fuss as possible.
- The original employs paragraphs that sometimes stretch over pages. I have noticed that other English translations of Roberto's work choose to re-paragraph. Seeing it as my goal to reproduce the original as fully as I can, I have left the original paragraphing intact.
- Now Roberto's rhetoric has some distinct peculiarities, the main one for the translator to take into account being that it often becomes what I would call 'telegraphic'. That is, as I hint above, he relies heavily on his accumulated/accumulating critical terminology to carry the weight of his analysis. (It decidedly does not mean that he writes short sentences.) One has therefore to bear in mind in reading that when Roberto establishes the precise meaning of a term in the given context he presumes that the subsequent re-use of that term will signal that specific meaning. What is more, re-use can also imply connections previously made with regard to the term. I have noticed that some English translations of his work approach the status of explanation rather than what we normally think of as translation. Indeed, sometimes the resultant 'translations', in order to render what the original

says, have entire phrases, even sentences, that have no relation to the actual verbal sequence of the original. For my part, especially since this publication comes in a specific book series with a specific implied readership, while I have occasionally – when I judged it necessary – 'explained' with an extra word or two (okay, sometimes more than that!), I have avoided wholesale 'explanation', save in a handful of cases where I thought meaning itself was at stake. Even there I have been as faithful as possible to the original. I have endeavoured to retain original sentence integrity, vocabulary, word order and phrasing whenever comprehension is not thereby diminished, so that comparison of original and translation is possible. The result is a text that cannot be termed 'colloquial' in English but does, I think, 'mean' in English at every turn – plus giving a good rendition of the texture and diction of the original. So – yet again – reading will have to be careful, now in a quite different way.

- A similar, though less intrusive issue involves verbs. Roberto uses a range of tenses and aspects that challenges translation into English. This is not an unusual problem, as the Portuguese language supports such a practice while English does not. In most cases I have relied on the simple present tense and forms of the past in English, in effect in this area rewriting Portuguese cultural criticism into something like English cultural criticism. To do otherwise would have run contrary to usual practice in working between the two languages in this register and, I suspect, would have frustrated the readership.

  I should note, though, that as a part of my practice I 'read through' verb tenses. The reader conscious of such matters will, then, have to accept the task of doing the same. That is, if a given passage in Roberto's text – likely but not necessarily his quotation from Machado – is in, say, past tense, but up to that point I have been working in present tense, I may choose to remain in present tense. Indeed, I change tenses on a purely situational basis as befits my translation rather than the original.

- As for problems in translating, there are several of which the reader should be aware. First, the gender of personal pronouns. Initially I attempted to use a more inclusive pronoun structure of the sort that I use today in my own writing – though I probably would not have in the 1970s either. While the problem has not been widely pervasive, after a while I found that with even occasional usage I was doing damage to an original not written that way – and violating my own commitment to sticking as close to that original as possible. I have reverted to the usage of the original, though I have purposely not been consistent in the choices I make from the array of options.

– A type of impediment that the reader without Portuguese will not be able to recognise at all is one that in various forms plagues translations of all sorts. I shall mention, as examples, only the two problems of this sort that recur with some frequency in what follows.

First, as I mention above, Roberto's style is 'telegraphic' in the sense that he relies heavily on his accumulated terminology to carry the argument. The problem is that, as with all languages, Portuguese words seldom carry a single discrete meaning but rather a field of meanings, usually closely related to each other. A key term in Roberto's argument is the Portuguese word 'arbítrio', which can signal everything from 'will', to 'choice', to 'being in a position that enables one to exercise one's will', to 'being recognised as occupying' such a position (in which case it has something akin to common-law force), to 'using that position to exercise that will and make a choice', all the way to being the word in Portuguese in translation of the Christian theological concept of 'free will' (usually 'livre arbítrio', though just 'arbítrio' suffices and is sometimes used). Those are just some of the variations within what is actually a comparatively small semantic field. And then there is the common word for 'will', namely 'vontade', which overlaps with some of the acceptances of 'arbítrio' (and on occasion is used by Roberto in approximately that way). As semantic fields in one language seldom map directly onto ones in another language, in translating I have, of course, had to render the word variously, according to the context. Which, also of course, runs counter to my effort to maintain in translation Roberto's very effective 'telegraphic' diction and tightness. And, obviously, 'arbítrio' is hardly the only term that presents that problem. In effect, I have occasionally been forced to sacrifice one area of 'meaning' to the needs of another. It is always thus, though in this particular case the problem is greater than usual; hence my 'choice' to bring this matter too to your attention.

And another, similar but almost opposite impediment that, with a couple of exceptions, affects only one lexical system: that of 'generalizar', 'generalização', and other lexically-allied items in Portuguese. Roberto uses those words a lot, almost always meaning with them 'make general', 'propagate', 'universalise', 'diffuse'. They convey a critical concept central to his analysis of the working of ideology. The last option, 'universalise', would normally be the closest possibility in English, save that in this particular context one would be 'universalising' only within Brazil, which would constitute a phraseology with an immediately-obvious surface contradiction about it. Now in English, 'generalise'/'generalisation' can mean what Roberto wants, but by far its most likely significance for English readers concerns the logical error of over-generalising ('now that's an argument from generalisation!'), and the contexts in which Roberto uses the term(s) can sometimes support that reading, thus potentially leading to confusion. This is my last plea for careful reading: I have chosen to stick with the cognates. So when you see 'generalise'/'generalisation' or allied items, think 'propagate/universalise/diffuse within Brazil'. There are other terms that have a version of the same problem (see, e.g., the verb 'to subject').

– One last category: the sense of humour in Roberto's writing (we don't know each other in person), which, in my reading at least, often functions as a wry commentary on what he is in the process of analysing. First, he several times uses three spaced periods (…) as a final comment on something he has just finished dealing with, meaning something like 'and we all know what is going to/likely to come of that'. You could think of it as his version of the long-sought-after 'irony mark,' albeit only for this specific sort of irony. The readerly task there is to differentiate between that usage and the standard usages of three spaced periods for ellipsis, suspension, etcetera – all of which also appear in the text.

Then there is situational humour in various forms. I have found it almost impossible to capture the various instances of it in translation, though when I found a way in a given passage I have made the effort. So if you come across something that you think might be a touch of humour (e.g. 'we, however, are dealing with Brazil') (p. 48), hopefully that is what it is – in my best attempt to have it show through the transfer of languages. Hopefully too, awareness of that dimension will help set for you something of the tone of the original, which is somewhat lost in my rendition … Enjoy!

Ronald W. Sousa
Professor Emeritus, U. Illinois Urbana-Champaign
Washington DC, January, 2019

Acknowledgements

The author and translator thank the Fundação de Amparo à Pesquisa do Estado de São Paulo, Brazil, for its generous financial and moral support for this project.

Thanks go too to the Department of Spanish and Portuguese of Georgetown University, USA.

A BBC Interview with Roberto Schwarz, on the Subject of Machado de Assis[1]

Q. – *Could you explain why you give so much importance to favour, and to dependants, in your account of Machado's fiction?*

A. – Well, I hope this importance is not an invention of mine, but a point Machado himself wanted to make. As you know, the key character in Machado's early novels is a poor girl who lives as a dependent of a wealthy family. To say it in another way, all that a good position in society may give and all that money can buy comes to the girl through the personal favour of people of property. What are the moral implications of this bond? Does the girl have the right to scheme and to manipulate the feelings of her benefactors? How much humiliation is it decent for her to stand in order to reach her goals? At the other extreme of the relationship, the wealthy of course are invited to all sorts of despotic nastyness and capriciousness, as they are under no obligation to the poor girl. Put together, these questions amount to a closely knit system of moral problems, full of subtleties and meanders, in which Machado specialised, in a manner of speaking. Yet, this is only half of the answer to your question. In order to understand the relevance of Machado's fiction one must consider still another aspect. Like every novelist, Machado was in search of significant plots, of private conflicts with far-reaching collective bearings. And in fact, scrutinising a poor girl's dependence on a family of means he aimed at one of the truly general and all-pervading features of Brazilian society. As you know, to put it succinctly, nineteenth-century Brazil rested upon slave labour. Which meant, for large numbers of poor whites, who had no slaves and no property, a situation of thorough deprivation. Since work was done by slaves, what should the poor free men do, as there was no labour market in which to earn a wage? Their access to necessary goods was dependent upon favour, upon the very personal favour of the propertied. We may then say that relationships of favour and personal dependency – all varieties of clientelship – were at the centre of the Brazilian social structure, where they remained to our day. They linked two of the country's basic social classes: the poor free men and the free men of property. To a large degree, the resulting tangle of interests and conflicts was

---

[1] The interview was conducted in 1991 for a Radio 3 programme titled *You, dear reader*. The interviewer was John Gledson and the producer was Judith Bumpus.

to determine for a long time to come the very fabric of the country's moral and cultural problems. Coming back to your question, let us say that the poor girl's manoeuvres inside a well-to-do family, a rather conventional literary situation, allowed Machado to deal in depth and in a very unconventional manner with a central question of national life.

Q. – *Does this have anything to do with his ability to understand certain aspects of human nature?*

A. – Critics always speak of human nature when discussing Machado's fiction. This comes quite naturally, since he himself was a great reader of French literature and philosophy of the seventeenth and eighteenth century and loved to invent witty maxims on 'man in general'. Yet, if you look closer at his prose, you will notice that the sayings on universal man always respond to very local and particular interests. Used in a devious and preposterous manner, the universalist phrasing does not lead us into the realm of human nature in the abstract, in the eternal; quite to the contrary, it gives comic evidence of the historical and changing ways in which different social groups think of themselves as being the only and true incarnation of mankind. At the root of these differences you will find the opposition between social classes. For example, if one looks at these novels' context, the effective meaning of a general statement on human egoism varies in the most extraordinary manner. If the statement is elegantly uttered by the narrator in the presence of a slave it may be, at first sight, a phrase on the nature of man; at second sight, it may work as an alibi, it may help a Brazilian nineteenth-century gentleman to show his civilised and literary self and to forget the annoying fact that he is a slave-owner, a character abhorred by the liberal opinion he so admires. At third sight it may be an apalling piece of cynicism. In fact, the social situation filters the somewhat outdated and over-literary talk on the unchangeable nature of man, so as to make it expressive – comically expressive – of historically conflicting points of view.

Q. – *How do you explain the change in Machado's fiction in 1880, the enormous change in the quality of his fiction which begins with* Epitaph of a Small Winner?

A. – Machado wrote his first great novel at forty. His new literary manner differed sharply from the earlier one, with which it seemed to have nothing in common. What had happened in-between? Biographers will tell us about serious illness, sudden maturity, loss of illusions, growing mastery, or, more straightforwardly, outbreak of genius. These explanations do not explain much. A good answer should tell us what had changed from the early and poor works to the late and great ones. Which were the changes in outlook and technique that made for the enormous difference in quality? We may ask as well about the steps that led from a backward and provincial literary tradition to one with contemporary relevance.

In the early novels the relations of personal dependence and favour are envisaged from below, from the point of view of the propertyless, in a civilising spirit. The point of these books is to show and to explain that it is in the best interest of the wealthy to help and to adopt the intelligent poor, who might enliven an otherwise empty and egoistical social life. The reasons for this co-optation are to be strictly paternalistic, since the poor are not considered as workers. In these circumstances, economic calculation would appear to be unchristian and indecent, the very obstacle to the generous favours on which the improvement of the poor would depend. The authoritarian and stifling character of this world and its incompatibility with critical thought are evident at first sight. One might even say that the suffocating atmosphere of these novels is their best and most instructive literary contribution, a sort of unwilling comment on the unreality of the hopes they tried to promote.

Be this as it may, sometime around 1878 Machado lost faith in the social solution his first novels worked upon. He no longer invested hope in the paternal goodwill of the propertied classes, who should raise the deserving poor, lifting them to their own higher sphere, the sphere of modern civilisation. By now Machado saw that the rich belonged to the world of bourgeois interest and property as much as to the world of paternal authority and responsibility. They would act upon one principle or the other according to their immediate interest, completely disorienting their dependants. These were alternately put to service as quasi-relatives or disacknowledged as strangers. The meanness of these shifts was to become one of the literary specialties of Machado de Assis.

In the *Epitaph of a Small Winner* the respectful and edifying manner of the first novels has disappeared. The double standard in the behaviour of the well to do is laid bare with an amazing frankness. Yet the technical solution devised by Machado is so unexpected – and blunt, in a way – that it becomes quite invisible. Instead of keeping to the point of view from below and criticising the despotic arbitrariness to which the poor were exposed, Machado would change the perspective. He now impersonates his class enemy, makes him into the narrator, the unreliable narrator of the novel, and lets him misbehave towards the characters and the reader in the most unacceptable and spectacular ways. The humoristic techniques of the eighteenth-century English novel, the capriciousness of Tristram Shandy, are put to new and unsentimental uses: they are to enact the terrible unconcern of the slave-owning classes towards the poor who depend on them. The thoughts that freely float into the mind of the narrator concerning the usefulness and the uselessness of the poor are really staggering, and a piece of great critical literature. Still, the perfection of the domineering mask that is to be exposed and denounced, and the habit that Brazilians have of admiring it, has lulled the readers into identification with the elegant figure of the *malfaisant*. These most devastating pieces of criticism of the Brazilian elite have worked until recently as enviable models of superior scepticism and *savoir vivre*.

Q. – *How does Machado treat the poor in his work – is there any truth in the accusation that he lacked real sympathy with them?*

A. – A striking feature in Machado's fiction is that the inner life of the wretched, of a miserable servant or of a slave, is not less complex and convoluted than the inner life of an elegant and good-smelling baroness. What is more, Machado tries to work out and to establish the strict complementarity between these worlds. In this – as in many other points – he is very similar to Marcel Proust.

This much said, it seems intriguing that so many critics would accuse him of lack of sympathy with the poor. This may be due to his sharp refusal of sentimentality and of romantic populism and patriotism, which to his contemporaries may have seemed like a sort of general lack in human feeling. In fact, I think that there are not many writers in world literature capable of a portrait of poverty as true and terrible as the one of Dona Placida in *The Epitaph of a Small Winner*.

Q. – *You said in a recent interview that Machado is 'getting younger every day': what is his relevance for Brazilians today?*

A. – As you have shown in your book on Dom Casmurro, there is something disconcerting about Machado's mature fiction. The novels are told by an elegant and enviable narrator, and yet they are written against him, so as to expose the untenable aspects of his social position. This is a tricky technical device. If we look at it more closely, we will notice that the elegance depends on the narrator's European, almost Victorian traits, especially on his very civilised rhetoric. While the other side, the side conducive to his indictment, depends on his entanglement with slavery and authoritarian paternalism, or, to say it in another way, with the remnants of the colonial past. Machado de Assis was the first Brazilian writer to be keenly aware of the moral problems and of the comic aspects of the alliance between the civilised pretense and the continuity of the colonial pattern. He did build his irony on these questions. However, it is a fact that the irony passed unnoticed, since that alliance seemed completely natural to the Brazilian elite, who would read Machado's fiction as a perfect manifestation of its own modernity and Westernism and not as its indictment and satire. Well, coming to our times we must notice that the contradiction between the first world aspirations of the Brazilian elite and the rather barbarous constraints put upon the poor continue to exist. Time has served at least to make them seem less natural than a hundred years ago and to render them more visible, a sort of early figuration of today's agenda. In this sense it is true that Machado has become younger as well as easier to understand.

CHAPTER 1

Misplaced Ideas[1]

All science comes grounded in principles from which it derives its systematicity. In political economy, one of those principles is the principle of free labour. In Brazil, however, it is the 'impolitic and repugnant' practice of slavery that has dominated.

That analysis – summary of the argument contained in a liberal pamphlet of Machado de Assis' time[2] – thus excludes Brazil from the realm of science. According to it we existed outside the reality to which it refers, being instead an 'impolitic and repugnant' moral datum – a huge throwback given that science was equatable to Enlightenment, to Progress, to Humanity and so forth. In the arts Joaquim Nabuco[3] expresses a similar orientation when he protests against the treatment of slavery in Alencar's[4] plays: 'If it offends foreigners, all the more does it shame Brazilians!'[5] Other authors of course made the reverse argument: given that they don't refer to our reality, economic knowledge and other such liberal ideologies are themselves what is repugnant, impolitic and foreign – not to mention foolish. 'Better good darkies from the African coast, for their benefit and ours, despite all the morbid philanthropy of the Briton that enables him to overlook his own house and let his poor white brother die of hunger, a slave without a master to take pity upon him, but has him cry, hypocritically or stolidly, over the destiny of our happy slave, thereby exposing himself to the ridicule of the true philanthropy'.[6]

Each in his own way, those authors reflect the disparity that existed between slavocratic Brazilian society and the principles of European liberalism. Bring-

---

1 [This essay exists in an earlier English version as the second chapter, entitled 'Misplaced Ideas: Literature and Society in Late-Nineteenth-Century Brazil,' pp. 19–32 of *Misplaced Ideas*, a collection of Schwarz essays in English translation. My rendering differs from the one published in that book, though the differences appear primarily in matters of terminology and expression.]
2 Torres Bandeira. Machado was a regular contributor to *O Futuro*.
3 [Joaquim Aurélio Barreto Nabuco de Araújo (1849–1910) was a prominent Brazilian writer and abolitionist.]
4 [The mid-nineteenth-century Brazilian novelist José Martiniano de Alencar (1829–77) mentioned in my 'Introduction.']
5 *A polêmica*, p. 106.
6 Statement made by a commercial firm, M. Wright & Cia., regarding the financial crisis of the 1850s. Cited by Nabuco 1936, p. 188 and again by Buarque de Holanda 1956, p. 96.

ing some to shame while angering others, who insisted on seeing them as hypocritical, those principles, in which neither opposing camp recognises Brazil, constitute the frame of reference for all. In sum, an ideological comedy is put on that is *simply different from its European counterpart*. It is obvious that economic freedom, equality under the law, and, generally, universalism, were an ideology in Europe, but there they corresponded to appearances, obfuscating what it was essential to obfuscate, namely the exploitation of labour. With us those same ideas would also be false but in, so to speak, a different and original way. For example, the Declaration of the Rights of Man, partially transcribed in the Brazilian Constitution of 1824, failed in that context to obfuscate anything, thereby debasing the institution of slavery even further.[7] The same with the professed universality of principles, which transformed the general practice of '*favour*' into a scandal. In that context what was the value of those great bourgeois abstractions of which we made so great a use? They did not describe our existence, but such is not the only role that ideas play. Along these same lines Sérgio Buarque observes: 'Fetching from distant countries our forms of life, our institutions and our vision of the world, and striving to maintain it all in an environment often both unfavourable and hostile, we were exiles in our own land'.[8] That inadequacy in our thought, which, as we shall see, is hardly a chance occurrence, was a persistent presence, cutting through and rendering awkward the ideological life of the Second Empire, down to the smallest of details. Sometimes overdrawn, sometimes trivial, ridiculous or crude, seldom accurate in tone, the literary prose of the time is one of the many social functions that witness that phenomenon.

While they constitute givens of Brazilian historiography, the reasons for this picture have been little studied as regards effects. As is known, we were an independent, agrarian country divided into large holdings; our production depended, on the one hand, on slave labour and on the other on the external market. More or less directly from those two factors come the singularities we have set out here. For example, a bourgeois economic logic – the priority of profit and its social corollaries – was inevitable for us given that it was the dominant logic in the international commerce toward which our economy was oriented. The ongoing practice of that commercial model taught no few of us that mode of thought. What is more, we had gained independence shortly before under the banner of a conglomeration of variously-liberal French, English and American ideas that therefore made up a part of our national identity. On the other side of matters and with equal necessity, that ideological bundle

---

7   Viotti da Costa 1968.
8   Buarque de Holanda 1956, p. 15.

would run into conflict with slavery and its defenders – and, what is more, have to coexist with them.⁹ At the level of conviction the incompatibility is clear – and we have seen examples of it. But it made itself felt at the practical level as well. Being property, a slave could be sold but not fired. In this sense one who sells his labour on the open market accords his boss greater freedom, not to mention tying up less capital. This aspect, one among many, is indicative of the limits that slavery imposed on rationalisation of production. Commenting on what he had observed at one plantation, one traveller wrote: 'there is no specialisation of tasks because the goal is to save on labour'. Citing that passage, Fernando Henrique Cardoso observes that in this context 'saving' does not mean accomplishing work in a minimum of time but rather carrying it out in a maximum of time. It was important to stretch out and organise the slave's day – the exact opposite of what modern methods seek to do. Founded on violence and military discipline, slave production was ordered more around authority than around efficiency.¹⁰ The rational study of the productive processes and their continual modernisation – with all the prestige that came to them from the revolution they ushered in in Europe, was pointless in Brazil. To complicate the picture still more, consider that slavocratic large-holding began as a commercial capitalist enterprise, so profit had always been its goal. Now profit as the subjective priority is common to older forms of capital as well as to more modern ones. So the uncouth and repugnant slavers, up to a certain date, namely when the form of production became less profitable than wage labour, were essentially more thoroughgoing capitalists than our defenders of Adam Smith, who in capitalism saw freedom more than anything else. In sum, for intellectual life the knot had already been tied. In terms of logic the roles were jumbled: science was fantasy and moralism, obscurantism was realism and responsibility, technical considerations were not practical, it was altruism that produced surplus value, and so on. And, more generally, in the absence of any organised viewpoint from the slaves, conflict between humanity and inhumanity, appropriate though it might have been, ended up finding a commonplace translation as conflict between two ways of investing capital – which was the view of the conflict found more suitable by one of the parties.¹¹

Constantly besieged by slavery, liberal ideology, the ideology of the young, emancipated nations of America, went off the rails. It would be easy to deduce

---

9   Viotti da Costa 1968.
10 Cardoso 1962, pp. 189–91, 198.
11 Alencastro observes in his doctoral dissertation that the true national question of our nineteenth century was the defence of slave trafficking in the face of English pressure. The question could not appeal less to intellectual enthusiasm.

the corresponding absurdities, true every one, many of which troubled the theoretical and moral consciousness of our nineteenth century. We have already seen a collection of those absurdities. They remained, however, curiously tangential. A reality test seemed unimportant. It is as though consistency and coherence didn't carry any weight, or the sphere of culture existed in a separate realm whose basic criteria of judgment were other. But 'other' in relation to what? By its very presence slavery showed up the inappropriateness of liberal ideas. But that does not mean that it changed their orientation. While it certainly was the basic relationship around production, slavery did not provide the functional core for Brazil's ideological life. The key lay elsewhere. To describe it, it is necessary to look at the country as a whole. In schematic terms one can say that colonisation, based on land holding, produced three classes of people: landowners, slaves and 'free men', who were in fact dependents. The relation between the first two is clear; it is the multitude of the third that will interest us now. Neither proprietors nor proletarians, their access to social life and the goods therein contained depended materially on *'favour'*, direct or indirect, by some landowner.[12] The *'agregado'* is the caricature of that figure.[13] 'Favour' is, therefore, the mechanism by means of which one of the principal classes of this society reproduced itself – through the involvement of another class, namely the one possessing wealth. It must be noted as well that it is in that interaction between those two classes that the national ideological life is produced, and it is governed by this relationship.[14] Thus, with a thousand different forms and names, 'favour' permeated and conditioned all of our national existence save the base productive relationship, which was safeguarded by force. 'Favour' was present everywhere in society, playing a role in the most various of activities, ones with which it had likely relationships and ones with which it did not: administration, policy, industry, commerce, urban life, the imperial court and so on. Even the liberal professions like medicine or forms of skilled labour like typography, which in the European model owed nothing to anyone else, with us were governed by 'favour'. Just as the professional depended upon 'favour' for the exercise of his profession, the small-scale proprietor depended on it for the security of his property and the bureaucrat for his position. *'Favour' was our almost-universal mediating factor*. Moreover, being more benign than the institution of slavery, the other relationship bequeathed us by colonialism, it

---

12   Carvalho Franco 1969.
13   ['Agregado' roughly means a man of no property, totally dependent upon a family with property, but still not a slave. (Note taken from Schwarz 1992, p. 31.)]
14   Concerning the ideological effects of the large-holding, see chapter III, 'A herança rural' [The Rural Heritage] of Buarque de Holanda 1956.

is understandable that writers would base their interpretation of Brazil on it – thereby involuntarily occulting the violence that had always ruled in the sphere of production.

Slavery, then, gave the lie to liberal ideas, and, more insidiously, 'favour', equally as incompatible with liberal ideas, absorbed and reconfigured them, giving rise to a very specific ideological pattern. The element of arbitrariness, the fluid interaction of worth and self-worth to which 'favour' submitted material interest, cannot be fully rationalised. In Europe the combat against such practices saw them as aspects of feudal privilege. In the process of its historical affirmation, bourgeois culture postulated instead the autonomy of the individual, the universality of the law, culture for its own sake, objectively-calculated compensation, work ethic, and so forth against prerogatives associated with the *ancien régime*. Point for point, 'favour' practices the dependence of the individual, the exception to the rule, culture at the service of privilege, the personalisation of services and their remuneration. We were, however, not to Europe as feudalism was to capitalism; to the contrary, in addition to never having been 'feudal', we were a function of European capitalism on every front – colonisation is, after all, a commercial-capital undertaking. Given the ascendant position occupied by Europe and our position relative to it, no one in Brazil was likely to have had the idea, not to mention the force of personality, to be let's say the Kant of favour, in order to do battle with his opposite number.[15] So the clash between the two antagonistic principles was an unequal one: in the area of reasoning *they* prevailed easily – or rather *we* readily adopted the arguments fashioned by the European bourgeoisie against arbitrariness and slavery. In practice all along, however, even on the part of the debaters themselves, favour supported by the sway exercised by the presence of the large-holding, reaffirmed again and again the feelings and ideas that came along with it. The same thing happened at the institutional level; for example, bureaucracy and justice, although ruled by clientelism, would proclaim the forms and theories of the modern bourgeois state. Beyond the inevitable debates, this antagonism produced, therefore, a stable coexistence that is interesting to study. Its novelty is as follows: *after European ideas and arguments were adopted, they could – and often did – serve as nominally 'objective' justifications for instances of what was ultimately arbitrary in the practice of favour*. Real though it was, the antagonism thus vanished in a puff of smoke, and incompatible quantities moved on hand in hand. The effects were many and they are pervasive in our literature. From

---

15 As Machado de Assis remarked in 1879, 'the external impact is what determines the direction of our movement; for the time being in our environment, the force necessary for the creation of new doctrines is lacking.' Machado de Assis 1959, vol. III, pp. 826–7.

the ideology – that is, an involuntary error well grounded in appearances – that it began as, liberalism came to stand for, for lack of a better term, the intentional desire to participate in a range of relationships with which it had no relationship. When he justified arbitrary choice with one 'rational' argument or another, the recipient of favour consciously aggrandised himself and his benefactor, who in turn failed to register any contradiction, rationality being, in this age of the hegemony of reason, the highest possible value. Under such conditions who would actually believe the justification? To what appearance did it correspond? But even that was not the problem since everybody recognised – and this really is important – the praiseworthy intention on the part of both patronage and gratitude. The symbolic compensation, even if somewhat out of proportion, would not be begrudged. It might be out of step with liberalism, which would be a secondary concern, but it would be perfectly in keeping with favour, which was the primary concern. And how better to give lustre to the people involved and the society that they constituted than the most illustrious ideas of the time – namely European ideas? In this context, therefore, ideologies do not describe reality, not even falsely, or work according to any law of their own. It is for that reason we shall label them 'second-degree ideologies'. Their logic is other, different from what they say it is; they deal in social prestige rather than cognitive-systemic issues. That logic derives easily from the blatantly obvious, known to everyone – the obvious 'superiority' of Europe – and comes linked to the expressive moment of self-esteem and of fantasy that are part and parcel of 'favour'. It is in this sense that we have said that a reality – or even coherence – test was not decisive beyond being acknowledged as available, invoked or ignored according to circumstances. Dependence is, therefore, methodically considered independence, caprice is considered utility, exceptionalism universality, kinship merit, privilege equality, and so on. Thus linked to the practice of what in principle it should be criticising, liberalism knocks the underpinnings out from under actual thought. Let us leave for later analysis all the complexities of this step: in becoming preposterous these ideas also ceased to deceive.

Clearly this was but one of many ways in which favour and liberalism could combine. For our ideological climate, however, it was key, in addition to being one in which the factors configured themselves in a complete and distinctive fashion. For now, let us look at a few aspects. We have seen that in the case of favour, bourgeois ideas, whose sober grandeur harkens back to the civic, rationalist spirit of the Enlightenment, take on the function of ... what can only be called ornament and aristocratic styling: they attest to and celebrate participation in an august sphere, namely that of Europe, a Europe in the process of industrialisation. There could not be an odder relationship between ideas.

The novelty lies not in the ornamental dimension accorded to knowledge and culture, which comes from Iberian colonial tradition; it lies in the absolutely incredible dissonance that 'modern' knowledge and culture give rise to when used this way. Is it as useless as some doodad? Is it a brilliant commendation? Is it our panacea? Does it shame us in the eyes of the world? It certainly is the case that, in the comings and goings of argument and interest, all those aspects have had occasion to come to the fore, with the result that in the minds of those paying close attention they must appear to be mixed together. Inextricably, ideological life both degraded and elevated those who participated in it, among whom there must often have been an awareness of that process. It was, then, an unstable mixture that could easily degenerate into hostility and the bitterest of criticism. To be sustained it required permanent complicity, a complicity that the practice of favour tended to guarantee. At the moment of favour's bestowal and counter-bestowal – particularly at the key moment of reciprocal recognition – neither party would have had any interest in denouncing the other despite the fact that each would all along have had everything he needed in order to do so. What is more, that ever-renewed complicity included the weight of social class: in the Brazilian context favour provided assurance to both parties, but particularly to the weaker, that no one in the arrangement was a slave. Even the lowliest of those being favoured saw acknowledged in that favour his status as a free person, which transformed the bestowal and counter-bestowal, however modest they may in fact have been, into a ceremony in recognition of social superiority, which itself had value. With the infinite harshness and degradation of slavery looming in the background, from which the two parties both benefitted and sought to differentiate themselves, that reciprocal recognition constituted an extraordinary collusion, one moreover multiplied many times over by adoption of the bourgeois vocabulary of equality, of merit, of labour and of reason. Machado de Assis would be the master of these intricacies. Let us look, however, at their other side. Immersed as we are yet today in the universe of capital, which never took on its classical form in Brazil, we tend to see this combination as having been completely disadvantageous for us, made up entirely of drawbacks. There may well have been no advantages, but to appreciate appropriately the complexity of the situation we should keep in mind that bourgeois ideas, initially directed against privilege, after 1848 increasingly took on an apologetic role: the wave of social strife in Europe demonstrated that 'universality' in fact occulted class conflict.[16] Therefore, in order to keep in mind its ideological gravitation we should bear in mind

---

16   Lukács 1965.

that our inappropriate discourse was also empty when used appropriately. And it should be noted in passing that this pattern would repeat itself in the twentieth century when on several occasions, believers in our own modernity, we have pledged allegiance to the most bankrupt ideologies on the world stage. For literature, as we shall see, the result has been unique, a sort of emptying of an emptiness. Here too Machado will be the master.

In sum, if we have persisted in looking at the directions that slavery and 'favour' imparted to the ideas of the time it has not been to dismiss those ideas but rather to describe them as regards those directions – off-centre with respect to their own reasons for being and, precisely in being so, recognisably ours. Thus, leaving aside the search for cause, what remains is that incongruity that was our starting-point: the sense that Brazil is made up of dualism and artificiality – unmanageable contrasts, disproportionalities, nonsensicalities, anachronisms, contradictions, accommodations and what have you – combinations that Modernism, Tropicalism and political economy have taught us to appreciate.[17] Examples abound. Let us look at some, less to analyse than to suggest the ubiquity of the picture and the variation of which it is capable. In the magazines of the time, be they comic or serious, the inaugural number is put together using both bass and falsetto: the first asserts the emancipatory purpose of the press according to the combative modality of Enlightenment tradition, the great sect founded by Gutenberg against generalised indifference; at the top the condor and the nation's youth glimpse the future while casting away the past and its prejudices, all the while the regenerative torch of the publication is dispelling the darkness of corruption. The second, according to the specific circumstances, declares its civilised intent to 'give to all classes in general and particularly to the honest families a means of delightful instruction and pleasant recreation'. So emancipatory purpose is of a piece with word games, calls for national unity, dress patterns, general knowledge and serialised sub-literature.[18] The doggerel that serves as the epigraph to *The Marmot*

---

17   Dealt with in a different way, the same observation can be seen in Sérgio Buarque: 'We may construct excellent works, enrich our humanity with new and unforeseen aspects, bring to perfection the type of civilisation we represent: still, what is certain is that the consequences of both our efforts and our laziness seem to take part in a system proper to another climate and a different landscape' (Buarque de Holanda 1956, p. 15). [Translation taken from Schwarz 1992, p. 32.]

18   See the 'prospecto' in *O Espelho*, a weekly magazine of literature, fashion, crafts and the arts, Typographia de F. de Paula Brito, Rio de Janeiro, 1859, no. 1, p. 1; 'Introdução' in *Revista Fluminense*, a weekly of news, literature, science, pastimes, etc., Year I, No. 1, November 1868, pp. 1 and 2; *A Marmota na Corte*, Typographia de Paula Brito, No. 1, 7 September, 1840, p. 1; *Revista Ilustrada*, published by Ângelo Agostini, Rio de Janeiro, 1 January, 1876, No. 1;

at Court can serve as a caricature of this entire procedure: 'Behold the Marmot/In his various features/He is to be esteemed/By every creature//He speaks the truth/He says what he thinks/Each and every one/He loves and respects'. When, in another entire area of life, we give our walls a little scraping, we find the same effect of compositeness:

> The architectural change was superficial. Over the earth-work walls raised by slaves European wallpaper was pasted or pictures hung to create the illusion of modern interiors, like those of houses in the countries undergoing industrialisation. In some cases the pretence reached a level of absurdity: Greco-Roman architectural motifs – pilasters, colonnades, columns, friezes and such – were painted, with perfect perspective and shading, to suggest a neoclassical ambiance that was unrealisable with the techniques and materials locally available. In other cases the walls were painted with windows showing scenes of Rio de Janeiro or of Europe, to suggest a faraway outside world and certainly one different from the actual one that featured slave quarters, slaves and work yards.[19]

The passage refers to rural houses in the Province of São Paulo, second half of the nineteenth century. As for Rio de Janeiro:

> The changes corresponded to changes in custom, which now included the use of more refined objects, of crystal, of china and porcelain as well as such ceremonial forms of comportment as formal manners of serving at table. All along they conferred upon the whole assemblage, which was endeavouring to reproduce the life of European residences, an appearance of veracity. In that way the social strata that benefitted most greatly from an economic system based on slavery and directed exclusively to agricultural production attempted to create artificially, for their own use, environments with European urban characteristics, the functioning of which required a distancing from the actual slaves and the importation of everything or almost everything.[20]

'Apresentação' in *O Bezouro*, a humorous and satiric periodical, Year I, No. 1, 6 April, 1878; 'Cavaco,' in *O Cabrião*, No. 1, Typ. Imperial, São Paulo, 1866, p. 2. [Translation taken from Schwarz 1992, p. 32.] [N.B., as these titles are not thoroughly bibliographed in the original and, what is more, are not readily available, I have not included them in the upcoming Bibliography.]

19   Reis Filho n.d., pp. 14–15.
20   Reis Filho n.d., p. 8.

This comedy is to be seen in live action in the remarkable first chapters of Machado's *Quincas Borba*. Rubião, recent recipient of an inheritance, is constrained to trade his black slave for a French cook and a Spanish serving-man, in neither of whose company is he comfortable. In addition to gold and silver, the metals that speak to his heart's desire, he loves the bronze statuettes – a Faust and a Mephistopheles – that too are valuable. Weightier but equally indicative of the times are the words to our Republican anthem written in 1890 by the decadent poet Medeiros e Albuquerque. Progressivist emotions that lack naturalness: 'We cannot believe that in another age/Slaves there were in so noble a country' (the 'other age' being two years before, given that abolition was proclaimed only in 1888). The proclamation of 1817 by the Revolutionary Government of Pernambuco sounds every bit as 'off' in diction but with opposite intentions: 'Patriots, your properties, even for those most opposed to the ideal of justice, will be kept sacred'.[21] The statement refers to the rumours of emancipation that had to be quashed to calm the landowners. The life of Machado de Assis himself provides us an example; in it follow closely upon each other the combative journalist, enthusiast of the 'proletarian intelligences from the lower classes'; the author of chronicles and of verses on the occasion of the marriage of the imperial princesses; and finally the Knight and later Commander of the Order of the Rose. Against all this Sílvio Romero would inveigh: 'we must found a nationality aware of both its merits and its defects, of its strength and its weaknesses, and not throw together a pastiche, a sham like the Judas of the popular entertainments that serves merely to shame us in the eyes of the foreigner … Only one cure exists for so great a desideratum: to throw ourselves completely into the vivifying course of naturalistic and monistic ideas that are in the process of transforming the old world'.[22] Seen from this distance the replacement of one sham with another is so obvious as to be amusing, but it is also dramatic in its pointing out of how alien the language had to be in which our desire for authenticity was inevitably expressed. The Romantic pastiche had simply given way to a Naturalist pastiche. In sum, in the magazines, in customs, homes, national symbols, declarations of revolution, theory, and almost everything else, we always see, to quote Mário de Andrade, the same 'Harliquinish' composition – namely dissonance between the representation and what, if we give it serious thought, we know to be that representation's context. Solidified by its important role in the international market and later in domestic politics, the combination of large-holding and forced labour weathered the

---

21 Viotti da Costa 1968.
22 Romero 1883, p. 15.

colonial period, the empire, regencies, abolition, the First Republic, and still today is cause for controversy and armed conflict.[23] The path of our ideological life has been different, however, it too having been determined by the country's dependency: in effect we accompanied at a distance the steps of Europe. We must note in passing that it has been the ideology of independence that has transformed that combination into a problem – stupidly when it has insisted on an impossible autonomy and profoundly when it reflects on the problem. Both the tenacity of base social relations and the ideological volatility of the elites were part – the part that fell to us – of the dynamic of that so-to-speak 'solar', and certainly international, system that is capitalism. As a result, a large-holding, little changed itself, has seen Baroque, Neoclassical, Romantic, Naturalist, Modernist and other styles pass through, styles that in Europe were part of and reflected immense transformations in the social order. It might well be supposed that here they would lose their specificity, which, in part, did happen. Nevertheless, we have also seen that the disjuncture to which we were condemned by the workings of the international system of colonialism was inexorable. Indeed, so that we can see its further-than-national reach, we must observe that those workings, as they produced us, condemned … themselves. It is a well-known, though weakly theorised, secret. In the arts, as opposed to cultural theory, solutions come easily: there is always a way to adore, quote, parody, ransack, adapt, or devour all the styles and modes so that they reflect, by their flawed aspect, the very cultural embarrassment in which we recognise ourselves. But let's go back a little. To summarise: liberal ideas could not be put into practice while at the same time they were not something that could simply be discarded. They had been located in a special constellation, a practical constellation that formed a system that would continue to modify them. Therefore it helps little to insist on their obvious falseness. It is better to study them in their functioning, of which it – that is, the falseness – is a true part. We see Brazil, bastion of slavery, embarrassed to face up to them, for they were the ideas of the day, the most advanced on the planet (or almost so, since socialism had now appeared on the scene), and resentful that those ideas were useless to it. But they had been adopted with pride, in a mode of ornamentation, as proof of modernity and distinction. And they were, of course, revolutionary when they accompanied abolitionism. Subjected to the influence of place, without losing the pretensions that came with their origin, they gravitated according to a new logic, the proprieties and disgraces, the ambiguities and illusions of which were themselves peculiar. To know Brazil was to know of these displace-

---

23 About the reasons for that inertia, see Furtado.

ments, practised and experienced by all as a kind of fatality, for all of which there was no name since the improper use of names was their nature. Broadly felt to be a defect, well-known but little thought about, that system of improprieties doubtless lowered the level of ideological life and diminished the chances for genuine reflection. On the other side of the coin, it facilitated scepticism in matters of ideology, at times a complete and self-assured scepticism and moreover one compatible with a lot of talk. Pushed a little, it would inform the astonishing power of Machado de Assis's vision. Now the basis of this scepticism is surely not to be found in any thoughtful exploration of the limits of liberal thought. It lies, if it can meaningfully be put this way, at an intuitive starting-point that spared us that effort. Inscribed within a system that they failed to describe even in appearance, from the very beginning bourgeois ideas saw their pretension to embrace all of human nature disproven by the weight of daily evidence. If they were accepted, it was for reasons that they themselves could not accept. Instead of functioning as the horizon of thought, they appeared against a much vaster background, namely, the vicissitudes of privilege and favour, which relativised them. Their pretensions to universality were attacked at their very core. Thus what in Europe would be a great critical achievement could among us have been ordinary disbelief. Utilitarianism, egoism, formalism and what have you amounted to just one more clothing style among many, fashionable but uncomfortably ill-fitting. Thus we see that this world has important consequences for the history of culture: a complex assemblage of features in which at every turn the hegemonic ideology of the West is shown up as inadequate, as one more mania among manias. All of which is also a way of indicating the worldwide reach that our national peculiarities could attain. Something comparable, perhaps, to what was happening in Russian literature. In comparison to it even the greatest novels of French Realism seem somehow ingenuous. Why? If I may risk a guess, it is that in the Russian Empire the psychology of rational egoism and Enlightenment ethics, in spite of their pretensions to universality, came across as constituting a 'foreign' ideology and therefore one that was localised and relative. From within its historical 'belatedness' the country imposed upon the bourgeois novel a more complex picture. The caricatural figure of the person putting on Western airs, Francophile or Germanophile, frequently given a ridiculous allegorical name, the ideologues of progress, of liberalism, of reason, were all forms of bringing to the scene the modernisation that came with capital. These 'enlightened' men reveal themselves to be in turn lunatics, thieves, opportunists, brutes, egoists, parasites, etcetera. The system of ambiguities thus linked to the local use of the terms of Western thought – one of the keys to the Russian novel – can profitably be compared to what we have described for Brazil. The social reasons for the similarity are obvious. In Russia too modernisation got lost in the immensity of the territory and of social inertia and came into conflict with serfdom and its entailments: a shock experienced as national inferiority and shame by many, though giving others criteria with which to measure the folly of the progressivism and individualism that the West was imposing – and imposes – on the world. In that exacerbation of the clash in which progress is a disgrace and backwardness is a shame lies one of the deepest roots of Russian literature. Without forcing unduly a comparison between unequals, we can say that there is in Machado – for the reasons that I have sought to point out – a similar vein, something akin to Gogol, Dostoyevsky, Goncharov, Chekhov and perhaps others of whose work I am unaware.[24] In short, the very debasement of thought among us, which we have felt so bitterly and still today stifles the student of our nineteenth century, was a knot, a key nerve centre through which world history passes and, in passing, is revealed.[25]

Throughout the course of its social reproduction, Brazil tirelessly affirms and reaffirms European ideas, always in inappropriate ways. It is in the light of that fact that they will be both material and problem for literature. A writer may not be aware of that fact, nor does he need to be in order to use the ideas. But he will achieve a deep, attuned resonance only if he feels, registers and develops – or avoids – the displacement and the dissonance. While there is an indefinite number of ways of doing that, the contraventions are palpable and definable. Among them are ingenuousness, loquaciousness, narrowmindedness, imitation, rudeness, etcetera, specific, local effects of an alienation with a long reach – the absence of social transparency imposed by the colonial nexus and the subsequent dependency that carried it forward.

---

24 For a rigorous construction of our ideological problem along lines somewhat different from these, see Beiguelman, in which there are various quotes that seem as though they came from Russian novels. For example, the following from Pereira Barreto (Beiguelman 1967, p. 159): 'On one side are the abolitionists, riding upon a sentimental rhetoric and armed with a revolutionary metaphysics, pursuing abstract types in order to turn them into social formulas; on the other side are the landowners, silent and humiliated, in the attitude of those who recognise their guilt or meditate an impossible revenge.' Pereira Barreto was the proponent of a scientific agriculture – in the avant-garde of coffee cultivation – and he believed that abolition should be an automatic consequence of agricultural progress. Besides, he considered negroes to be an inferior race; it was a disgrace to depend upon them.

25 Antônio Cândido sets forth some ideas in this vein. He tries to identify a 'malandro' ['roguish'/'rogue'] lineage within our literature. See 'Dialética da malandragem' [Dialectics of Roguishness] in Candido 1993 as well as his paragraphs about anthropophagy in 'Digressão sentimental sobre Oswald de Andrade' [Sentimental Digression on Oswald de Andrade], in Candido 1970, pp. 84 ff.

With all this in place, the reader has heretofore learned precious little about our literary or general histories and could not yet even situate Machado de Assis. What good, then, are these pages to him? Instead of a 'panorama' and the correlative notion of environmental impregnation, always true and suggestive but always also vague and external, I have tried a different solution, namely to specify a social mechanism in the form in which it makes itself an internal and active element of the culture: the inescapable difficulty that Brazil over and over again forced upon its intellectuals in the very process of cultural reproduction. In other words, a kind of analysis of the historical ground of intellectual experience. I have sought to see in the gravitation of ideas a dynamic that has set us apart. My starting-place has been the common observation, almost a sensation, that in Brazil ideas were out of focus in relation to their use in Europe. And I have presented a historical explanation for that displacement, one that involved the relations around production and parasitism in the country, our economic dependency and its partner, namely the intellectual hegemony of a Europe revolutionised by capital. In sum, in order to analyse a national originality, sensed in everyday life, I have been constrained to reflect on the process of colonialism as a whole, which was international. The ongoing interplay between liberalism and favour are the opaque, local effects of a planet-wide mechanism. Now the daily circulation of practical ideas and points of view has been the immediate and natural material of literature once fixed forms lost their validity in the arts. It has therefore been the material for the novel, especially the Realist novel. What I describe, then, is the manner in which world history, structured and expressed over and over again in the form of its ever-varied local products, passes into writing, over which it now exercises an internal influence, whether the writer is aware or not, wishes it be so or not. In other words, I have defined a huge, heterogeneous but structured field that is a historical outcome and can be an artistic origin. As I have studied it I have seen that it differs from its European counterpart while using the same vocabulary. Therefore difference, comparison and distance form part of its definition. It is an internal matter, the displacement I have spoken of so much in which at one moment the logic seems to be ours, at another someone else's, but always exists in an ambiguous light, outcome uncertain. The result is a similarly singular chemistry the attractions and repulsions of which we have observed – and, to an extent, set forth in examples. It is natural, of course, that such material should pose original problems for the literature dependent on it. Without getting ahead of ourselves at this point, we can say only that, contrary to what is generally believed, artistic material thus shows itself to be far from formless: it is historically formed and in one way or other registers the social process to which it owes its existence. In forming it, in turn, the writer superimposes one form over the other, and it is on the success of that operation, that relationship with the pre-formed material – in which History lies unseen – that the profundity, strength and complexity of the results will depend. There is nothing automatic about those relationships; we shall see in detail how hard it was for our literature to arrange them in such a way as to produce the novel. And, to vary the same theme one more time, one can see that, sitting at a writing desk anywhere in Brazil facing the modest day-to-day goings-on, our novelist has always had as material, to be formed as well as he can, questions of world history. Yet he doesn't deal with those questions, if by 'deal' we mean 'deal directly.'

CHAPTER 2

The Importation of the Novel and Its Contradictions in Alencar

The novel existed in Brazil before there were Brazilian novelists.[1] When they came into being it was only natural for them to follow the models, good and bad, that Europe had instilled within our reading habits. A banal observation that nonetheless is replete with consequences: our imagination had been fixed into a form the basic presuppositions of which in great part were not otherwise to be found within the country or were to be found in altered form. So, was it the form – after all, the most prestigious at the time – that didn't fit, or was it the country? An example of this ambivalence, characteristic of peripheral nations, is given us by Machado de Assis' contemporary, the American Henry James, who would choose to emigrate to England attracted by its social complexity, which seemed to him more conducive to the imagination.[2] But let us examine the question more closely: to adopt the novel was to accept the way it dealt

---

1 As regards this point, read the suggestive study by Meyer.
2 Theobald, an assertive American in the Henry James short story 'The Madonna of the Future' (1873):
> 'We are the disinherited of Art!' he cried. 'We are condemned to be superficial! We are excluded from the magic circle. The soil of American perception is a poor little barren artificial deposit. Yes! we are wedded to imperfection. An American, to excel, has just ten times as much to learn as a European. We lack the deeper sense. We have neither taste, nor tact, nor power. How should we have them? Our crude and garish climate, our silent past, our deafening present, the constant pressure about us of unlovely circumstance, are as void of all that nourishes and prompts and inspires the artist, as my sad heart is void of bitterness in saying so! We poor aspirants must live in perpetual exile.' (James 1962, pp. 14–15.)

On a return to America to visit in Boston, James notes:
> I am 37 years old, I have made my choice, and God knows that I have now no time to waste. My choice is the old world – my choice, my need, my life ... My work lies there – and with this vast new world, *je n'ai que faire*. One can't do both – one must choose ... The burden is necessarily greater for an American – for he must deal, more or less, even if only by implication, with Europe; whereas no European is obliged to deal in the least with America. No one dreams of calling him less complete for not doing so. (I speak of course of people who do the sort of work that I do; not of economists, of social science people.) The painter of manners who neglects America is not thereby incomplete as yet; but a hundred years hence – fifty years hence perhaps – he will doubtless be accounted so. (James 1961, *Notebooks*, entry for November 25, 1881, pp. 23–4).

with ideologies. Now we have seen that among us, the fact that they preserved their original name and gravitation notwithstanding, they were out of place – an involuntary difference, the practical effect of our social formation. It fell to the writer, in his search for adaptation, to reiterate that out-of-placeness on a formal level, without which he would have been out of step with the objective complexity of his material – no matter how closely he followed the lessons of his masters. Achieving that goal would be Machado de Assis's great accomplishment. In sum, the very global dependency that forces us to think in inappropriate categories also induced us to create a literature in which there was no way for that inappropriateness to be brought to the fore. Put another way (and jumping ahead in my exposition), instead of constituting a constructive principle, the difference appeared, as it were, through the cracks, involuntary and unwanted, like a defect. One instance of the inferior intellectual level alluded to in the preceding chapter. Recalling the years of his intellectual formation, Alencar would write about the soirées of his childhood when he would read aloud to his mother and female relatives until the room was awash in tears. The books were *Amanda and Oscar*, *Saint-Clair of the Isles*, *Celestina* and others.[3] He mentions as well the reading rooms and his colleagues' literary libraries in the fraternities of the University of São Paulo: Balzac, Dumas, Vigny, Chateaubriand, Hugo, Byron, Lamartine, Sue and, later, Scott and Cooper – and the impression created in him by the success of *A Moreninha*, Macedo's first novel.[4] Why should he not try to write as well? 'What regal diadem could compare with the worth of that halo of enthusiasm that would encircle the name of "writer"?[5] There was no shortage of grand models, and beyond that there was the overall prestige and the patriotic desire to bestow upon one's country another of the advances of the modern spirit.[6] Nevertheless the immigration of the novel, particularly in its Realist vein, would present difficulties. No one would have felt uncomfortable frequenting in thought the salons and barricades of Paris. But to bring to our streets and drawing rooms the whole procession of sublime viscountesses, ruthless opportunists, renowned thieves, eloquent minis-

---

3 [The reference is one to prominent titles of the so-called 'female Gothic' popular novels of the late eighteenth and early nineteenth centuries. Similar in some respects to the American Harlequin romances, they were usually written by women, took up multiple volumes, were published inexpensively, and circulated in Europe sometimes in translation. The respective authors of the three mentioned titles, along with the dates of the titles' first known publication, are: Regina Maria Roche (1796), Isabelle de Montolieu (1831) and Charlotte Turner Smith (1791).] [These titles too are not included in the upcoming bibliography.]
4 Alencar 1959, vol. I.
5 Alencar 1959, vol. I., p. 159.
6 Cândido 1969, vol. II.

ters, imbecilic princes and visionary scientists, even if just their problems and the atmosphere that would come along with them, would seem totally out of place. But could the 'novel' exist without them? The great themes that provide the novel with its energy and in which its form is anchored – social climbing, the corrupting power of money, the clash between aristocratic and bourgeois modes of life, the antagonism between love and convenience, vocation and the need to make a living, how would such things work in Brazil? In modified form no doubt, but they did exist – beyond existing powerfully in imaginations; they existed with the same reality that the set of European ideas had for us. There was not ready to hand, however, a system for their modification and even less so for the effects that such a system might impose upon literary form. Such things would have to be discovered and developed just as, moreover, the aforementioned themes were not just there, waiting since time immemorial for the advent of the European novel. They arose, or took on their modern form, in the soil of continent-wide secular transition from the feudal era to the age of capitalism. In Europe too it was necessary to explore those themes, isolate and combine them, until there emerged a kind of inventory-in-common upon which all could draw, the bad, the mediocre and the great. It should be observed in passing that it is this cumulative and collective, although individual, aspect of literary creation that would enable the multitude of acceptable novels that Realism produced. At the forefront of current ideas and solutions, even if they did not go deeply into them, those books gave the impression of complexity and sustained readerly interest just as a good film does in our days. It was an accumulation that was difficult for Brazilian literature, whose motivations came – and come – from outside, to achieve. A disadvantage that today, on the contrary, has its advantages, converging very naturally with the bankruptcy of the grand tradition (to which the European intellectual has great difficulty adjusting) and arrival – as though at a key expression for our time – at the cultural discontinuity and arbitrariness which in Brazil, completely against our own will, has always obtained.

Reflective and resourceful writer that he was, Alencar responded to this situation in varied and often profound ways. His work is one of the treasure-troves of Brazilian literature down to today and, although at first glance it may seem otherwise, has points of continuity with Modernism.[7] Something of

---

7 ['Modernism' (Port. 'modernismo') is the name given to the various literary, artistic and general intellectual movements, centred in São Paulo, that flourished in Brazil in the period between the world wars, with considerable influence still today. Literary history sees it generally as a breaking-free of inherited models and the creation of truly Brazilian-voiced cultural production.]

Iracema finds its way into *Macunaíma*: the wanderings that interconnect with the adventures, the geographical specificity of the representation of Brazil, the mythological material, the Indian place-naming and white history. Something of *Grande Sertão* was already to be seen in *Til*, in the pacing of Jão Fera's exploits. And our imaginary iconography – of young maidens, of Indians, of forests – owes much of its social construction to Alencar's books. More generally – to avoid adding overly to the list – the resourceful, Brazilianizing vitality of his prose still today remains capable of inspiring us. That acknowledged, it is necessary as well to acknowledge that his work is never, strictly speaking, successful: it always contains something a little bit out of tune and – the adjective having been chosen after due deliberation – silly. It is interesting to observe that these weak points, looked at in a different perspective, are exactly his work's strong points. They are not accidental, nor are they the results of a lack of talent; to the contrary they constitute important, though failed, evidence of artistic breakthrough. They signal the places where the coming-together of the European mould and the local material, with which Alencar was an ardent sympathiser, ended up producing nonsense. Points that are therefore critical for our life and letters, manifesting as they do the objective discord – the ideological incongruities – that resulted from the transplantation of the novel and European culture to this country. In order subsequently to examine the solutions that Machado de Assis would give to those incongruities, we shall be looking in detail at instances of them in Alencar's urban novels. A curious commentary about those points of impasse is to be found in Nabuco, the pro-European intellectual, who understood them very well and detested them. As opposed to what is usually said, his dispute with Alencar – a tête à tête of giants according to Afrânio Coutinho – is poor in thought and lacking in substance. (The two even argue over who knows more French.) But it has the interest of having captured a specific situation. Alencar's Realism elicited a dual aversion from Nabuco: first for failing to keep up appearances and second for not ridiculing them with, let's call it, the refined and presentable license of French literature. It's like someone who has been away and, returning to his city, is mortified by the existence there of a house of ill repute – and its lack of chic. To Nabuco, Alencar's young women with all their airs seemed both improper and stupid, neither Romantic nor Naturalistic, which is well observed, although it focuses only on the weight side of the scale. His observations about the topic of the slave and about the Brazilianisation of the Portuguese language have a similar tenor. If Alencar had accepted such a critique he would have written either moralistic novels or European ones. Nabuco puts his finger on real weaknesses, but in order thereby to elide them; Alencar, by contrast, persistently includes them, guided by the sense of reality that enabled him to see in them precisely the new issues and the Brazilian element in them. In pointing them out without resolving them he doesn't make great literature, but he establishes and cultivates elements that would inform such literature – a further example of the tortuousness of the process of literary creation.

Studying the work of Macedo,[8] in which our novel tradition begins to take hold, Antonio Candido observes that it combines the Realism of detailed observation 'sensitive to the social conditions of the time' and the apparatus of Romantic emplotment.[9] Those are in fact two aspects of the same point of conformity, each of which merits separate discussion: one a pedestrian adherence 'to the humanly- and socially-lacking sphere of the carioca bourgeoisie' and a second aspect, which 'we might call "poetic" and ends up being the use of patterns more appropriately linked to the concept of "Romantic", as has just been suggested: tears, darkness, betrayal, and conflict'. The final product fails to meet the test of verisimilitude: 'So much so that we end up asking ourselves how it is possible for people so flat to become involved in the agonies to which Macedo submits them'. As we shall see, this same analysis, lightly adjusted, works as well for Alencar's urban novel. First, however, let us return to its basic elements. The verist touches and local colour expected of the novel of the time lend seriousness and a literary air to figures and anecdotes of our day-to-day world. The plot – the very principle of composition – finds its central motive in the ideologies of Romantic destiny, in potboiler versions for Macedo and some Alencar and in Realist versions for the Alencar of the stronger urban novels. Now, as we have seen, our day-to-day life was regulated by systems of favour, which were incompatible – in a sense we shall make clear further along – with melodramatic plots that are the stuff of Realism with Romantic influences. Being subject at the same time to both trivial realities and literary convention, our novel thus sets out in two canoes going in opposite directions, so it was inevitable that it would undergo stumbles in its own fashion, stumbles not of a sort to be seen in French novels, since the social history that gave life to the latter could be fully explored by that type of plot.

---

8 [Joaquim Manuel de Macedo (1820–82), was a Brazilian writer and educator. His novel *A moreninha* (The Little Brunette) of 1844 is considered by many literary historians to be the first Brazilian novel to seriously tackle Brazilian material.]

9 Cândido 1969, pp. 140–2. One should, indeed, consult the chapters in that title that deal with the novel. Their totality constitutes a theory of that genre's formation in Brazil and can be read as an introduction to Machado de Assis. Although not figuring in the 'formative' phase that the book deals with – and he is mentioned only a handful of times – Machado is one of its central figures, its vanishing point: the tradition is thought of, in part at least, with an eye to the use that Machado would make of it.

Seen from the point of view of origins, the disparity between plot and Realist notation makes manifest the juxtaposition of European mould and local setting (it matters not in this case that those appearances have already been transformed into literary material through the influence of that same Romanticism). Step number two: let's go on from origin-in-the-world map to the ideas that corresponded with it; we shall have returned, with a much clearer sense of underlying forces involved, to the problem of *composition itself* – in which Romantic ideologies, it matters not whether liberal or aristocratic but always with reference to the mercantilisation of life, figure as the pass key to the universe of favour. Faithful to observed (Brazilian) reality and to the model of the (European) novel, the writer without knowing it will be reinscribing a central incongruity in our mental life – without resolving it. Note that there is no simple consequence to be derived from the duality; in a country like Brazil with a dependent culture, its presence is inevitable and its consequences can be good or bad. It is a matter of judging case by case. Literature is not reasoned judgment, it is figuration: the movements of a renowned key that in point of fact opens nothing at all may perhaps have great literary interest. We shall see that in Machado de Assis it is the lock that opens the key.

Senhora is one of Alencar's most careful novels; its composition will serve as our starting point. It is a novel whose tone varies markedly. We can say that it is more relaxed at its periphery than at its centre: Lemos, our heroine's unscrupulous, self-serving uncle, as round as a Chinese vase and with looks like a piece of popcorn; old Camargo, a bearded farmer, coarse but straightforward; Dona Firmina, the heroine's maid and factotum, who gives her mistress's cheeks great loads of kisses and, when she sits down, is presented as accommodating 'her half-century of flesh'.[10] In other words, a simple, familial sphere in which there might be suffering and conflict without the sphere's continuity being brought into question, legitimated as it is by the characters' natural and sympathetic ability to get along on a day-to-day basis. The businessmen are scoundrels, the younger sisters selfless, the relatives self-serving, vices, virtues and flaws are openly admitted, so the prose that describes them doesn't overstep an accommodating propriety. It isn't conformist because it does not seek to justify, nor is it really critical, since it makes no push for change. The register rises when we pass to the more sophisticated social circle, which is limited to youth of marriageable age, a fact that presents no small interest, as we shall see. Here rule monetary calculation, consideration of appearances, and

---

10   Alencar 1959, vol. I, pp. 958, 966, 969, 1,065–6.

the course of love. Here too hypocrisy, complex by definition, combines with the ethical pretensions common to this sphere as well as with spontaneity, typical of Romantic feelings; they saturate the language with moral implications. Those implications lead the reader spontaneously to normative reflexion at the expense of simple evocative pleasures. The distant sources are the salon and the prose of Balzac. Finally, at the centre of this centre the voltage hits the roof when Aurélia, the book's heroine, is on stage. For this beautiful heiress, intelligent and much-courted, money is strictly a cursed intermediary: she casts an exacting eye on all men and on all things because of the fateful suspicion, from which nothing escapes, that they all have their price. Symmetrically, her sense of purity becomes exaggerated, a sense articulated in terms of the most conventional morality. Veering between the extremes of purity and degradation, one perhaps feigned, the other intolerable, Aurélia creates a dizzying trajectory of great ideological import, for it traces the 'reach' of the 'modern god', namely money. At the same time that movement is a bit banal: its two poles lack complexity. Wealth is reduced to a problem of virtue versus corruption, which is inflated so far as to become the measure of everything. The consequence is a prose dense with disgust on one hand and deep conformity on the other – self-righteous indignation, which is by no means original with Alencar. It is one of the complexes of the century, the mark of the Romantic melodrama, of the future radio soap-opera, and not long ago it could be seen in UDN railings against the corruption of the times.[11] But let's go back and readjust the previously-made distinction in tone between the peripheral characters and the central ones. The question isn't one of degree, it is one of kind. In the case of the former, Alencar tries to highlight the evidence of consensus, localist and often burlesque, just as tradition, habit, affect, in all their various manifestations, had consolidated them. This world is what it is; it doesn't aim toward another world different from it into which it might be transformed. Or, put another way, it is unproblematic: it excludes normative-universal intentions, part and parcel of Romantic-liberal prose – and of the Aurélia sector of the book. We shall see that such is the tone as well of another important novel in our literature, *Memoirs of a Militia Sergeant*. And let us be clear in passing: there is nothing that would hinder that consensus from itself bearing the imprint of literary traditions. By contrast, in the second case, namely that of the central characters, the present is perceived as a problem, as a state of affairs to be rejected. That accounts for the greater weight, the 'seriousness' of its passages – even though, literarily speaking, it is always a relief when Alencar returns to

---

11 [The UDN was a Brazilian political party.]

the other mode, which contributes many pages of wit and narrative power. Nevertheless, it is with the second mode, laden with principles, polarised by alternations between the sublime and the vicious, that the novel joins the uncompromising line of the Realism of the time, dedicated precisely to showing the present day in all its contradictions – instead of local difficulties, the tensions inherent in bourgeois society looked at from a universal viewpoint. The latter is the style that would prevail. By way of summary, let us say that in *Senhora* reflexion derives its pith and its style from the worldly sphere of money, of social-climbing, giving it, therefore, primacy within the composition. Like the great characters of the *Comédie humaine*, Aurelia experiences her torment and seeks to express it, by transforming it into an intellectual element of her day-to-day existence and a formal element – as we shall see when we turn to the plot – responsible for the novel's denouement. That reflexive and problematic tone, however, albeit well designed in itself, is not wholly convincing and comes off badly next to the other sector of the novel. It seems pretentious, has something ill-fitting about it, and is in need of more detailed analysis.

It must be taken into account in this connexion that in *Senhora* formal predominance of the characters and their social importance do not coincide. If it is only natural that the worldly scene should stand in opposition to impoverished provincial life, it is strange that the former should include minor civil servants and the daughters of well-off businessmen. And it is even stranger that the adults should be marginalised: in the court parties the mothers are never anything more than respectable ladies who keep an eye on their daughters and never tire of criticising Aurélia's uninhibited ways, 'unfitting for well-brought-up young ladies'.[12] The same with the men, who, unless they are young, are all caricatures. In short, the up-to-date tone is used, in a mode of adornment, for the nubile and fashionable youth, but it is hardly the synthesis of the experience of a social class, aside from becoming problematic if it is carried out very far. It has no currency among characters already serious; they are excluded from the literary focus and from the movement of ideas that has to sustain the novel through to its end. In terms of composition, therefore, the book stays within the confines of frivolity – which compromises its ambitious construction. Such discord is not to be found in the model; to see the difference one has only to recall the importance that middle-aged adultery, politics and the arrogance of power have in the worldly scenes in Balzac. Alencar preserves his tone and a variety of the verbal techniques, but they are displaced by the local scene required by

---

12   Alencar 1959, vol. I, p. 952.

the need for verisimilitude. We shall return to consideration of that difference. For now, let us look at the complexity, the variety of dimensions, of this borrowing. First it is necessary to remove, but not completely, the pejorative sense of the very notion of borrowing. Consider what it meant in terms of audacity and air of contemporaneity to have a character – and a woman to boot – deal freely with issues that at the same time or not much earlier European Realism was dealing with. In a very clear sense it is an accomplishment, no matter the literary result. Something similar for our generation that turned twenty in the 60s, when they jumped from reading handbooks of philosophy and sociology in Spanish to the books of Foucault, Althusser, Adorno. Caught between an old alienation and a modern one, the well-formed mind does not hesitate. Small-scale and subaltern imitation fell by the wayside, and the novelist forced himself to enter upon an overall conceptualisation of the world, establishing a contemporary horizon for his reflections. The novel was attaining the seriousness that Romantic poetry had gained for itself some time before. Finally, consider the very act of this imitation, which is more complicated than it seems. In his preface to *Sonhos d'ouro* [Golden Dreams] Alencar writes: 'to accuse these books of being foreign in conception is, if the critics will pardon my saying so, not to know Rio society, which is out there enjoying itself in the streets and the halls in Parisian ribbon and bows, speaking the universal argot, which is the language of progress, a jargon bristling with terms from French, English, Italian, and now German as well. How could one presume to photograph such a society without copying its features?'[13] The first step, therefore, is taken by social life and not by the literature, which will then end up imitating an imitation.[14] But inevitably progress, and Parisian finery, inscribed themselves here under another head; if we pick up again our term from earlier, we can call it 'second-degree ideology'. The novelist arrives on the scene, him- or herself a part of this bemusing social state of affairs, and not only copies the new ways copied from Europe but copies them according to European practice. Now this second copy disguises, but not completely, the nature of the first, which, for literature, is unfortunate – and it emphasises the ornamental element. Adopting the form and tone of the Realist novel, Alencar honours its tacit understanding of the sphere of ideas. Therein lies the problem: he treats as serious the ideas

---

13   Alencar 1959, vol. I, p. 699.
14   The situation is comparable to that of Caetano Veloso singing in English. Accused by the 'nationalists,' he said it was not he who brought the Americans to Brazil. He had always wanted to sing in that language, which he had listened to on the radio since he was little. And of course, singing English with a northern Brazilian pronunciation, he provided a substantive moment in our history and imagination.

that have taken a different form among us. He treats second-degree ideologies as though they were first-degree. Which adds up to an exaggerated and a-critical style despite the scandalous subject matter – and one devoid of that malice without which the modern tone, among us, becomes absence of historical consciousness. Again we stumble across the knot that Machado de Assis will untie.

In sum, even in the realm of letters foreign debt is inevitable, always complex, and not merely a part of the specific work in which it appears. It occurs in the culture generally, to variable benefit, and the borrowings can easily be moral or political audacities – or ones of taste – at the same time as they are literary blunders. Which of those contexts is of greatest importance? Nothing, unless it be professional conditioning, requires us to have recourse only to the aesthetic criterion. We are seeking to illuminate a moment of de-provincialisation, the argumentative disposition within the tone that predominates in *Senhora* – without, however, failing to include its negative aspects or hiding its structural weaknesses. But let us again go back: in its self-disposition the book's tone is daring and aggressive; it would like to be regarded as a voice of its moment in time. But its place in the overall composition makes us see in that serious impulse a mere drawing-room ornament. And that is the last word on the subject. For some reason – one that the reader should by now be beginning to glimpse – the harsh moral dialectic of money lends itself to description of the frivolous youth but does not touch the rich landowner, the man of business, the middle-class mother or the poor governess, whose lives remain oriented by the rules of favour or of simple brutality. Nevertheless, these are the characters who make the novel feel populated; although secondary, they constitute the wider social milieu within which the central figures circulate and of whose importance they serve as the measure. In other words our procedure has been the following: after characterising the structure of the novel's plot, we have related it to the specific circle that it describes – all in the terms that the novel itself sets out. Then we have seen what that restricted circle is like considered in relation to the place it occupies within the societal space, albeit a fictional space. What authority does its discourse have? What decides is the ebb and flow within our second look, at the background characters: it subverts the tone of the book and its intentions. Diction contradicts composition, which is the exact opposite of what is to be seen in the model: Balzac's sensationalistic and generalising style, so artificially constructed, correlates with an extraordinary effort of *condensation*, to the extent that the style gradually becomes less and less uncomfortable as we convince ourselves of its deep continuity with the innumerable occasional profiles from the 'periphery' that displace, reflect, invert, modify – in sum, play a part in – the central conflict, in which they are all involved in one way or another.[15] Let's take the example of the discourse, disillusioned and 'very central', of one of the Balzacian *grandes dames*: it is defiant, suggestive, vulnerable, opportunistic and overbold just as are, when they 'casually' appear, those of the criminal, the seamstress, the pederast, the banker, the soldier.[16] The novel's dizzying course departs from the natural, borders closely on the ridiculous, but balances that distance – that level of abstraction – with a large counterweight of knowledge and experience that far exceeds those of any individual and is not merely a literary fact: it is the sum of a social process of reflexion from the viewpoint of, let us say, a man of spirit. This is the experienced and sociable fifty-something who, according to Sartre, is the narrator of French Realism.[17] We shall speak later of the historical presuppositions underlying that form. For now suffice it to say that this manner of reflexion derived from a real, and new, process, itself somewhat dizzying and hardly 'natural', that was turning European society inside out, visiting similar results upon Brazilian society as well, while not succeeding in transforming the latter's core: we are speaking of the diffusion – with its infinite effects – of the commodity form, of money, as the basic nexus of all social life. It is the gigantesque magnitude, simultaneously global and local, of this movement, that supports the changeability, the theatrical variety of Balzac's work – permitting free passage across areas with apparently incommensurable social experiences. In summary, we inherited along with the novel, but not only through it, a posture and a diction that do not accord well with the local circumstances, that indeed clash with them. Machado de Assis would exploit mightily that misfit, which is naturally comic. To address the point directly, the main thrust of our argument is that Alencar's peripheral and localist agenda will come to the centre of the

---

15 Commenting on habits of consumption in Brazil at the end of the century, Warren Dean notes that import commerce had transformed products that industrialisation had made common in Europe and the United States into luxury items for us. See Dean 1971, p. 13.

16 'Compared to other forms of representation, the multiplicity of Balzac is what comes closest to objective reality. Nevertheless, the more it approaches that reality the more it moves away from the habitual, common or average manner of directly reflecting that reality. In fact, the Balzacian method abolishes the strict, customary, routine limits of that *immediate reproduction*. Thus it contradicts the habitual ways of considering reality, and therefore it is felt by many to be 'exaggerated,' 'overworked' etc. ... Moreover, his ingenuity is not limited to his brilliant and spicy; rather it manifests itself in the well-phrased revelation of the essential, in the extreme tension among the contrary elements that compose it.' Lukács 1965, p. 483.

17 Sartre 1948, pp. 176 ff. For a comic condensation of Balzacian tics, see the incomparable imitation of them that Proust does in *Pastiches et mélanges*. The ridiculous, sedative aspect of Balzac's generalisations is mentioned by Walter Benjamin in his study on the *flâneur*, in Benjamin 1969, pp. 39–40.

Machadian novel, and that relocation affects the 'European' motifs and the serious grandiloquence central to Alencar's work – which don't disappear but take on a grotesque tonality. In Machado the problem is solved. But let us return to *Senhora*. Our argument has perhaps seemed arbitrary: how can a few secondary characters occupying a small part of a novel determine its tone so decisively? In fact, if they were eliminated altogether from the text the dissonance would disappear. But what would be left would be a French novel. That is not the intention of the author, who, much to the contrary, wanted to nationalise the genre. Nevertheless, that small secondary world, introduced as local colour and not as an active, structural element, something like a decorative border albeit one without which the novel would not be taking place in Brazil, dislocates the weight and effect of the course of action on the primary plane. That is the issue: if the local feature has the power to locate the novel, it also has the power not to leave its diction unsettled. For the reasons we have already seen and others we shall see, that arrangement strikes a false note. In other words, the artistic problem, the problem of formal unity, has its root in the specificity of its ideological grounding and, in the last analysis, through it, in our dependent-independent position in the concert of nations – even though the book itself doesn't deal with any of this. What it does is express literarily the difficulty of integrating localist and European tonalities commanded respectively by the ideology of favour and that of liberalism. Not that the novel could in fact eliminate that opposition, but it could have sought an arrangement in which those elements do not constitute an incongruity but rather a regulated system with its own logic and its – our – problems dealt with in their viable dimensions.

What we have done up to here, rather than explain, has been to set out attributions: one tone for us, another for them, a European plot, Brazilian anecdotes, and so on. To escape the accidents of paternity, however, the contingent factor of geographical origin needs to be replaced with the forms' stable and ineluctable sociological underpinnings. More precisely, let us say that of the more or less contingent set of conditions under which a form is born it retains and reproduces some – without which it would not make sense – that *become its literary effect*, its 'reality effect',[18] the world it signifies. This is what interests us: from the transfer to the status of sociological presupposition a part of the original historical conditions now reappears, with its same logic, but on the fictional plane and therefore formal. In this sense forms are the abstracts of specific social relations and that is how, at least in my view, the difficult passage from social history to properly literary questions, questions of composition –

---

18   An expression from Althusser, but with a different philosophy.

that have to do with an internal logic and not a logic of origin – is carried out. We said for example that there are two dictions in *Senhora* and that one predominates inappropriately over the other. The astute reader probably recognises, sensing the similarity, that one of them comes from European Realism while the other is more akin to family and localist orality. As explanation, however, that recognition does not get us fully to the issues. Why shouldn't the two modalities be compatible if incompatibility is a formal problem rather than a geographical one? Why can't the form of European Realism be Brazilian? The latter question has the merit of turning perspective upside down: once we have seen that origin is not argument we can also see how decisive its real weight is in the matter. In the final analysis, a few important formal borrowings; indication of the presuppositions that a borrowed form brings with it, which have come to be its effect; description of the materials to which this form is being applied; and finally the literary results of this displacement – these will be our topics.

To begin, let us look at how the story develops. Aurélia, a very poor, virtuous young woman, loves Seixas, a modest, and slightly weak-minded, young man. Seixas asks her to marry him but then backs off in favour of another young woman who has a dowry. Aurélia suddenly receives an inheritance. She would have pardoned Seixas's inconstancy but cannot pardon his pecuniary motive. Without revealing her identity, she offers her ex-boyfriend a marriage in secret [in the dark], one with a large dowry but against receipt. The young man, who is in debt, accepts. That is where the principal plot line actually starts. To humiliate him and avenge herself upon him, but also to test his resolve, not to mention for reasons of simple sadism – there is a little bit of each of those motives – Aurélia begins to treat her recently-purchased husband like a possession: she reduces the marriage of convenience to its mercantile dimension, the implications of which reduction dominate the plot. To the point that the four stages of the story are entitled 'The Price', 'Settlement', 'Possession' and 'Redemption'. As this rigour in the structuring of the conflict indicates, plot and characters have Balzacian lineage. With much suffering and reflection, they carry this great theme of contemporary ideology to its ultimate and improbable conclusion (although there is a reconciliation at the end, which we shall talk about later). Aurélia derives from that strict and unyielding family of avengers, alchemists, usurers, artists, social climbers, and so on, in the *Comédie humaine*; like them she latches onto an issue – one of those that captivated the imagination of the century – without which her life is devoid of meaning. As a consequence, the logic and historical destiny of a prominent issue become determining elements in the organisation of the plot, taking on the force of a formal principle – among other things. It is not that the characters incarnate an abstract notion like Harpagon incarnates greed in Molière. It is an abstraction that can combine with all kinds of specifics of biology, psychology and social position – a voluntary and problematic element of personal make-up: it dictates the destiny of those other factors. Like a flash of light across the night sky, these reflective and emphatic characters cut across the social landscape and leave behind, in addition to wonder at their impetuous actions, the implacable trace of the contradictions that show society at odds with its own ideals. Taking back up the thread of our exposition, we can say that what we are dealing with is a narrative model in the material of which ideologies of the first degree figure – certainties such as equality, republic, the redeeming power of science and of art, romantic love, merit and social mobility – ideas, in fine, that in nineteenth-century Europe support unequivocally the value of human existence.[19] In this sense the Realist novel was a huge illusion-crushing machine. To understand its importance it is necessary to see it as a whole, an active movement crossing national borders, disrespecting the hierarchy of things: one after another it sets up the dearest convictions of the time, links them to the time's strongest and most gifted characters, and lets them be broken apart along the plot's course by the pitiless machinery made up of money and social class. Hence the intellectual weight of this movement, its daring posture as friend of truth – which is taken up by Alencar. Here we come to our problem again: Brazil was importing a model whose involuntary effect was to give standing and scope to ideas – tone, energy, drama – that were at variance with what Brazilian life conferred upon them. Or, from the point of view of composition: without coordination with the construction of the secondary characters responsible for local colour. What does Aurélia's universalising and polemical discourse have to say to those characters, who are above all else interested simply in survival? We shall see how in such circumstances Realist audacity will have its meaning transformed.

For another example, consider Aurélia's 'Machiavellianism', the self-confident way with which she takes advantage of the machinery of her society. The girl who had the good fortune to inherit, is at first upset by the venality of her male counterparts. After giving the matter more thought, she makes a plan and buys the husband she loves. The victim of money in effect goes to its school and finally puts her trust in it – its odious mechanisms – to achieve happiness. She thus joins the illustrious number of those 'superior' creatures who

---

19   As an example see the pages by Lukács on the role of Romanticism in the Realist novel. Being a spontaneous ideology arising from the nonconformist anticapitalism of the nineteenth century, the Romantic vision was novel material obligatorily, so to speak: ideology of characters and literary climate that the plot tears apart. See 'Balzac, Critic of Stendhal,' Lukács 1965.

escape the empire of fortune and social mobility to the extent that they succeed in understanding it and manoeuvre to their advantage with respect to it. In their proper time and place those characters, with whom Realist fiction is full, were figures of truth. They freed themselves from obsolete traditions, they were not deceived by morality, and they purchased their farsightedness with the hardening of their hearts. It is a basic situation of the nineteenth-century novel; the vagaries of love and of social position, brought about by the bourgeois revolution, butt up against inequality which, although changed, continues being a fact of life; those desires must be put on hold, calculations made, one must manipulate oneself and others … only finally to discover, when wealth and power have been acquired, that one is no longer fully the hope-filled youth from the first chapters. In a thousand variations, this formula in three acts would be fundamental. Between the ardours at the beginning and the disillusionment at the end there is always the same interlude in which the principles of modern life have unrestricted sway: the machinery of money and 'rational' self-interest, anonymous and decisive, does its work, thereby putting a contemporary seal on the journey through trial after trial that is the destiny of heroes since time immemorial. Such are the consequences, from the viewpoint of bourgeois individualism, of the general victory of exchange value over use value – also referred to as alienation – which becomes the touchstone for the interpretation of the times. The literary effect and social presuppositions of that plot line, at the first moment of calculation that is its central lever, lie in the autonomy – are sensed as a congealment of the emotions, as reification – of the economic and political spheres, which are seen to function separately from the others according to an 'inhuman', mechanical rationality. As regards the economy the cause lies in the automatic nature of the market, in which objects and the workforce are considered the same thing and which acts, from the viewpoint of personal merit, as an arbitrary rollercoaster. As regards the political sphere, in the historical period begun with the advent of the modern state, according to the teachings of Machiavelli, its rules have nothing to do with moral norms. In the two spheres, as well as in regard to social mobility, which in a certain sense is an intermediate area, social life is affected in a negative and implacable way, and it is only by confronting it that something is saved.[20] This and no other is the backdrop against which the novel's disen-

---

20   'It is only with the eighteenth century and within "bourgeois society" that the different forms of social relation present themselves to the individual as simple instruments for the attainment of his or her private goals and as external necessity.' Marx, 'Einleitung' [Introduction], p. 6. See as well *Die Theorie des Romans* (Lukács 1971b) and 'Geschichte und Klassenbewusstsein' (Lukács 1971a, ch. 4). Also Goldmann 1964.

gagement – sometimes exhilarating, sometimes sinister – between individual and the social order, becomes poetic. Solitary and free, purpose stamped on their forehead, the characters of novels plan their financial, amorous or worldly moves. Some succeed by intelligence and toughness, others by marriage or crime, still others fail, and finally there exist the symbolic ones who make a pact with the devil. In all of them a certain grandeur, let's call it 'satanic grandeur', derived from their radical loneliness and firm commitment to use their head to achieve happiness. Even Seixas, a watered-down grandchild of Rastignac, makes a calculation of this sort: he is treated as merchandise? well then, he accepts the role, and with such rigour that Aurélia, exasperated and finally defeated by his obedience, ends up imploring him to return to behaving like a human being. In terms of our problem: these are fables that owe their symbolic force to a world that never existed in Brazil. Its form is the tacit metaphor of the society that has been demythified (*entzaubert* [disenchanted] in the terminology of Max Weber) and mystified – a society that has resulted from bourgeois rationality, or rather from the generalisation of mercantile exchange.

Those matters thus established, we can say that only in theory can direct comparison between a literary form and a social structure take place, since the latter, being at the same time both impalpable and real, cannot appear in person between the covers of a book. Literary experience proper is other, and it is to it that good theory should direct itself: it lies in the agreement or disagreement between form and the matter to which that form is applied, matter that is marked and formed by real social forces, of whose logic it becomes the more or less awkward representative within the literary piece. It is, therefore, the form of that material that will occupy us in working between the two. What, then, are those formal embryos that establish localist accuracy and contrast with the certainties in which the model – which we imitated – of the European novel is based? We spoke some pages back of a 'more relaxed tone'. Let us return to the problem, now with regard to the plot. The first part of the novel, entitled 'The Price', ends in suspense and climax on the wedding night: Seixas is 'singing his love song, that sublime ode of his heart' when Aurélia interrupts and declares, receipt in hand, that he is a 'bought man'. Face to face 'the chaste first fruits of holy conjugal love' on the one hand and the intolerable 'hundred *contos*' in dowry on the other. Within the confines of the stark either-or opposition consecrated by Romantic ideology, the antagonism between ideals and money could not be more highly charged.[21] There the chapter ends. The second part opens simply and casually, in another register, greatly benefitting from the con-

---

21   Alencar 1959, vol. I, pp. 1,026, 1,028–1,029.

trast. It goes back in time in order to tell the story of Aurélia and her family, from its modest origins up to the thousand-*conto* inheritance. In the process, we leave the elegant sphere, the scene is now poor, in an outlying area or in the country's interior. It will be seen that the stories here – subplots that do not play a role in determining the form of the book – are of another sort. Pedro Camargo, for example, is the natural child of a well-off landowner, whom he fears worse than death itself. He goes to Rio to study medicine. He is attracted to a poor girl, doesn't have the courage to tell his father, marries her in secret, she too having to run away from home since there is opposition in her family as well, on the grounds that Pedro is illegitimate and might not receive an inheritance. From that marriage are born Aurélia and a simple-minded boy.[22] With his fear of confessing to his father, the student returns to the plantation, where in the course of time he dies. He leaves his wife and children in Rio in an awkward position, as a family with no known father. The women sew to make a living, the son becomes a clerk, etcetera. Observe in this summary that although elements of the Realist novel are present, they are presented in a completely different way: the grandfather – from whom Aurélia will later inherit her fortune – does not come across as reprehensible because he has had illegitimate children nor is the son condemned, either because he didn't move mountains in the name of love or in the name of medicine, which was not his vocation, nor is his wife depreciated for having disrespected family and propriety, nor is her family, which after all is large and poor, condemned because it doesn't take in a penniless student. In other words, love, money, family, decorum, profession are not there in that absolute sense of secular priesthood in which they are cast in bourgeois ideology, the imperative exigencies of which dramatise and elevate the tone of the main part of the book. They do not constitute first-degree ideology. The formal consequences of this situation are many. First, the tension is lowered, which relaxes normative stridency and its central position as the dividing line between what is acceptable and what is not. Not being an obligatory moment for the collective destiny, the ideological conflict does not centre the narrative economy but rather appears to play an incident-related, circumstantial part. And it does not permit that amalgam of individualism and Declaration of the Rights of Man upon which the classic plot of the Realist novel depends for its vibrancy. The solutions are not ones of principle, they are ones of convenience, and they conform to immediate circumstances. Arrangements that would have been considered degrading in the bourgeois world are, in this sphere, the stuff of life. Note as well the episodic character of the story, the

---

22   Alencar 1959, vol. I, p. 1,038.

dispersed nature of its conflicts, which in fact presuppose the aforementioned 'relaxed' state, without which the poetry of erratic movement – so Brazilian – would end up being clouded over with moralism. As for the prose, it turns out that its literary quality is derived not from its critical force and its depiction of a problem but instead from verbal felicity, a keen eye, pacing, all of which are directly mimetic virtues that keep easy and sympathetic company with common speech and trivial ideas. A stream of events evoked with no inconsiderable art and infinitely extendable that form something like a repertoire of the thinkable destinies in this world of ours. Thus we are close to orality and perhaps close as well to the 'causo' [tale for its own sake, 'yarn'], simpler in structure than the novel but in tune with the illusions – themselves individualistic – of our social universe. A literary complement to the ideological predominance of favour: the absence of normative absolutes reflects, if we can put it this way, the arbitrariness of the will, to which we all have to conform. Hence the attractiveness for moderns of this mode of narration in which the absolutes that still today suck away our energy and morale appear relativised, because they are linked to a motile and human grounding – illusory, we repeat – for interpersonal relations. To fully appreciate the ideological distance traversed in that change of register, let us say that it turns on or off like a switch the fetishism inherent in the civilised world of capital: a fetishism that isolates and makes absolute what we call 'values' (art, morality, science, love, property, etcetera and, above all else, economic value itself) and in separating them from the whole of social life makes them both irrational in substance and depositories, for the individual, of all available rationality: a kind of insatiable taxman to whom we owe our existence and whom we continue conscientiously to pay for it.[23]

---

23   For a construction of the contrast between pre-capitalist narrative and novel carried out against the background of the transition from artisanship to industrial production – a transition that did not take place in Brazil – see the admirable essay by Walter Benjamin on the narrator, in *Schriften* [Writings], vol. II. Ideally – and with some sense of peril – we can say that the 'causo' submits to the experience of its hearers, and to the tradition in which they make their lives, the inexhaustible simplicity of an anecdote. Experience and tradition, themselves composed of anecdotes, into the store of which this most recent, before it is completely told, is beginning to be incorporated. A story that stands out for the skill that informs it against the backdrop of the varied repertory that constitutes the common wisdom is the poetry of this genre – from which conceptual knowledge is banned, knowledge that has no lived collateral and no translation into another anecdote. It is the opposite of what happens with the novel, the adventures in which are permeated and explained by the general but counter-intuitive mechanisms of bourgeois society. The poetry of this form is to be found in the 'modern' – and artistically difficult – combination of lived experience, rendered, naturally, through mimetic effort, and abstract and critical knowledge referring principally to the social predominance of exchange value and the thousand varieties of

Just one novel but two incompatible yet superimposed reality effects, that is the question. Aurélia is bizarre, her trajectory will be that of the novel and her reasons, which, to be taken seriously, must presuppose the classic order of the bourgeois world, are transformed into a formal principle. But around her the

---

the contradiction between formal equality and real inequality. Harshness and logical consequences are among its marks of quality. Let's therefore say that in the novel the incident is permeated by generalisation but that its generality is referred to a particular type of society, or – better – to an historical moment in such a society encoded in the central conflict. Now in the 'causo' the incident is free of explanation and therefore will be inscribed – despite its total localism – in the a-historical and generic treasure trove of the motivations and destinies of our species, seen according to the idea of the diversity of men and peoples, and not of the transitory nature of social regimes. The 'causo' contributes to a case by case repertoire of human situations and regional traditions: it serves to provide information and to entertain; it fortifies the person who knows how to hear it and shows him how to live. While the novel, which on the contrary knows only how to disillusion, has a commitment to the truth about life in a specific social formation and plays a part in a movement of criticism, even when it does not wish to. A most historical form – into which is freely incorporated that knowledge called scientific, particularly history, psychology and economics, in addition to the intentions to portray an era and to denounce – among us the novel was able up to a certain point to obstruct the literary figuration of the country. Such is the paradox. While the 'causo', incomparably less differentiated, bathed in the all-but-eternal and unspecific outpouring of the oral narrative, combines an a-historical outlook – the snares of life – and an unfettered appreciation for the reproduction of circumstance, which allows it to achieve a realism that among us the Realism of literary tradition not only did not attain but actually hindered. Nevertheless, it is clear that Alencar is not a teller of 'causos' but a writer. Because of one of those happy errors of Romantic literature he combines the authentic popular vein with modern Romanticism, restorative of the past, the broad, sustained rhythm of which constructs the symbiosis of meditation and spontaneity – the profound and natural connection with nature and community, feigned in his 'visionary' posture – that is this school's poetry and the sense of the world that it contrasts with bourgeois society. In a pure state this second movement of the imagination is seen in *Iracema*, in which the world being evoked never allows itself to be in the indifferent distance of objectivity. From sentence to sentence, or even less, the image is always passing, approaching, disappearing in the distance, compensating for another prior one, in space, in time, in affection – 'inspired' changeability that undoes the sclerosis of pure objectivity and restores the interested and thrilling element in memory and perception. In this sense see as well *O guarani* [The Guarani] and the beautiful opening description in *O tronco do ipê* [The Trunk of the Ipê Tree]. Everything taken into account, it is the rhythm of the grand Romantic meditation, in which by dint of silence and mental intensity the world's complexity is apprehended and retained, to be recomposed – in minutes of exalted plenitude and clarity – according to the flowing, unmutilated order of the imagination. Note, however, that in such visions, affirmative though they may be, in the English poets or in Hölderlin for example, the world composed is always unreal – the shaky, unstable world of a visualisation governed by the inner sense – whose plenitude 'returns' to men the sense of nature and of life that modern society has taken from them. On that score there is an important distinction to be made: Alencar's nature contains

environment is one of patronage and protection. Old Camargo, Dona Firmina and Mr. Lemos, the decent Abreu and the honest Dr. Torquato, Seixas's family, the ease with which Seixas arranges sinecures for himself, are all characters, lives and styles implying an entirely different order. Formally, what predomin-

much of that world, it is effectively permeated with nostalgia, but there are times when it becomes the Brazilian countryside and nothing more. Where the Romantics, polemicising against their own time, imaginarily worked to renew perception and nature, Alencar contributed to the glory of his country by singing its countryside and teaching his countrymen to see it. The magic of Romanticism enabled him to value his land, not to rediscover it in opposition to his least sensitive contemporaries. Thus among us Romantic exaltation lost its negative force and ended up establishing the pattern of our patriotism on the matter of countryside. The prestige of a modern literary school consecrated the land that others considered primitive, and the discovery of our land consecrated the truth of the literary school (see Cândido 1969, vol. II, p. 9). With great satisfaction and sense of progress our elites caught up with the sentiment that mandates despair of civilisation. That is what is called being a young country. Hence the odd superposition in *Iracema* of the poetry of distance, gilding with Romanticism the Indian names and geographical accidents and of properly informative and propagandistic intention – a superposition that creates room for a zone of indifferentiation between literature and national chauvinism, nostalgia and the post card, a vein retrieved humouristically – and only in that therefore true – in the early poetry of the Modernists. In an ignoble version, because deprived of its ingenuousness, the confusion of paradise and empirical country – the 'gentle lie fest' of which Mário de Andrade spoke – is now the source of official publicity. Be that as it may, the whiff of Romantic meditation reached the Realist novel as well, albeit diluted by the extension of the form's prose and contradicted by the mundane subject matter. In place of nature and the village, the whole developed totality of the social world: in order to offer the equivalent of the contemplative plenitude of the poet, the novelist is obligated to merge in his prose the necessary mass of factual knowledge, his critico-analytical elaboration, and, lastly, a synthesis that completely contradicts the tendency of the century in which the three requirements should squabble among themselves, as they continue to do. Once again, the prime example is Balzac. His visionary posture, practised but not always convincing, presents itself as the awesome faculty of encompassing in a single spiritual look the France of the capital; of sounding out its complex dynamic on the basis of any suggestive detail; of being able to fantasise freely with respect to it while always saying rare, authoritative and original truths, etcetera. The nature of the content, however, gets in the way: only with great difficulty does reflexive intimacy with the bourgeois world provide support for a climate of meditation – transactions are not countrysides nor are they destinies – whence the occasional impression one gets that the visionary titanism of Balzac is also an oversized impulse to gossip. Alencar, who seeks the same atmosphere, gets good results when he is retrospective: leaving the foreground conflict in suspense – which he is not good at – he goes back to sketch in, from its origins, the history of one of its elements, which he does with a sure, interesting, economical – and also poetic – eye. See, in addition to the prior history of Aurélia, that of Seixas as well as Part I, chapter 10 of *O tronco do Ipê*. Brief and informative by definition, the retrospective limits ideological reflection on the part of the character or the narrator – which is detrimental in the problematic urban novel and to farfetched adventure stories, which are detrimental to more adventurous books. It

ates is the order of the plot. Artistically, however, that same primacy does not materialise since Alencar does not complete the formal pre-eminence of bourgeois values with a critique of favour, of which he is an admirer and friend. Thus the form not only is left unproductive but finds itself restricted in its operations: the negative sign that logically, albeit perhaps implicitly, it should attach to material with which it disagrees is overridden, counterbalanced merely by fine words. *So the alternation of incompatible presuppositions breaks apart the fiction.* A divided base, which will generate on the literary level a corresponding incoherence, artificial tone and especially lack of proportion. If in Balzac the mid-level characters stare petrified at the Medusa-like features of the radical ones – the 'types' that Lukács speaks of – who are their truth in concentrated form, in Alencar they look with dismay at Aurélia, whose vehemence seems preposterous to some, a drawing-room stunt to others, and imported literature to both. The programmatic aspect of her suffering, which should provide her with a dignity that transcends her individual case, instead seems to them an isolated whim, a young girl's fancy. Now love, money or appearances not being absolute and exclusive, there is nothing more reasonable than to take those three aspects into account, along with others, at the time of marriage; the conflict that turns them all into absolutes seems unnecessary and unnatural. The

---

is realistic by definition: its norm is the clear, suggestive linking together of acts with an eye to the situation back where the flashback started. The result is a calmer figuration, one interested in the description, rather than criticism, of the issues that will be decisive. It is a solution in which a talent for mimesis, the Brazilian culture and Alencar's overall vision shine, and at the same time the disconnects in our ideological life are minimised. An occasional technique in *Senhora*, it is central to *Til* and *O tronco do Ipê*, Alencar's plantation novels. They are books of abstruse intrigue linked to a subliterary notion of destiny and the expiation of sin, a notion that nonetheless lightens the prose in the same way we have seen in the flashback. In place of analytical complexity in the problems, the force of destiny. Both cases deal with rich planters who have to pay in detail for the forgotten misdeeds of their youth. At the outset, however, when the focus falls on the mortals, the weight of their guilt coincides in large measure – and advantageously – with the weight of the past, with the linking-together and purgation of the objective antagonisms of the real world of the plantation: illegitimate children, slaves crazy with fear, embezzled property, hired thugs and murders, fires, superstition, uprisings in the slave quarters, etcetera. In *Til* read the chapters surrounding the fire (Part IV, chapters I–IX) to get an idea of the strength and scale of this sort of action. Moreover, it is the unity of the construction of long, varied sequences like this one that attest to the Romantic, 'subjective' power of the narrator. It is there as well in the spontaneity with which the words and images occur to him – a spontaneity that does not preclude some verbosity – that Alencar's diction converges with common, pre-literary speech. The novel's movement in turn can be taken apart into brief episodes, comparable with the traditional popular narrative. To me, as regards what could have been, these two are his best books.

prose as well, which seems exaggerated. And even from the point of view of linear coherence there are difficulties, for while she is a good person, compassionate and unselfish, Aurélia gives off sparks of satanic fire and applies the ethic of the contract with total rigour. Some might say that this is dialectical, Shylock and Portia in one character. That is not the case, however, for while there is movement between the terms, indeed a frenetic movement, that process does not transform them – Alencar adheres to both, one because of a sense of the local customs involved, the other in appreciation of modernity; they each exit the book the same as when they entered it. See also in this regard the uncertain significance of Aurélia's cynical comments: if they were fitting (as they would be if their formal power were functional within the text), the ladies who don't like them because they find them improper should come off looking like hypocrites; but they don't, they are just well-intentioned mothers. The trendy young men, who find her risqué, and are not offended thereby, are accused of moral insensitivity. Seixas himself, who had chosen for romantic reasons to humble himself in order to return to the good graces of his beloved, ends up giving, among the reasons for his obedience ... faithfulness to the bargain – thereby highlighting the commercial nexus, critique of which is the central motive of the plot.[24] To see the damage perpetrated upon the very texture of the prose, one has only to study the opening pages. Polite Rio society is referred to successively as elegant, backward and vicious without the contradictions being called into question. Also, the narrator does not remain stable. At one moment he speaks the language of the complicit social chronicler, at another he speaks as an expert in the laws of the heart and of social life, at yet another as an unflinching moralist, then as a sophisticated man aware of Brazilian provincialism, then finally he is someone who respects the customs in force at the time. In sum, for the purposes of the novel, where might the truth reside? Yet a bit of self-critique and humour would transform this incoherence among attitudes, visible from sentence to sentence, into the vertiginous fickleness of Machadian narrative.

Similar cases of disorder appear in a more ingenuous vein in *A pata da gazela* [The Gazelle's Foot] and in *Diva* [Diva]. In the latter, which starts out comically, the general climate – as in *Senhora* – involves family, social proprieties, parties and little flirtations. The plot, however, soon explodes: the heroine's apparent prudishness and reserve, common-enough-sounding and convincing at the outset, increase to the point of extreme tension and are expressed in the most extreme and exalted Romantic rhetoric – of total purity, doubt and disillusionment – all ending up in marriage. Between the banality of social life and

---

24   Alencar 1959, vol. I, p. 1,203.

plot movement, then, an abyss. They really are not even talking about the same things. Nevertheless, albeit ever short of the level that only artistic coherence can provide, the story does project a certain energy: it has something crude and blunt about it despite its conformity, something peculiar to the violent, prolix stories stocked with delicious punishments and abject triumphs with which the humiliated imagination compensates for the resentments and uncertainties of life. In *A pata da gazela* the imbalance occurs in the opposite way: instead of the Romantic monumentalisation of small conflicts, we witness the rapid deflation of the initial Romantic situation, which, nonetheless, remains the main element of interest in the book. Horácio, dissolute man-about-town, is set up in opposition to Leopoldo, a modest young man on the outside and enlightened on the inside – opposition, that is, carried out to the point of absurdity. Horácio to Leopoldo: 'You love the smile, I the foot',[25] which is both figurative and literal. In fact, in the novel materialism and forbidden fixations are counterposed to love of moral beauty – all with regard to a foot. As long as it is beautiful, Horácio cares little for the lady herself; but Leopoldo, if the lady speaks to his soul, will marry her even if her foot is a 'deformity', 'an elephant foot', 'covered by protuberances like a tubercle', 'a mutton leg, a stump!'[26] Little by little, however, the perverse and cruel element is tempered, leaving the field to the conventional contrast – and one with a predictable outcome – between the frivolous young man and the sincere one. Gradually – perhaps a bit more than gradually – that matter gives way to another. The brashness of the ideological conflict is like a false support that captures the reader's attention but in the final analysis cannot bear the weight of the narrative. Because they are not metaphors for the whole of Brazilian society, perversion, the mundanity of life, tedium, the high-fashion tailors and cobblers and so on, are all reduced to the status of decoy, superimposed, without much effort at disguise, upon Brazilian common routine, to provide it with prestige. Not that the result is without depth – as Machado de Assis would demonstrate. But that depth would have to be given a structure. For now, we are back to the picture we have studied previously: the touches of up-to-dateness confer modernity and importance upon the narrative, which however is such as to undermine those very touches: they are neither necessary nor superfluous. Or better, while it is necessary to make narrative literature *presentable*,[27] when the attempt is made to incorpor-

---

25   Alencar 1959, vol. I, p. 650.
26   Alencar 1959, vol. I, pp. 608, 652.
27   Expression and problem are suggestions by Alexandre Eulálio, who sees Alencar's diction as a rearrangement of the juridical-political prose of the student communities of São Paulo that never left off its hold on his fiction.

ate the local element to it, the pieces do not fit together. The same with the conflict of moral ideologies, which at one moment is daring, serious à la Balzac, and at another is pure excess, sometimes intentionally humorous and at others unintentionally so. Needless to say, with every one of the latter bumps, the credibility of whatever of the former is in the process of being constructed is undercut. The pieces that are capable of being salvaged, which are many, here again owe their existence to the author's mimetic drive, which shows through the incongruities of the composition. Even the question of the foot, legitimated for the field of letters by the Satan thematic in Romanticism, comes to function in an unexpected, low and direct but lively area, following the example we have seen in the development of *Diva*. It is the source not only of an insipid debate between body and soul but also of more intimate and spontaneous thoughts, expressed, for example, in the names given to the physical defect or in the way its discovery affects a lover. Through the generalities, then, there percolates something more piquant that makes up a part of a tradition in our literature, the tradition – if we can speak of it as such – of the vulgar moment, intended in some cases, spontaneous in others. To document it, let us recall the episode of the haemorrhoids in Macedo's *A moreninha*; the odd sensation experienced by the hero of *Cinco minutos* [Five Minutes], Alencar's debut novel, when he realises that the veiled female passenger in the back of a night bus on whose shoulder he had placed 'his hot lips', could turn out to be ugly and old; the terrible chapters about Eugenia, the lame girl, in *Memórias póstumas de Brás Cubas*, the multitude of gross words in Parnassian-Naturalist literature, a combination that has something vulgar about it; and in our days Oswald's[28] jokes, Nelson Rodrigues's[29] intentional rottenness, the tone of meanness in Dalton Trevisan,[30] in addition to a well-established line in popular music.

Alencar's Realist fiction is inconsistent at its core, but its inconsistency reiterates in concentrated and developed form the essential difficulty of our ideological life, of which it is the effect and the repetition. Far from being incidental, this inconsistency is substantive. Now, to repeat ideologies, even in a concise and lively manner, is, from the point of view of theory, merely to repeat ideologies and nothing more. But from the point of view of literature, which – at this level, at least – is imitation, not rational assessment, it is half the battle won. From there to conscious, careful representation is only one step further.

---

28 [José Oswald de Souza Andrade (1890–1954) was a highly influential writer and publicist and one of the founders of Brazil's 'Modernist' literary-cultural movement.]
29 [Nelson Falcão Rodrigues (1912–80), in addition to being a prominent novelist and journalist, was one of Brazil's most important playwrights.]
30 [Dalton Jérson Trevisan (1925) is a highly acclaimed short story writer.]

Although I have dwelled upon one side only, my analysis shows that there are two. Let's go to the positive side. Alencar himself must certainly have sensed something of what we have been describing in these pages. In explaining himself with regard to *Senhora* and the character of Seixas, which was being criticised for its minimal moral stature, Alencar answered that he '[modelled his] characters to the size of Rio society' and expressed pride 'precisely in [their] national stamp'. 'Your colossuses', he said to his critic, 'in this (Brazilian) world of ours, would look like stone guests'.[31] So everything depends on knowing what that shrunken measure is, that 'Rio size' in which the true nature of the country can be seen. Why should a Rio social climber be smaller than a French one, at the risk of seeming a ghost? If we take a closer look at the question, it must be noted that the stature of Alencar's heroes isn't stable. Are they mediocre? Are they exceptional? Now one and now the other. They oscillate between the titanic and the familiar according to the needs of dramatic development on the part of European-style and localist characterisations respectively. Thus Aurélia, who lives in the most exalted of absolutes – sensuous as a salamander, singing arias from *Norma* in a bellowing voice, trampling society 'as though it were a poisonous snake'[32] – asks Dona Firmina if she, Aurélia, is more beautiful than the Amaral girl with whom she goes to the parties;[33] a bit later, to emphasise her intelligence, we find praise of her knowledge of arithmetic.[34] The same occurs with Seixas, who, when Romantic purposes are involved, is 'a superior nature' and 'predestined',[35] but the rest of the time is a young man like any other. In *Diva* medicine is represented as a priesthood, but the doctor spends his time courting a moody adolescent who spurns his overtures.[36] Also the heterodox adorer of women's ankle boots in *A pata da gazela* early on shows himself to be in fact a respectful young man who feels 'a rush of contentment' when his beloved's father welcomes him into their home.[37] In truth, then, 'Rio size' results from the unresolved alternation between two different ideologies. Its cause, if we may now return to our own terms, lies in the damaged validity, emptied so to speak, that European ideologies had in Brazil, dislocated by the mechanisms of our social structure. That with regard to reality. As regards fiction, it is necessary to take with caution Alencar's own statements, distin-

---

31 In a note accompanying *Senhora* (Alencar 1959, vol. I, p. 1,213).
32 Alencar 1959, vol. I, p. 955.
33 Alencar 1959, vol. I, p. 959.
34 Alencar 1959, vol. I, p. 968.
35 Alencar 1959, vol. I, p. 1,054.
36 Alencar 1959, vol. I, p. 527.
37 Alencar 1959, vol. I, p. 609.

guish between constructive planning and justification of an effect – that is, between degrees of intentionality. We have seen that – contrary to what their author says – the characters are not lacking in extremism, particularly in *Senhora*; what gives them their stature, however, to the detriment of their intended grandeur, is the network of secondary relations, which lessens the value and grounding of the central conflict, which then comes out relativised. Thence the sense of disproportion, of formal duality, that we have tried to point out and that constitutes both the aesthetic result of these books and also their profound consonance with the Brazilian experience. Erased at the first level of composition, which is determined by the acritical adoption of the European model, our national difference comes in through the back door in the form of literary implausibility, *which Alencar nonetheless values for its mimetic merits*. Thus the tribute paid for the inescapable inauthenticity of our literature is recognised, fixed, and then capitalised on as an advantage. It is that transition from involuntary reflex to conscious elaboration, from incongruity to artistic truth, that we must study. We are at the beginnings here of a different dynamic for the composition of our own novel. Take note, therefore, of a problem: where we see a *compositional defect* Alencar sees *an imitative success*. In fact, the formal defect upon which we have concentrated – and that Alencar insisted on producing, guided by his sense of 'Rio size' – has extraordinary mimetic value, and nothing is more Brazilian than this ungainly literature. The difficulty in this case is only an apparent one: in all literary forms there is a mimetic aspect, just as imitation always contains the germs of form; a lack of formal coordination at the level of construction can be an opportunity for imitation – as we have already seen it to be in this case – which, without redeeming it, gives it artistic relevance as potential future material or as food for thought. Let us see how this can work. Alencar does not dwell upon the contradiction between European form and local societal characteristics but he persists in including them both – in which respect he is merely a member of his class, which appreciated progress and the current cultural goings-on to which he had access, and also appreciated the traditional relationships that validated his own position of eminence. It isn't a question of indecision but rather one of simultaneous adherence to completely heterogeneous terms, ones incompatible as regards principles but aligned within the practice of Brazilian 'enlightened paternalism'. We are in the presence of an early figure in that conservative modernisation the history of which has not yet ended.[38] It is the problem outlined in our first chapter reappearing on the literary level: what is the logic of this bizarre

---

38   Gilberto Freyre registers the problem, with finesse as regards its permanency and with class blindness as regards its difficulties, and especially without the least distancing –

but real combination? In repeating acritically the interests of his class, Alencar makes manifest a crucial fact about Brazilian life – the conciliation of clientelism and liberal ideology – all the while not recognising its problematic nature, which is the reason he shipwrecks on another kind of conformity, namely that of common sense, the falsity of which the literary incoherencies are the symptom. In other words, let's say that European form and local society are taken just as they are, with talent but without any reworking. Face to face in the narrow, logical space of a novel, they contradict each other in principle, but that contradiction is taken no further because of ... a sense of reality. Neither reconciled nor in conflict with each other, they do not engage in the communication that they would need to in order to undo their conventionality and achieve artistic integrity: the former is without verisimilitude, the latter without importance, and everything is shrunken and imbalanced. It is in the whole, however – and here is the surprise – that successful imitation occurs, producing the 'national stamp' that leads Alencar to repeat the formula, stabilising it as a feature of our literature. It is his profoundest legacy to the tradition of our Realism. Formal failure and mimetic force are thus brought together. The reader must realise that in saying this, we are re-reading the book through a different lens. Inconsistency is now viewed not as a weakness in a book or in an author – not as mere repetition of ideologies – but as imitation of an essential aspect of reality. It is not a final effect but an asset or crossing-point toward another, larger effect. This is a second-degree reading that recuperates for further thought the not-always voluntary truth of 'Rio size'. Take note that the formal defect is an ingredient here in the same way as are the ingredients that have produced that defect. Thus formal inconsistency becomes subject matter. So much so that instead of the combination of two elements – European form and local material – a combination that turns out to be unstable – we have a combination of three elements: the precarious results of the combination of European form and local material, which combination turns out to be amusing. Replacing the first effect, which is lowered to the status of element, a second, different and

---

despite the almost one hundred years that have passed: 'So we have to be attentive to this contradiction in Alencar: his modernism, anti-patriarchal on some points – including the wish for a 'certain emancipation of the woman' – and his traditionalism on other points, including his liking for the purely Brazilian figure of the sinhazinha [mistress] of the patriarchal "big house"'. 'It is as if Alencar, through this lens at one and the same time traditionalist and modernist, familyist and individualist, had anticipated the attempt to renovate Brazilian culture upon a basis both modernist and traditionalist that was, in our time, the Movimento Regionalista do Recife [Regionalist Movement of Recife], alongside the more grandiose Modernismo of São Paulo, one wing of which indeed made the attempt to combine those contraries.' Freyre 1951, pp. 15, 27–8.

less programmatic effect comes to the fore, the humour of which resides in the clumsiness of the first effect. It is true that the intellectual and artistic potential of this second effect goes almost completely unrecognised in Alencar. For its appreciation it will be necessary to await second-phase Machado de Assis. Nevertheless, it is the very substance of 'Rio size', available to be developed. In the abstract, the argument would run as follows: if the jumbled effect is an initial and anticipated dimension of the construction, the elements that produce it can be reassessed and described, and their interrelationship re-defined. The overblown demands of European thematics must be put in perspective, the innocence bred of marginality removed from the localist thematics, and calculated comic sense given to the narrative unevenness that signals the disconnects among the premises of the book. By now, the reader is, I hope, recognising Machadian tonality. Perhaps he can be further convinced by considering a question of scale: if, as in the case of Alencar, imitative power is the result of the breaking of the whole, which weakens all its parts, on which, however, reading focuses, then reading will be tedious – as in fact it is – and there is an error in literary economy. To make the most of the end result, it is necessary to concentrate it so as to give it presence throughout the narrative – transform the effect of an architecture of writing into that of a minute chemistry of writing. Now Machadian prose pretty thoroughly depends on the prior miniaturisation of novel circuits by Alencar, whose entire ideological space, inconsistencies included, it pervades seemingly phrase by phrase. Reduced, routinised, stylised like a rhythmic unit, the disproportion between the grand bourgeois ideas and the to-and-fro of favour is transformed into a diction, into a sardonic and familiar music. From formal inconsistency to a deliberate and humoristic incoherence, the result becomes departure point, more complex material, that another form would exploit. I am not suggesting with this that the Machadian novel is the simple product of critique of the Alencar novel. Literary tradition does not run separate from life like that. The fact is that Alencar's problems were, with minimal modification, the problems of his time, as can be documented quite easily by reference to speeches and periodical material, which suffered from the same disproportions and contradictions. Machado can be seen as redressing many of them. Nor are we really talking about influence, though it is definitely present and cases are not hard to identify. What needs to be examined more closely here is the formation of a literary substratum with sufficient historical density to be able to support the creation of literary masterpieces. Let us go back to the mimetic power of the formal impasse. According to our analysis it results from the acritical incorporation of an ideological combination – normal in Brazil – subjected to the demand for a unity characteristic of the Realist novel and modern literature in general. In repeating ideologies, which themselves are repetitions of appearances, literature itself is ideology as well. Second moment, the impasse is considered to be characteristic of a Brazilian national life. As a consequence it becomes an effect consciously sought after, which is the same as relativising the combination of ideologies and forms that produces it, since they no longer have value in themselves but rather because of the weak outcome of their contact with each other. *The ideological repetition of ideologies is interrupted* in the cause of mimetic fidelity. 'Rio size' is thus a name for this little hiatus that, without being a full break, is virtually sufficient to redistribute emphases and shift points of view, making it possible to glimpse the field of a possible literature that would not be just the reconfirmation of established illusions – a step that Machado de Assis would take. For the writer there may be many reasons for this modification. From the objective point of view, which is what is important for us right now, it leads to incorporation into the field of Brazilian letters, *as something in and of itself*, of that moment of incongruity that European ideology has with us. In other words, the process is a complex variant of the so-called dialectic of form and content: our literary material reaches sufficient density only when it includes on the level of content the failure of European form, without which we remain incomplete. There remains, of course, the problem of finding the appropriate form for this new material, an essential part of which is the inanity of the forms to which by necessity we have been constrained to adhere. Before form, therefore, it has been necessary to produce the raw material itself and enrich it with the degradation of the European-style formal universe. Concerning this operation, it should be noted that its motive force is purely that of mimesis. Similarity to day-to-day reality is thus not a merely superficial element. The work of adjusting the imitation, at first glance apparently limited by the chance nature of appearances, prepares the course of a new river, as it were. Its consequences for composition, determined by the logical – that is, historical – demands of the material being used for the purposes of imitation, infinitely surpass the restricted circle of mimesis, which, however, brings those consequences to light. In this sense, for the use of writers, 'Rio size' can be a vague nationalistic and imitative criterion needing no further definition; objectively, however, it produced something like an amplification of the internal space of the literary material, an added space that went on to include a permanent transatlantic reference that will be its piquancy and its truth. In other words: to construct a true novel it is necessary that its material be true. That is, in the case of a dependent country like us, there has to be a synthesis that regularly includes the mark of our diminished position in the nascent imperialist system. By virtue of imitation, of fidelity to the 'national stamp', the ideologies of favour and of liberalism are permanently intermixed, forming a puzzle that, upon being furnished with logic rather than only with mimesis, will produce a new, non-diminished form of the diminution of our bourgeoisie. It is a development that interests us yet today, given that its cycle is not yet ended.

The most obvious defect of *Senhora*, namely its sugar-sweet ending, has been kept for last. With regard to it, imagine a different ending, one that the 'mysterious hymn to holy conjugal love' had not ruined: the novel would have one fewer defect but wouldn't be any better. None of the problems that we have been dealing with would have been solved. The rosy, or at least morally edifying, close is not particularly linked to Brazilian literature but rather to the novel of social reconciliation, to Feuillet and Dumas fils, for example, who were direct influences for it. Those authors indeed ruined their own literature through calculated conformity. Take the former's *Le Roman d'un jeune homme pauvre* [Romance of a Poor Young Man] and have the contradictions that it minimises pointed out instead: then we would be in the presence of a good Realist novel.[39] It is that Feuillet, like Alencar, was heir to a formal tradition grounded in the critical assumptions of the bourgeois revolution. *Senhora* and *Le Roman d'un jeune homme pauvre* both oscillate between the modest garret and the villa, the city and the provinces, the businessman's office and the beloved's gardens, aristocratic sentiment and bourgeois sentiment, etcetera. In Feuillet's book the antagonisms involved in that disposition of spaces and themes are like shadows of doubt and subversion defeated by the virtue of the positive characters. An exemplary league of egalitarian aristocrats and altruistic bourgeois characters triumphs. Nevertheless, the problems of the bourgeois revolution not only are formalised in the basic structure of the Realist novel, to which Feuillet subscribes, but work especially with reality, the social body of Europe, which is the living material of this literature. So for Feuillet to disguise social contradictions and negate their literary importance are one and the same thing. The matter is different with Alencar, who reconciles only at the end and along the way is not conformist but rather audacious, an ally of the contradictions.[40] What is one to do with this form if the opposing principles that compose it do not work with the material to be organised? If old

---

39   Paul Bourget makes the same observation with intentions contrary to mine: 'Reading [Feuillet's] books one feels a singular esteem for this noble spirit who, dismissing truculent analysis and dangerous curiosities, knew how to retain the cult of the chivalresque, of the woman and of love' (Bourget 1912, p. 113). Perhaps impressed with the Paris Commune, Dumas, fils is more direct: 'The time is past to be witty, amenable, libertine, sarcastic, sceptical and fanciful; it is not the moment for that. God, nature, work, marriage, love, children are the serious things' (Dumas n.d., p. 325).

40   The distinction between conformity and compromise in Alencar was made for me by Clara Alvim.

Camargo's plantation is not the site of provincial and aristocratic virtues but instead of capital and the dissolute customs of the slaves, what can possibly be the outcome of its contrast with the greed and the frivolity of Rio? Be the answer to such questions as it may, it cannot fit with the central conflict, nor respond to it. Analogously, when he moves from his poor room to his wife's great-house Seixas does not really move in social class and especially not in ideology, as the contrast in places would have us suppose; he moves only in standard of living (as we would call it today), which takes poetic force away from the contrast in sites of action. Etcetera, etcetera. If the oppositions that define the form do not govern as well the social milieu to which the form is applied, then formal rigour will be accompanied by artistic imbalance, and the very boldness with which those conflicts, said to be monstrous – but prestigious – are related will itself be conformist. Thence, moreover, the odd effect these novels have: trained as they are on contemporary history, they produce no impression of historical rhythms whatsoever. Precisely because the poetics of such rhythms depends upon real-life periodisation, that is, it depends upon the correspondence between the material of conflicts precisely located in time and the historical contradictions that organise the movement of the work as a whole. Thus, now that we have shown that Alencar's biggest contribution to the formation of our novel resides in the weak points of his writing, let us see as well how the weaknesses can come to function as really strong points, ones that, taken in isolation, become Alencar's writerly merits. Regarding *Senhora*, Antonio Candido observes that its subject – the purchase of a husband – not only gives form to the plot but has repercussions within the book's metaphorical system as well. The question is precisely one of formal consistency, the effect of which merits scrutiny. The heroine, hardened by her desire for vengeance, which was made possible by the possession of money, inures her soul as though she were the agent of an operation intended to crush the other by means of capital, which will reduce him to something merely owned. The very images of the style manifest the hardening of her personality as the result of its being touched by the dehumanising effects of capitalism, until the Romantic dialectic of love recovers its normal conventionality. As a whole and in the detail of each part, the same structural principles shape the material.[41] In fact, the dramatic movement transforms the rich young lady, besieged by the 'mob of suitors',[42] into a vehement woman in full revolt. Once she has the initiative, Aurélia looks at the world through the lens of money, with the inten-

---

41 Candido 1965, pp. 6–7.
42 Alencar 1959, vol. I, p. 954.

tion to pay back doubly every humiliation she has suffered. On the other side of the coin, when she sees herself as the person exposed to the gaze of that same lens, marbled lividity, frozen lips, cheeks mottled like jasper, spells of tension, hoarse and metalicised voice, and so on, take over in her.[43] Up to then, we see the moral dialectic of money and the evil it perpetrates upon people. Nevertheless, as the references to marble and jasper have suggested, the movement is more complex. The mineralisation to which Antonio Candido refers stands at the intersection of many narrative threads: it is the hardness necessary for her to manipulate the other, it is her visceral refusal to lend her own humanity to others' plans, it is the worship of pagan, statue-like material, it is rejection of the body, it is the prestige of expensive substances, etcetera. In sum, the object of economic critique exerts a sexual attraction. 'And the world is such that the satanic radiance of that woman's beauty is her great allure. In the acerbic vehemence of her rebellious soul, one can sense depths of passion – and as well that this virgin bacchante's love must contain tempests of sensuality'.[44] Explicit message: money curbs natural emotions; latent message: money, disdain and denial form an eroticised set that opens up more exciting horizons than conventional life. In other words, money is deleterious because it separates sensuality from the existing family picture and it is attractive for that same reason. Thence the convergence in Alencar of wealth, female independence, sensual intensity, and images drawn from the sphere of prostitution. As one can see, the development is carried out with considerable boldness and complexity, though it clearly relies upon Dumas, fils' *La Dame aux camélias* [The Lady of the Camelias]. Thus the formal logic with which Alencar develops his subject matter, instead of eliminating the formal duality that we have been studying, strengthens it: it locates at the novel's centre the bourgeois reification of social relations. Where Antonio Candido points to a virtue – which does exist – there is a weakness as well. Extreme manipulation and therefore absolute antagonism here constitute the model of individual relationships. Now that is one of the essential ideological effects of liberal capitalism, just as it is one of the merits of the Realist novel to manifest it in its very structure. But it was not the formal principle that we needed, though it has proven indispensable to us – as a theme.

---

43   Alencar 1959, vol. I, pp. 1,028, 1,044.
44   Alencar 1959, vol. I, p. 955.

CHAPTER 3

Paternalism and Its Rationalisation in Machado de Assis' Early Novels

1   General Considerations

The problem we have been studying presents itself in a different way in Machado de Assis' early novels.[1] To be sure, they too bear in their composition the mark of Brazilian national dependency. They lack, however, the sympathy that ingenuousness – to today's eyes – lends to Alencar's outspoken production. Machado's first novels are deliberately and disagreeably conformist books. Where Alencar had followed the lead of Realism, treating questions posed by individualism and money, questions alive and critical down to today, Machado aligned himself with the narrow apologetics of the European Reaction, Catholic at its core and focused on *the sanctity of families and on the dignity of individuals* (as opposed to their rights). Hence the novels' musty atmosphere, to which the modern reader is particularly allergic having lost the custom not so much of authoritarian regimes as of their moral justifications. We are, however, dealing with Brazil. The replacement of the liberal reference with conservative paternalism had the advantage of bringing to the fore some of our more crucial issues. And we should recall as well that an authoritarian doctrine in which the family provides the paradigm for society came naturally entwined with our Catholic and patriarchal traditions. Slavery and the system of favour did not present themselves as a problem. With regard to beliefs, the ragged was exchanged for the tattered, notwithstanding the repellency of the options, which in Europe were used to confuse workers.

It must be noted that, ten years before, Machado had adopted liberal ideas and assimilated the rhetoric of progress and equality:

> The newspaper is the true form of the republic of thought. It is the intellectual locomotive on a trip to unknown worlds, it is the common literature, universal and highly democratic, produced daily, bearing fresh ideas and the fire of conviction … The emancipation of the intelligentsia is being completed and that of peoples is beginning. The right of force,

---

1 Much of what will be said in this chapter was pointed out by Lúcia Miguel-Pereira in her remarkable *Prosa de Ficção*; see Miguel-Pereira 1973. For a different interpretation, stressing continuities rather than contradictions, see Castello 1969.

the right of bastard authority consubstantiated in dynastic individualities will fall. Kings no longer wear purple, they wrap themselves in constitutions. Constitutions are the peace treaties celebrated between popular power and monarchic power ... Energy is rising within the common voice; industry is elevating itself to the status of institution; and the popular titan, everywhere shaking off ingrained governing principles, slashes with the sword of reason though the cloak of new dogmas. It is the light of a fecund dawn that is spreading across the horizon. To prepare humanity for the sun that is going to be born – that is the work of modern civilisations.[2]

The illusion did not last, and Machado's convictions would change, moved by reasons that are best left to his biographers to elucidate.[3]

Later, when he comes to write his first novels, they draw upon anti-liberal ideology. For Machado, therefore, it was not a matter of rejecting an incipient, unconsidered position that he once held but rather the result of experience with that part of realism – if not of truth – that inhered within the disillusionment. What is of interest is the depth of his turnabout, which, for his literary material, had the effect of a veritable vaccine. The Rights of Man and the libertarian generalisations proper to Romantic individualism are almost absent from his books, in which there is no lack of impasse and injustice but not a whiff of social revolt. Or, more precisely, such things are relegated to the margins. And if by chance they come onto centre stage, the efficacy of the vaccine is further confirmed by the highly caricatural way they are depicted. See, for instance, the idiotic Byronism of Estevão, the unhappy ladies' man in *A mão e a luva*, or the sudden patriotism of a certain lady who sends her son off to the Paraguayan War to avoid a marriage she considers inferior (*Iaiá Garcia*). We shall see in detail the advantages that this retreat – the conservative affiliation as relates to European tradition – brought to Brazilian literature. For now, let us merely observe that it is responsible for the essential timidity of these novels set in Rio, the nation's capital. In fact, that ideological restraint is also a restraint on subject matter and choice of conflict: questions of individualism, the current goings-on in bourgeois civilisation, and with them the thematics of modernity, appear infrequently and occupy a secondary position. They couldn't be altogether absent, being indispensable to the novels' nineteenth-century 'perfume'. Top hats, cigars, elegant manners and gentlemen of few scruples updated the

---

2 Machado de Assis 1959, vol. III, pp. 955–8.
3 Massa 1971, especially pp. 299 ff., calls attention to the problem and suggests that Machado had become frustrated in his political ambitions.

terms of a problematic with which we are already familiar. In *Senhora* local colour discredited the dramatic nexus involving the new civilisation of Capital. Inversely, in Machado's first novel phase, although infrequent and filtered, modern colour provides a contrast and renders evident the narrowness of the central conflict, in which rearrangements in the domestic sphere are made to pose as solutions to social conflicts. As we have previously concluded, Alencar's localist accessory becomes a formal force in his work, and the cosmopolitan audacities of his central conflict are reduced to what they always were, namely elements of fashion. In Machado's hands they become steps in the more credible redistribution of themes and emphases, a redistribution brought about far from unproblematically. Their literary result is initially negative, for it voices Brazil's historical belatedness, the effect of which, since it does not produce any analytical distancing that might open society up to examination, could only be provincialism. Picking up our thread again, let us observe that the exclusion of references to liberalism avoided the latter's misplacement – of which we have spoken so much – but at the price of cutting ties with the contemporary world. To evaluate the ambiguities of that path we have only to take Machado's anti-Realist militancy: in his words Realism 'is the very negation of the principle of art'.[4] There are echoes there of the doctrines of the *Revue des Deux Mondes* [Review of the Two Worlds], for which Realism, democracy, common people, materialism, slang, dirt and socialism were part of a single detestable continuum.[5] The norm is anti-modern on all counts. The rejection of low material leads to the search for elevated subjects – that is, material from which the practical aims of modern life have been purged. The nullity of the explanations in that regard has a programmatic character: 'Our aim is to see the Brazilian muses cultivate the literary novel, the novel that conjoins study of the human passions with the delicate and original strains of poetry'.[6] Nevertheless there was on Machado's part a Realist intent within this conservative anti-Realism, if we look at it as an expression of experience and scepticism – which was not the case with the European version, in which it represented an intellectual retreat – about the suitability of liberal ideas in Brazil. Aimed at watering down the antagonisms of the bourgeois regime, anti-Realism did not go into

---

4 Machado de Assis 1959, vol. III, p. 826.
5 See Du Val. Among the *Revue*'s mentors on such subjects is Charles de Mazade, who authored studies in literature and politics and especially the 'Chronique de la Quinzaine' [Chronicle of the Fortnight] in which one finds, it seems to me, one of the rhetorical models for the Machadian 'crônica'. For Machado's anti-Realist pronouncements see his principal essays: 'Instinto de nacionalidade' [The Instinct of Nationality], 'A nova geração' [The New Generation] and '*O primo Basílio*' [Cousin Basil].
6 Machado de Assis 1959, vol. III, p. 859.

them and spared us the illusion of being France ... Even the exclusion of coarse material, particularly the miseries of modernity occasioned by capital, was for us the exclusion of a topic filled with frivolous tropisms. And the choice of decorous topics – paternalism instead of money – was closer to the actual life of the people than was the dialectic of so-called capital. There was no way to escape such confusions, genuine marks of the inauthenticity of our cultural processes. On that point the twentieth century did not bring with it total change; the very history of our assimilation of Marxism shows many comparable things. For Machado at this point, all that was lacking was disillusionment with the disillusionment, namely to become disillusioned with paternalist conservatism as well. Be that as it may, despite his intelligence and talent, which we shall not forget, there remain four stuffy, insipid novels of the sort required by the myths of marriage, purity, father, tradition and family, to the authority of which they, the novels, respectfully submit themselves. To echo Oswald de Andrade, they are running on a non-existent track.[7] And in fact one of the hallmarks of the second and great phase of Machado's novel will be its large-scale reintegration of liberal and modern thematics, of social doctrines, of science, political life and the new material civilisation – all done in his own distinct way, of course.

Ressurreição [Resurrection] (1872) is the story of a marriage that would be good for all parties but does not come off because of the fiancé's unfounded jealousies. In the three succeeding novels the issue is one of social inequality. The heroines are young women born below their deserts, and it falls to affluent families to repair nature's 'error' by elevating them.[8] The issue is dealt with approvingly to the verge of bluntness in *A mão e a luva*, from the viewpoint of susceptibility in *Helena* and with great disenchantment in *Iaiá Garcia*. Despite that evolution, the common denominator in the four books is the emphatic affirmation of social, moral, and familial conformity, which orients their reflexion on the destinies of the individuals involved. A type of reflection that neither amplifies nor generalises the set of contradictions to which it directs itself but to the contrary considers them as constituting specific cases that require equally specific solutions. What Félix, the indecisive fiancé of *Ressurreição*, lacks is the energy necessary to constitute a family and become a contributing member of society. Analysis – that destructive force – is applied not to the institution of marriage but to deploring the character's wavering

---

7 'My mistake lay in measuring my progress on the metrified and nationalistic leads of two remote idiots: Bilac and Coelho Neto. The error was having run on the same non-existent track'. The constellation is other, though the problem is the same. Oswald de Andrade 1971, vol. II, p. 131. ['Bilac' refers to the very prominent poet Olavo Brás Martins dos Guimarães Bilac (1865–1918). 'Coelho Neto' to the poet Henrique Maximiano Coelho Neto (1864–1934).]

8 Machado de Assis 1959, vol. I, p. 142.

will. Next Guiomar in *A mão e a luva* adapts herself with praiseworthy sagacity to the wishes of a baroness whom she values very highly and who ends up adopting her. The girl's calculations and malleability constitute the novel's raison d'être. In *Helena* the heroine, after a great effort to have herself accepted, prefers death to the idea of being thought badly of by the family on whose good will she depends. And even the prideful Estela, an *agregada*[9] whose 'cup of gratitude is full up', does not extend her sense of independence to the placing of limits on the authority and the institutions that diminish her.[10] Her merit lies in the decorum that she is able to maintain under adverse conditions. In other words, *the family, preferably wealthy, is the unquestioned depository of order and the meaning of life*. As opposed to the egoism of celibacy and the waste of widowhood, to the sterility of passing relationships and the brutality of unequal ones, to uncertainty in general, to the obscurity of poverty, to the aridity of labour, and the many other of the country's disgraces, family life is the sphere of mending, the sphere in which social and natural disparities find solace and sublimation. Civilising agent or refuge of the civilised, it is the criterion for the morality and the rationality of human actions; the disconnects that may occur – which are mere difficulties rather than problems – form the reflective centre of these books confined almost entirely to its circle. Its transcendental purity has the weight of premise, but it is a spurious premise that, in this context filled with observed realities, acts rather like a law – which does not keep it from being a formal principle. Its un-truth is glaring and repels any sympathetic reading. Furthermore, the conflicts that it contains are not very heroic or Romantic, for it is up to the characters, necessarily a company of altruists, to adjust to the established order, from which, basically, they cannot diverge. A space riddled with good feelings and tensions, in which the conflict is never declared since to declare it would be to deny the agreed-upon general good will of the family members. It is a limit in the face of which the characters stop on pain of breaking the formal regulation and thereby of slipping into a different novel-world entirely. Thence the strange climate of the novels: of passions virtuously contained and resignations little more than uneasy at worst, a climate not without poetry; we shall speak further about it.[11] We shall speak as well of

---

9   'Agregada' is the feminine form of 'agregado'. For the social location of *agregados*, see n. 13 to ch. I.]

10 Machado de Assis 1959, vol. I, p. 315.

11 In some of his better mature-phase short stories Machado will give another version of that same family recess. See 'A missa do galo' [Midnight Mass], 'Uns braços' [A Pair of Arms]. Also the novel *Dom Casmurro* [Dom Casmurro]. The same matter took Alencar to the most Machadian of his works, the small, very promising fragment 'Escabiosa/Sensitiva' [Scabietic/Sensitive] (Alencar, vol. I) [the novel-to-be was left unfinished; the two words the fragment is known by today were apparently alternative possibilities for a title].

the exceptions, of the villains who have no respect for the institution of the family – such will be the definition of villainy in the novels. They are marginal characters who share the concepts of French Realism as regards money and love. One more case for the contrast with Alencar, in whose novel such questions would be at the centre. It is clear, then, that wealth and social inequality are not lacking. But the resulting problems, in contrast to European Realism, are inscribed within the narrow, pious orbit of domestic sentiment.[12]

To no apparent literary advantage, Machado linked his novel to problems narrow in scope, which problems would, however, yield a different and credible combination of local themes – the importance of which, as we move on, will appear in reference to the formal and ideological changes that we shall be studying.[13] The obscurantist aspect of his position is obvious, since the family is a taboo subject for analysis. Analysis itself, however, is held in high regard. It is cultivated with all the more ardour because it is one of the essential hallmarks of the modern spirit, the same spirit whose external dimensions Machado is involved in dismissing. The contradiction is insoluble but not irreconcilable. Reflective thought and conformity are less incompatible than is usually believed, and it is necessary to look to nuance. In the middle of the nineteenth century bourgeois reason had become the normal basis of thought – of both its opponents and its proponents. As Sartre observes, at that time even Romantic aristocratism, contrary in principle to its own nature, saw the need to have recourse to analytical explanation.[14] Something analogous takes place

---

12   I base myself on the observations of Szondi 1973, pp. 89–90, about bourgeois sentimentalism in the eighteenth century. Schematically, in the lachrymose comedy of the Enlightenment, bourgeois familial intimacy is valorised as the site of true humanity and of exemplary feelings, in contrast to political submission to the despot, the heartless manipulations of the libertine, the genealogical obligations of the nobles, and also the hardness necessary for the economically-based life of the bourgeoisie itself. Hence the dignity of that intimacy as antithesis of the unhuman. See as well Habermas 1969, pp. 60–9. Then in the nineteenth century the Realist novel would show sentimentalism on the defensive, victim of the great economic and political transformations. In the second half of the century it is again propounded as a model, now by apologetic literature and so as to impede the growth of horizons necessary for the formation of a class consciousness. In parallel, good literature comes to see it through Naturalist fatalism or in perspectives, akin to Freud's, that see it as a form of oppression and repression.

13   With Ponsart, Augier and Jules Sandeau a good-bourgeois and anti-Romantic literature is created. For those authors art should moralise. They condemn passion in the name of utilitarianism. That is what Dumas fils does too, after an incipient Romantic round. See Sartre 1972, vol. III, p. 203. It is probable, according to Massa, that Machado found support in this line of thought. It would be necessary to do the research to locate the possible borrowings; in the absence of such, this exposition remains incomplete.

14   Sartre 1972, vol. III, pp. 138 ff.

in Machado's first novels. While the sanctity of order and that of family are affirmed, this is not the larger nor the best part of the novels. It is as if conformity on the essentials authorised, for general benefit and edification, the investigation of the sometimes anomalous, real grounds of family life. Thence the freedom in the 'transcription of customs',[15] the disposition to see much and complexly, from which really new and noteworthy considerations might result. This is where Machado's writerly power, albeit somewhat hampered by reverence, leaps to the eye: in the number and quality of his observations, the formulations and even the vocabulary, only partially restrained by the straitjacket of good principles. That development is unexpected, and it enters as a variant into this scene of our perversion of importations. Over against the materialism of 'a certain French school',[16] he sees it as necessary to spiritualise the bases of the social order. Delving with power and gusto into the mire of the soul (spiritual material par excellence), thereby proving his qualities as a modern writer, Machado carries out, in one sense, the work of an apologist. But in another sense he is also exploring the territory of personal domination and submission dear to conservative taste, to the economy of which he should have been adhering. Looked at carefully, the latter would be no less materialistic than the former. It is, however, one of the true pillars of our social life.

As regards the reorganisation of novel material, the procedure is similar. If the family is not to be reduced to less sacred dimensions, then its values will be final and respected. It will become the origin of the analytical impulse. Now inspiration from family does not produce the same literary results as inspiration from individuals. There is a gain in Brazilian verisimilitude on the most intimate level, the level of the elaboration of the analysis and construction, and a loss in critical vitality – a loss, that is, if we agree that the uninhibited and daring diction of individualism, of which Alencar possessed a bit and the French Realists and the second-phase Machado demonstrated much more, was and continues to be an aesthetic ideal. Thus we can see that the ideological valuation of a theme can have consequences on the formal level ... We are at the pole opposite to *Senhora*. As we have seen, the individualistic viewpoint, linked to the effects of money and competition, dwelt upon the progressive degradation of everything and everybody. Machado, however, insists on a respect and a decorum by means of which problems should find solutions. Conformity? Most certainly. Sense of reality?

15   Machado de Assis 1959, vol. II, p. 702.
16   Machado de Assis 1959, vol. III, p. 818.

That too, since the generalisation of commercial exchange that is the basis of the critical radicalism achieved in the French novel had not been effectuated among us. Now, once it is believed that 'family' is untouchable, that it is sacramental, plural and proprietary by definition, there will always be people and things that are 'authentically' valuable, in relation to which instrumental calculation cannot occur – thus would universalisation of the latter be prevented.[17] The difference is clearly shown in the way social advancement is regarded: in one case the price that has to be paid is focused on even when all turns out well, the person advancing having transformed both himself and others into mere steps in a career; in another case the conditions are examined under which the advancement, desirable in and of itself, is carried out with dignity to the benefit of the person and that of the good families that benefit from his abilities, and finally to the benefit of our Brazilian society, which needs to curtail its irregularities and draw upon the human element available to it. Instead of absolute opposition of individual and society, of generalised manipulation and the corresponding critical radicalism, there is the community of customs, of interests and beliefs, the desire to improve, and 'accommodation'. Favour, co-optation, the subtleties of conformity and obedience replace, at the core of Machado's novel, the combativeness that comes with the ideology of liberal individualism. These are calculations of another sort, covered over, to their great artistic detriment, by the narrator's zeal. In his mature phase, comfortably ensconced in this different logic, Machado will examine it in its turn – from a viewpoint we have yet to examine – leaving its sanctity stripped bare. Even then he does not deny its efficacy: to the end he will keep exploring its implications for literary form. Was he condemning himself to being an out-of-fashion writer? We shall return to that question. For now, let us see how distancing himself from the strong tradition of Realism – in which Alencar found his inspiration – and finding support for himself in recent second-category French literature, Machado created a literary method closer to the reality that Brazil presents. In fact, the ideology of family permeates society along lines that European evolution had made obsolete and deceitful, which is why only the apologetic novel based itself on it. In Brazil, far from disguising the process of proletarianisation, which was minimal anyhow, the idealisation of family moves the narrative along lines that maintain contact with the multiform and all-but-universal practice of paternalism. It did not cease being deceitful, but for the novel it worked as a nucleus to which material gleaned from observation could be added suggestively and without apparent artifice, benefitting from the infinity of recognisable connex-

---

17   Goldmann 1964.

ions that the real process weaves together. In the final analysis, the challenge of any novel is the same: to develop a formal principle capable of taking in empirical detail.[18]

2 *A Mão e a Luva*

A good strategy ... every bit the offspring of the heart[19]

To judge by its design, *A Mão e a Luva* is a light, indulgent pastime – one with the sort of indulgence in which members of good families engage among themselves. A girl of humble origin, who is adopted by a wealthy baroness her godmother, deliberates among three suitors: the first is Romantic and weak; the second, nephew of the baroness to whom the girl owes her position in society, is dull; the third is strong – and also the one who has won the girl's heart. The requisite setbacks are overcome, and the ending is a happy one. The book separates itself from the status of commonplace pastime, however, in the analytical work it undertakes. It seeks to formulate and poetise – therein the surprise! – the well-understood interests of the several parties in questions of co-optation, in which operation it proceeds with daring and reflection. The result produced is a kind of brash, expedient conformity, the forerunner of the reactionary modernisation of our own days, in which intelligence, vitality and antipathy join together. Close to practical reality, distant from innocent idealisations, this outlook cannot be reconciled with, much less subordinate itself to, the sense of pastime, from which it differs both in gravity and in maliciousness. The coexistence of those two outlooks cannot produce a good effect. We witness in this novel, though, the consolidation of a portion of the material Machado will treat in future work.

Using 'intelligence and smarts',[20] Guiomar tries to take the place in her godmother's eyes of the latter's own deceased daughter. She succeeds in that undertaking and thereby ceases being 'the simple heiress to her parents' poverty'.[21] But how are we to understand her conduct? Guiomar reciprocates the emotions of her second mother, though there might just be in her otherwise sincere affection a kind of emotional overreach that could look like pretence.

---

18 Machado de Assis 1959, vol. I, p. 116.
19 Machado de Assis 1959, vol. I, p. 116.
20 Machado de Assis 1959, vol. I, p. 130.
21 Machado de Assis 1959, vol. I, p. 127.

The affection is spontaneous; it is the overreach that may be intentional.[22] The reader may well sense the questionability of the exposition, which includes the expectable antagonisms – between spontaneity and calculation, sincerity and simulation, genuine feelings and self-interest – but denies them relevance: after all, the heroine's calculations do not stand in opposition to her heartfelt emotions, of which they are merely the extension, and if perhaps they incite an effusiveness that is a little exaggerated, they do no harm, indeed they do good. The book's rhetoric, however, stands in contrast, for it reassigns to the girl's thinking the negative connotations that the plot has taken away. This ambiguity is frequently repeated, sometimes in a highly freighted manner. Is Guiomar a cold person, overly shrewd, given to pretence and tactics? If so, then always in the interest of her good nature.[23] 'Imposture say I, as long as it is understood that she is honest and upright, since her intent has been nothing more than not to distress her godmother but rather to remove the motive for any affliction that might otherwise occur'.[24] Honest imposture, sincere pretence and other paradoxes, repeated over and over again, amount to the suspension of Romantic oppositions, *after having brought them up*. Does Guiomar (calculation) use her stepmother (emotions in mourning) as a springboard to fortune? No, since she 'reciprocates the emotions of her second mother' and one who does that exists in the sphere of reciprocation and naturalness, innocent of that manipulation that characterises those who 'use'. But Guiomar nonetheless proceeds with intelligence and smarts … The same with her marriage, which is the result of 'cold-blooded, reasoned selection',[25] the choice falling to a rich and ambitious gentleman, who in addition will become a Deputy.[26] Calculation in such matters, which would seem to the Romantics contrary to genuine sentiment, was in truth 'every bit the offspring of the heart',[27] since ever since she was little she has had an attraction to the elegant life, which fits well with her basic instincts.[28] But why is her choice 'cold-blooded?' At first, because that premeditated behaviour is revealed through the lens of conventional Romanticism, which condemns it. But then this condemnation is mistaken, since it presumes an antagonism that in practice – that is, in terms of the novel's central conflict – does not exist (Guiomar's behaviour is foresightful, not premeditated). And

---

22   Machado de Assis 1959, vol. I, p. 129.
23   Machado de Assis 1959, vol. I, pp. 145, 171–172, 176 ff.
24   Machado de Assis 1959, vol. I, p. 172.
25   Machado de Assis 1959, vol. I, p. 165.
26   [The Chamber of Deputies (Câmara dos Deputados) is the lower house of the Brazilian National Congress.]
27   Machado de Assis 1959, vol. I, p. 116.
28   Machado de Assis 1959, vol. I, p. 130.

then, third (and this step gives the book its piquancy, by holding the first two options in suspension): the behaviour that has seemed reprehensible, although it might even have been commendable, in the end will be evoked in words that incriminate Guiomar (her behaviour is said to be premeditated, although it might have been foresightful). The terminology of cynicism and of virtue are made to coincide, and the reprehensible behaviour is exactly what was needed. In sum, the movement of co-optation combines calculation and feelings in a single aspiration, all the while retaining their conflicting nomenclature, thus complicating the terms of the problem. The ignoble dimensions of this 'harmony' will figure among the favourite materials of second-phase Machado. This first phase now has such 'harmony' as an ideal. *Thus the rebuttal that reality gives to Romantic judgment has come to be a formal element, something like the tone of prose.* Its affinity with the order of reality is clear, it must be remembered that at the time the literary-sentimental dimension of the country lay in the area of Romanticism while social mobility and marriage were inscribed in the sphere of co-optation. Looking more closely, we note in Machado's rebuttal a very pronounced, if not insolent, stridence. The solution is a bit facile but far from superficial: it is a conscious position in which the reality of local relations finds vindication over against 'literary' sentiments coming from Europe. With apologies for the anachronism, a kind of corrective is imposed upon the alienated culture, an ambivalent corrective that holds together both the attack upon an illusion and an acquiescence to the social inequality that sustains that illusion. On the level of the characters one finds a similar attitude in expressed sympathy for low but strong ambition, in Guiomar's earthy and conformist appetites – a shocking heroine custom-made for Brazil, from the race that Romanticism never softened and tradition did not intimidate. In fact, she – whose ideals can be summed up as maintaining appearances in polite society and owning a good house with good furniture and a husband with a good position – contrasts to advantage with Estévão's weepy emotionality as well as with the inertia of Jorge, the baroness' nephew who just sits back and waits for the benefits that will derive from his last name to appear. In opposition to ideas floating in the ether – and foreign ideas to boot – and in opposition to blind traditionalism as well, Machado defends what he considers the best interests of Brazilian society: it is necessary to promote a modern people, with initiative, resolute if necessary, in order to … build a family, according to positive principles, in the interests of the rich and the better-prepared among the poor. The same thing is observable on the dramatic level of the work with regard to the conflicts in which Guiomar is involved. Romantic love, indifferent to material benefits, appears in the person of Estévão, but only to be set aside. He evokes from the heroine 'some sympathy to be sure but it is slight and inconsequential'.[29] The core dilemma belongs to another order: whether to comply passively with the baroness' wish, which is to marry her goddaughter to her nephew Jorge or to manoeuvre in the direction of Luís Alves, Guiomar's preferred option, who would also be acceptable to the godmother, as well as being an even better match. Social and familial conformity would not be threatened by either of the two, for they are both unassailable on that score. What is on the line, however, is the concept of favour. Does the young woman owe unquestioning obedience to her benefactress or does she have the right to take her own wishes into account, to seek a compromise between her interests and the debt of gratitude? In more general terms, Machado sets authoritarian and traditionalist paternalism over against an enlightened paternalism that takes into account the beneficiary's natural gifts and initiative instead of sacrificing them. A national line of progressivism, the platform of this book ... And finally, observe that from the very first pages Estévão's Romantic sentiments are comical, presented as they are as preposterous, foreign Byronisms, and, in particular, as superficial in contrast with the grasp of the real that both Guiomar and Luís Alves value so highly. Now the classical, taut arc of the European Realist novel, which is completed only with its final step, can be summed up as the more-or-less gradual loss of illusions: the facts of bourgeois life demonstrate the unviability of Romanticism, which even so is not seen as foolish and does not lose its power to expose the iniquity of those facts. From the outset understanding Romanticism as a second-degree ideology, Machado avoids the implications of that arc – which then remains in a weakened state. In this he includes an essential datum of Brazilian life, and in so doing finds himself grappling with a new and capital problem for which only later will he find a solution. That problem: what is the trajectory appropriate to the lives of his characters? What is the form proper to the plot?

From this quick review we can see that the number of literary innovations is large, in emphases, characters to study, ideological content, and the dramatic structuring of conflicts. The reader will have noted their affinity, as far as reality is concerned. A collection of realistic solutions, all of them complex in that they invoke the universe of favour and the liberal universe regularly conjoined. What in Alencar was a sporadic coexistence with no internal necessity, is in Machado a problem, and, more than that, a premise located within the very fabric of the novelistic construction: it is no longer merely a question of now and again running across the incongruity between Romantic ideas and the texture of local society but rather one of bringing those terms together on the exacting and

---

29   Machado de Assis 1959, vol. I, p. 145.

generalising level of forms, where the dissonance between them would itself be an element of life. As regards the author's motives, detailed evidence is not available, but the case does not seem mysterious. That fine society should open itself up to the talents of the disadvantaged would naturally seem appealing to Machado, since that was his own story. Under the circumstances, it is understandable too that Romantic norms might have seemed to him obstacles rather than profundities. These are positions with clear practical grounding that were widely disseminated at the time. Machado's merit lay in seeing their disconnect and transforming them from isolated facts in current life into the germs of novel construction and of the interpretation of existence. In other words, the relationships involving 'favour' come to be much more than free-floating data. Pulling liberal ideas into their field of gravity, they engender an area with its own problems, conflicts, priorities and vicissitudes. This logic repeats a real logic – without, needless to say, reproducing reality in toto. There lies the basis of that singular, non-picturesque Brazilness widely recognised as Machado's creation – one that he strove to achieve.[30] But it is obvious as well that only in the second phase will this logic be developed unimpeded. *A mão e a luva* works through some of its elements and benefits from so doing, but they are subordinate to the rigid inconsequentiality of light literature. Thence the dubious impression left by the first-phase novels: they are no better than their predecessors, albeit considerably more substantial. Their density is owing to the forms of which we are speaking, which are genuine in the simplest sense of the word, representing as they do generalisations upon social practice. It was natural that scattered pieces of Brazilian daily life (images, ways of speaking, ideas, customs, material culture, etcetera) that were part of the native soil should respond to those forms by creating with them a more meaningful literary substance with a higher relational content, not one that is merely picturesque. Nevertheless, because of the irony inherent in artistic endeavour, the truth is that the outcome was worse. The formal adjustment that we have seen has solved prior inconsistencies but also produced new ones, the difference being that the latter are serious and lack the ingenuousness of the former. Carried out well, the assimilation of social contradictions into the novelistic framework

---

30   See the famous passage about national instinct: 'What should be asked of the writer above all else is a certain inner sentiment that makes him a man of his time and of his country, even when he deals with subjects far removed in time and space. Some time ago a notable French critic, in analysing a Scots writer, Masson, said quite rightly that, just as one could be British without always talking about gorse, Masson was thoroughly Scots despite saying not a single word about thistle, and he explained what he meant by adding that there was in Masson an inner Scottishism different and better than if it had been merely superficial'. Machado de Assis 1959, vol. III, p. 817.

creates a more demanding context, one element of which is the rationality of real processes – an element that infuses it with a seriousness particular to the Realist novel. In this case, inconsistencies become questions of literary – as well as social – logic, and with this mixed quality they become intolerable. The irritation left behind by first-phase Machado novels is linked to this more substantial kind of inconsistency and also signals, in addition to the defect, the constitution of a Brazilian Realism.

Let us examine a passage from the novel that is representative of this problem. Almost at the end, when the heroine's social-climbing tendencies are fully recognised – 'there is no doubt: she is self-serving'[31] – Luís Alves senses in his heart a confirmation of his old feelings. He declares himself and finds his sentiments requited, as Guiomar's heart has been touched as well. Read the narrator's commentary, in which prior observations are taken up anew and at this point form a conclusion of sorts:

> Guiomar loved truly. But up to what point was that emotion involuntary? It was – up to the point of not attenuating our heroine's chastity of heart and of not diminishing the power of her affective faculties. Only up to there; from there on cold-blooded deliberations of the spirit came into play. I do not wish to present her as a soul that emotionality blinds and drives mad nor to have her die from a silent and timid love. She was, and would do, nothing of the sort. Her nature required and loved those heart-flowers but shouldn't be expected either to go gather them from bare, wild places or on the stems of modest bushes planted in front of a country window. She wanted them, beautiful and luxuriant, but in a Sèvres vase placed upon a rare piece of furniture set between two city windows, that vase and those flowers flanked by cashmere curtains whose ends must just brush the carpet on the floor.[32]

No one will claim that the passage is pretty, but it has a certain undeniable force linked to apprehension of its elements in their contradictory and concise whole, and especially linked to the ambiguity of its construction, in which moral restrictions constitute praise and vice-versa. To fully appreciate its complexity one has only to repeat yet again that Guiomar is a positive figure, indeed much more so than the above passage would seem to indicate. A dissonance in which the reader will recognise the movement that we have spoken of before:

---

31 Machado de Assis 1959, vol. I, p. 153.
32 Machado de Assis 1959, vol. I, p. 165.

insinuation of a Romantic outlook followed – or preceded, according to the case – by the depreciation of that very outlook. Mad, blind passion, involuntary emotionality, silent and timid love are all expressions that bring to the stage the viewpoint of Romanticism, for which affect (nature), if it is not unconditional, is degraded (by the coercion of conveniences). Guiomar loves truly, but without madness, blindness or timidity, and her emotions are involuntary only in part. Repeating a bit: spontaneous emotion and cold-blooded, wilful choice are not opposites like positive and negative but rather are allied, and their conciliation is not a matter of fortunate happenstance. On the contrary it is representative of the reciprocity natural to the practices of paternalism, in which spontaneity is not all good, calculation is not all bad, and each is indispensable. In terms of novel composition, their conciliation is sanctioned by the central conflict: within the specific frame of familial co-optation, to struggle for good terms of conciliation does not diminish, but rather elevates, the person – indeed gives them the opportunity to prove their value – while the absolutes of Romantic ideology simply miss reality. Over against the false dilemmas to which mental marginality (on a world scale) disposes us, Guiomar is an affirmation of local life and intelligence. The piquant note to that effect comes in the perverse rehabilitation of highly-charged notions: cold-blooded will, disdain for modest, rustic modes of life, desire for wealth and comfort are converted into qualities that possess extra saliency from having emerged from a combat in which they have represented clarity as opposed to acritical imitation. A turnabout that is not fully convincing itself, for at the critical moment another factor is added that renders the whole specious. In fact, speaking generically, in the absence of liberal individualism the stigma that Romanticism had attached to social calculation loses its foundation, and calculations go back to being what they had always been, one of humankind's greatest strengths. With blame removed, the intelligence directs itself to that which it spontaneously desires – *but at that point in pre-bourgeois Brazil it so happens that the elements of life were taking on bourgeois form*, that very form whose detestable aspects Romanticism points out with profundity. This is a multi-consequential fact in regard both to reality and to literature, and it signals the limits of our national difference. Thus, let's say that Guiomar's ambitions are of the very type to which Romantic critique applies, which contradictorily does not apply to her because her universe is ruled by reciprocity. Where does that leave us? The problem relates to the whole of the book: the distanced use of Romantic vocabulary, the praise of a character immunised against its tensions, the secondary position of Romanticism in the dramatic geography, centre stage being occupied by a conflict in the sphere of paternalism, the treatment of Romanticism as fashion rather than problem – are all energetic forms of mental unblocking and affirmation of Brazilian difference; and once Romantic constraints are set aside its eternal enemies – price, property and social status – come in through the front door, enemies that the plot had led us to think were absent. And they come with the additional advantage of impunity. In other words, material civilisation was breathing the very same individualism the inexistence of which was being proved. Furthermore, the vindication of paternalism seems to go hand in hand with vindication of modern style, that is, urban, wealthy, assuming the commodity form and with no ties to tradition, precisely the wealth that had given rise to the Romantic revolt – and this in addition to not being the expression of the universe of paternalism. This doubtless constitutes a compositional error, but one that is there to complete the novel's overall ideological framework, which loses in literary coherence and human sympathy and gains in representation of the nation. The thesis is simple: since Romanticism has no raison d'être among us as we are not a bourgeois country, long live bourgeois opulence since we aren't Romantics! The sophistry is obvious and is made viable by a kind of deliberate foreshortening of the moral horizon, which despite its innocent tone is one of the principal intentions of *A mão e a luva*. With this support, consideration of Romanticism in the light of our reality surpasses the status of critical procedure – which it is – to become an ideological piece. Argued with respect to the sphere of paternalism, dismissal of Romantic concepts is established and extended disproportionally, providing, as a secondary effect, moral and rational cover to bourgeois property and prestige that, being too a part of our reality, are unreservedly legitimated and, so to speak, advised. When it comes to saying what we are not, namely European-style bourgeois, the argument's anti-Romantic line calls all the attention to itself and redeems what we are; paternalistic relations are analysed with finesse but not in a critical vein, which too is a form of legitimation. From the point of view of our elites it would be impossible to ask for more: paternalism is seen as subtle, flexible, not out of date, the new forms of property are not immoral and the two spheres do not clash with one another – rather each completes the other, intimately associated as they are on the subject of the ineptitude of Romantic criteria. In sum, criticism of critical fantasies – fantasies in which Brazilian ideological belatedness is in fact reflected – ends up as pure and simple acquiescence to the real order, albeit a complex and somewhat cynical acquiescence. An intelligent conformism that seeks to give coherence and increased refinement to the expression of our ruling classes. Such is the ideological sense of *A mão e a luva*. With that established and the scant and 'interested' character of this 'solution' indicated, let us recognise that the problem exists and look at the impact that it has. In our analysis the element that bears the contradiction and the literary incoherence has been bourgeois luxury. Its presence is not fortuitous, and nor are the questions that it raises. As is well known, Europe's cultural hegemony was not limited to ideas. Rather it resided in the consumer goods that we imported and which, in their way, were also vehicles of ideology, and what is more ones more difficult to criticise and impossible to do away with, being part of normal economic flow – Guiomar herself can serve as an example, for she is a sceptic with regard to Romanticism but a true believer when it comes to Sèvres vases. Reproduction of the international economic system fixed the eyes and the desires of the Brazilian elite on things and ideas that had no continuity with our base social relations, which remained relatively silenced, without completion within material and ideological civilisation. An incongruity with enormous effects – one that was a daily fact in our life, an appropriate symbol of our location within the international division of labour and the insoluble ideological problem for the beneficiaries of the Brazilian order, which at that time, just as now, sought to partake of the combined advantages of social belatedness and material progress.[33] Picking up our thread once again, we can

---

33 In a recent study, Celso Furtado further develops the analysis of this disconnection not only with respect to discontinuous imitation but also as a causal element for underdevelopment. The steps are as follows: with its base in expanded international commerce, a new international division of labour develops, driven by England, between industrialised countries and countries that provide raw materials and foodstuffs. With the latter, the dominant groups are led to use their wealth to import the new consumer goods produced by the industrialised economies. In this sense they modernise at the expense of the extractive and agricultural production, which stays just as it has been (hence the incongruity we have been speaking of: 'The local elites are thus empowered to look to the patterns of consumption in the centre – to the point of losing contact with the cultural sources of their respective countries'). The consequences will appear later, during the phase of so-called import substitution, when these countries try to produce what they had previously been importing: the 'constellation of goods consumed by the modernised groups' will dictate the direction of the industrialising undertaking, because the 'ruling classes who have taken on the forms of consumption present in the centre countries do not perceive a question in choosing between that constellation of goods and any other.' Now those goods imply specific modes of production that have no relation to the local level of capital accumulation. As a consequence 'the productive apparatus tends to divide itself in two: one segment connected to traditional productive activity geared to export or to the domestic market (rural and urban), the other constituted by industries that require high capital density and produce for the modernised minority.' Because to survive this second segment needs part of the surplus generated by the first through international commerce, modernisation and the development of productive forces are complementary to the oppression and hyper-exploitation of a large part of the population, which remains at a subsistence level. And finally, at a later phase the accelerated and expensive evolution of the technology will render useless the importation of isolated technical solutions, which soon become obsolete, and it becomes necessary to associate with the actual flow of innovation, that is with the great international firms, who retain

say that the little story of Guiomar brings together in highly distilled form those elements from the totality necessary to a problematised representation of the country's life, minus the picturesqueness. Despite the specific sphere it represents, it is a condensed and detailed transposition of our real process, and the reflection that it invites is substantial. Nonetheless, we are once more facing an artistic achievement that is unconvincing, for the distance between the modesty of the tale and the ambition of the analytical framework with which it is associated is one of the book's obvious defects. Be that as it may, the adjustments performed are considerable: Romantic-liberal concepts are disqualified as superficial forms of conformity – a just conclusion – but in favour of a more pervasive conformity that asserts a modernised version of paternalism, flexible in its co-optation and open to the advantages of the modern world. A paternalism that unites the old injustice and the new into a whole that wishes to see itself as progressive and prejudice-free. Compared to Alencar the solution is considerably more thoughtful and more in line with reality. But it is far from pleasing, and one would have trouble arguing that this book is better than *Senhora*. To be specific, let us say in the case of *A mão e a luva* that the search for ideological clarity discredits an inadequate fashion, but in order to accredit a socially substantive inconsistency that responds to the particular and exclusive interests of a paternalistic league of the wealthy and the gifted. And if it is true that the perception of social rationality and of its incorporation into literary form has made progress under those circumstances, the novel produced is even less recommendable. Between generous illusion and cynical realism ... A hundred years later the elitist critique of liberalism retains similar aspects, albeit without the streak of mental independence. Today as well, those who insist upon the ineptitude of liberal demands for Brazil, which is not Europe, are right – which enables them to practice, in unapologetic and violent ways, social injustice, in the name of progress and modernity of the spirit.

But let's return to the words 'Guiomar loved truly' cited earlier. In our analysis of the passage we have traversed the road that leads from defence of the intelligence to desire for a luxury house. In the light of the overall movement of the book, that path is conceived as positive and exemplary. And we have also pointed out the contrast between that concept and the progressive shamelessness that constitutes the movement of the passage itself. A contrast that contains some dose of literary coquetry but above all the formal idea and the scope of the novel's problematics. In its overall lineaments we have seen the

---

their monopoly. National dependency caps off underdevelopment. See Furtado 1971, esp. ch. II, 'Subdesenvolvimento e dependência: as conexões fundamentais' [Underdevelopment and Dependency: The Basic Connections].

social grounding of this constellation and in that sense its accuracy as a reflexion of reality – greater than we might have supposed. Let us now look in detail at its overall elaboration, which one could also call its novelistic productivity, in which, up to a certain point, the intimacy of its premises is revealed. On this plane the logic of the composition – faithfulness to the premises, which, as we have seen, are national – and the exploration of Brazilian reality are attuned to each other. Or, better, the depth of the latter depends on the coherence and viability of the former. Let us begin yet again with the lengthy and convoluted set of moral considerations that is a factor of intrinsic interest and also reveals an objective complexity that had not previously found its literary manifestation. Reconstruction of the formal structure along apparently less-than-glorious lines gave Machado's prose – and identified in our society – what within the universe of the novel is true stature: a complex, closed, logical social fabric, not to mention an original one. There are more examples of what I am describing, of the increase in literary and mimetic density, without overall qualitative gains. Guiomar loved truly, *but* up to what point was that emotion involuntary? It was – *up to the point* of not attenuating our heroine's chastity of heart and of not diminishing her affective faculties. *Only up to there; from there on* cold-blooded deliberations of the spirit came into play. Let the reader observe that doctrine and grammar are not saying the same thing in this passage. One (which, clearly, is not thus analysed on the basis of this passage alone but rather by reference to the whole book) declares the harmonious partnership of spontaneity and will within love, while the other, with its '*but*', '*up to the point of*', '*only up to there*', '*from there on*', carries water to the mill of Romanticism and has us supposing that the part given to the will represents harm to the other part, which remains in a subordinate position. Hence affirmation of an emotion without flaw and suggestion of doubt in that same respect, all in the same development. 'I do not wish to present her as a soul that emotionality blinds and drives mad nor to have her die from a silent and timid love. She was, and would do, neither of those things'. Like Guiomar, who 'was, and would do, nothing of the sort', the narrator is not going to make concessions to Romantic fashion. He too is one of those positive spirits that the book recommends. He is going to say the truth without adornment, even if it is not pleasing. In this sense there is something emphatic in '*I do not wish to*' and '*she was ... nothing of the sort*' that is like a lesson in toughness, which continues his prior suspicions regarding the naturalness of Guiomar's motives, by confirming those suspicions, and which, especially, labels as misleading what had been positive only two lines before. Furthermore, if we go back to 'I do not wish to present her ...' and emphasise the first person, the reader will perhaps agree that the narrator says not only that he is not going to lie but also 'I am not the one who is going to lie in this material', in the saying of which he enlists himself within the group of those whom the experience of life has disabused. Disappointment's part within the 'positive' attitude becomes more palpable in the following phrase in which Guiomar shouldn't be expected to like poor people. Disdainful praise of conservative common-sense, finding of fact, veiled lamentation, homage to the powerful? it contains a little bit of all of them. 'Her nature required and loved those heart-flowers but shouldn't be expected either to go gather them from bare, wild places or on the stems of modest bushes planted in front of a country window'. The reader will say if I am forcing the argument by thinking that in 'shouldn't be expected' there exists something like 'let no one expect ... he who is saying this to you is one who expected'. In any case, observe that the sphere of spontaneity, a little while back indispensable 'to the power of [Guiomar's] affective faculties', now is included among the 'heart-flowers', an expression that in context is also unencumbered and somewhat disdainful and in which both the flowers and the heart are discredited, reduced as they are to superfluities that merely give perfume to life. The inversion is complete: Romantic spontaneity has become a lovely artifice, and the true naturalness is Guiomar's, which takes advantage, that is, which avoids, what is wild, bare, modest or 'country', and demands – emotion notwithstanding – the more emphatically, *that* vase and *those* flowers, in an insistence that sweeps away what little remained of illusion, therein performing the transformation of vase and flowers into conventional signs of the bourgeois good life – the life that it would constitute a lack of naturalness not to appreciate. It is clear that this sentiment unconditionally aligned with the wealthy constitutes mockery of the other. With regard to the narrator, from being hardened by deception he graduates to the position of thorough cynic. On the other side, the paragraph opens: 'Could Luís Alves give her this kind of love? He could – she felt he could'.[34] Taking the passage as a whole one can say that with every new corrective brought up to allay a prior suspicion the overall picture grows worse, the explanations being more worrisome than calming. It is a pattern of development that appears to be sarcastic, but that remains suspended and does no harm since it presupposes a Romantic distribution of emphases in which emotion is positive in opposition to merchandise, which is negative – an order that in this book is set up as illusory. But it is also the case that that development is not completely dismissed but rather counts when it is convenient that it do so. Thus, within the few lines of a paragraph Guiomar's excellence finds its ground in the most varied of authorities, such as her vibrant nature, her cold-blooded

---

34   Machado de Assis 1959, vol. I, p. 165.

will, her controlled passions and attraction to wealth. They are all credible reasons that can comfort whoever accepts them. Guiomar justifies herself with all of them, without ever foregoing conformity – which is possible given that Machado does not point out the contradictions among them. And it matters little that the narrator is obliged to keep recanting line after line, since he too always has the security of an authority – he too is a kind of Guiomar. In the passage we have studied, this inconsistency takes on a so-to-speak demonstrative character, which heightens its literary interest. As Machado himself would later laugh – with respect to others, of course – at the smell of merit and virtue that comes along with this gallery of sophistry, we can discount him: the reader will see that he is moving from the bad to the excellent and that here he is in the presence of the good literature of Machado's maturity. In an effort to impart coherence and literary standing to the ins and outs of co-optation, Machado creates a process in which spontaneity is, successively, highly valued, confined, ironised and denatured, in which ambition is seen as baseness, necessity, naturalness and as an eminent social quality – without there seeming to be a conflict among those positions. But one has only to separate them from their edifying premise to recognise the literary capturing of a lively, mean opportunism that, in matters of ideology, paternalistic liberal-slavery could not but lead to – and which will be one of the dominant themes of Machado's second phase.

To bring to a close, finally, the parallel with Alencar, we see that the experience of paternalism and its primacy on the formal level are explored and systematised within these solutions without their giving a satisfactory account of the other half of the material, namely that which originated in the modern world of bourgeois individualism and mercantile society. As in Alencar, those are not contingent failings, connected as they are to the effort to impart rationality and lustre to the situation of our elites, and, also as in Alencar, the artistic impasse has mimetic value providing excellent literary material. It is precisely in those failings that social interest finds its true transcription. As regards Machado's intent, the merging of the two spheres is, so to speak, an ideal of pragmatism and progress and is dissonant only in appearance: counter to what Romantic doctrine claims, the family scene benefits from the resourcefulness of the individuals within it, at the same time that it subordinates it, removing its sting; the family is the token of altruism, egoism is the token of intelligence, and the two together are perfection. But we have seen that the context urges a reading in another direction. Far from redeeming the characters' calculations and the bourgeois luxury to which those characters aspire, familial order reveals itself and appears to be what it is, namely another form of particularism. The overall picture is as follows: the pragmatism and progress recommended by Machado do exist but they are for the few, and the efforts to combine them with justice and the general good is all-but-obvious sophistry. Consequently, the moments when the book's intention acquires its greatest visibility are absolutely horrible (albeit vibrant, while the rest, besides being bad, are dull). They are passages in which the social partiality of the logic is undisguised, in which the novel loses the respectability proper to the search for intellectual and formal coherence. And involuntarily they are examples of second-phase Machado's best comicality. Such is the case when Luís Alves tells himself 'There is no doubt: [Guiomar] is self-serving'[35] and then says to her 'You have a great and noble heart', words that 'were particularly arranged to leave a deep mark in her memory'[36] – in all seriousness, without the slightest intention to mock. Another example is the detestable close of the book, in which the recently-married couple confess to one another about their appetite for social prominence: 'Guiomar, who was standing before him with her hands in his, let herself slowly fall over her husband's knees and the two ambitions exchanged a fraternal kiss. Each then adjusted him- or herself as though that glove had been made for that hand'.[37] The same can be said for the title image, *A mão e a luva*, in which too there is no reticence. And finally let us consider Guiomar's reaction before Mrs. Oswald, the house's English governess, who to please the baroness tries to exert influence within the heroine's nuptial machinations. What irritates Guiomar is not so much the pressure as 'the person exerting it – an inferior wage-earner'.[38] In a prior passage, when Guiomar had not yet ceased to be 'the simple heiress to her parents' poverty'[39] – an expression that is an example too, coming as it does from the lips of the good baroness herself – she, Guiomar, allows that she will have to work to make a living. 'These last words pass through her lips as though being forced, red crawls up her cheeks, as if her soul had covered her face with shame'.[40] Thus, by a mere hair's breadth had Guiomar escaped being an 'inferior wage-earner' herself; all the more reason for keeping her distance: 'She looks coldly and distantly at the English woman with one of those looks that are, so to speak, a gesture from an indignant soul. What irritates her is not the allusion, which was of little importance, it was the person who had made it – an inferior wage-earner. Mrs. Oswald understands all this; she bites the tip of her tongue but compromises with the girl'.[41] What is more,

---

35 Machado de Assis 1959, vol. I, p. 153.
36 Machado de Assis 1959, vol. I, p. 157.
37 Machado de Assis 1959, vol. I, p. 180.
38 Machado de Assis 1959, vol. I, p. 135.
39 Machado de Assis 1959, vol. I, p. 127.
40 Machado de Assis 1959, vol. I, p. 130.
41 Machado de Assis 1959, vol. I, p. 135.

it should be observed generally that Mrs. Oswald is treated with a goodly dose of xenophobia. Having explored this museum of horrors, the careful reader will have noticed how much our examples are close to great moments in Machado's second phase and will be re-encountered there. The 'kiss of two ambitions' is precursor to the marriage as a Limited Company of scoundrels illustrated by the Palha spouses in *Quincas Borba*. Luís Alves' esteem for Guiomar's social ambitions is repeated in the enthusiasm that Brás Cubas feels for Nhá Loló when she rejects her so-to-speak excessively 'popular' father.[42] The general development of the paragraph we have analysed in which the emendations keep making the sonnet worse, is the same as Brás's brother-in-law Cotrim's extraordinary eulogy, one of Machado's most devastating pages.[43] Etcetera, etcetera.

Elevated to norm, the unconditional commitment to the realities of life brings them to the forefront and sets the novel on the track of reality. Hence the paradox of a steadfastly pedestrian book that simultaneously is enhancing: wealth, social protection and high society are entirely desirable and do not bear any contra-indication – except in one brief moment of delicacy in which Guiomar says she prefers not to have the 'benefits received' thrown in her face.[44] Social climbing is envisaged through the eyes of those on top by someone who is coming from below. Climbing may present difficulties, which it is the task of the strong to circumvent, but it does not disclose injustice, nor is it, properly-speaking, a problem. Now in his next novel, which is considerably more idealised in several ways, Machado will be less optimistic and more profound on this point. Co-optation will be seen from the perspective of susceptibility.

3   *Helena*

... the wings of favour are all that protect me ...

Comparable in subject matter to *A mão e a luva*, *Helena* is a book written in a completely different spirit. In this book, too, Machado seeks to contribute to the perfecting of paternalism. But the point of departure has changed, and his position is now a defensive one. *Left to itself, the interplay of co-optation and bourgeois interests produces results that are degrading*. Such is the new thesis, according to which it is necessary to engage in moral watchfulness. In place of

---

42   Machado de Assis, *Memórias póstumas de Brás Cubas*, chs. CXXI–CXXII.
43   Machado de Assis, *Memórias póstumas de Brás Cubas*, ch. CXXIII.
44   Machado de Assis 1959, vol. I, p. 171.

the prior confidence – albeit somewhat cynical – in the appetite and the flexibility of the strong appears the vigilance of Christian precept.

To mark the difference, let us say that in the new novel *A mão e a luva*'s Guiomar would figure among the negative characters. The social landscape is the same: the 'good' families, wealth and political interest stand in opposition to the erratic and obscure world of the poor. But only the less 'good' (Dona Ursula and Eugênia) and the openly bad (Dr. Camargo) adhere unreservedly to temporal gain and let themselves be guided by it, like Guiomar. In this book's terms, they, 'lacking in elevation of feeling', give in to 'considerations of a lesser order'.[45] The good are highly exacting in this area, and the least insinuation about their motives is enough to lead them to pull back. As we shall see, Helena prefers death to being suspected, and Mendonça breaks off a marriage for the same reason. This does not mean that familial prerogatives, wealth and influence are the objects of criticism. In fact, Machado seeks to legitimate them, creating a frame in which they don't undermine individual dignity. More precisely, they are not criticised as institution but as motive. The problem does not reside in inequality but in the people that seek to use it to their advantage. For Christian sentiment, wealth and poverty, illustrious birth and anonymous birth, the regular and the irregular are secondary, which, paradoxically, is the reason – following the lines of apologetic Catholicism – for accepting them. The contrary would be immodest and constitute a lack of decorum. Thus, if it is true that Helena moves from a poor family to a wealthy one, such was not her objective as it was for Guiomar. She was obeying her father. And while she fights to become accepted, she does so to be worthy of her new relatives. It is Dr. Camargo, who plots a rich and illustrious marriage for his daughter Eugênia, who is the villain. In other words, it rests with the severity of familial and Christian love to moralise social differences and cleanse them of the low behaviour that they may bring forth. Such, then, is the book's ideology, the insipidity of which goes without saying. With that established, we can say that it is not an inapposite ideology, since it merely extends the Catholicism that is infused into paternalistic relationships, without which those relationships would not be understandable – a dimension that *A mão e a luva* cynically prefers not to bring up. Insipid as solution, the Christian outlook is determinative as presence and comes to complete the space of favour and to reorganise it along more nearly realistic lines, according it a less utilitarian economy of its own. In sum: the absolute dignity of the individual and of the family, superior to life's contingencies, compensates in principle for the inequalities in real social

---

45   Machado de Assis 1959, vol. I, p. 189.

relations, which in this way are legitimated – above all else freed from the bitterness of humiliation. Now in practice it was only natural for that connexion to be taken in another sense as well: at the slightest setback those involved could become upset and consider themselves wounded in the sacred core of their being. According to the attitudes of the moment, the transcendence of the individual person could provide a logic for prudence or for susceptibility. Thus we shall see that, literarily, the Catholic environment brings out the aspects of paternalism that, according to Machado, it is supposed to restrain: oppression, disrespect, venality, lack of trust, permanent disposition toward violence, etcetera. From the point of view of secularisation, the book is a step backward – but to that step is linked the exploration of a system of real, controlling contradictions that *A mão e a luva*'s more nearly materialist posture leaves in shadow.[46]

Such is the underlying movement of *Helena*. Its correct, civilising intent alternates with the characters' turbulence, for they can unexpectedly give up on everything, abandon good sense, go back on their word, and become abject – always temporarily, without the tether of decorum and morality breaking completely. Similarly, the climate among the 'good people' is one of great virtue, although at every turn they expect to suffer the worst of indignities – which never ceases to surprise. As we shall see, there is thereby created a rhythm in which the relations of favour become manifest in a complex and interesting way.

At the outset of the narrative, we encounter the wishes of the recently-deceased Counsellor Vale, a man who belonged to 'the leading classes of society'[47] and whose life 'had been far from a page out of a catechism'.[48] In his will the Counsellor reveals to his family the existence of his illegitimate daughter and stipulates that she be received 'as though she had come from the marriage'.[49] Pretty, intelligent, and lowly-born, Helena finds herself in a situation

---

46 In this respect, read Maria Sylvia de Carvalho Franco's beautiful study of the place of the free, property-less man within the slavocratic order conditioned by capital. She analyses the practical complementarity between personal recognition, which is a form of equality, and the relationships of personal dominance into which political and economic inequality are translated. They are relationships in which violence has a regular and systematic place. The book deals with the rural world and especially with the Caipira [person from rural and/or remote areas in the interior of south-central Brazil], which lie outside the sphere of Machado's work. But with some adjustment, the complex of interrelations in those very different fields is the same – which leads to reflection about the underlying unity of the social process and, for our interests here, about the clarifying reach of literary work the scope of which exceeds that of the specific issue. See Carvalho Franco 1969.
47 Machado de Assis 1959, vol. I, p. 185.
48 Machado de Assis 1959, vol. I, p. 189.
49 Machado de Assis 1959, vol. I, p. 188.

of needing to win the affections of a family and a social sphere previously unknown to her, just as was the case with Guiomar before her. Such is the basic situation of the novel, to which other conflicts will be added.

The first reactions are three. Dona Ursula, the Counsellor's sister is 'eminently severe with regard to customs'.[50] She judges her brother's act in recognising the natural offspring to be 'a usurpation and an awful example'.[51] What she finds most repugnant, though, is having to receive 'within the bosom of the family and her own chaste affections' a creature about whose mother nothing is known. Dona Ursula can't imagine that her brother might perhaps have atoned for 'an indiscretion gone wrong',[52] which would constitute a 'mitigating circumstance'.[53] In her view, not only the law but also sentimentality are to be condemned when they violate traditional family structure. In the scale of the novel, it is a narrow-minded rigour, one attached more to the letter than to the spirit, excusable given the age of the good Dona and given that, with her, material reasons do not occupy centre-stage. Different is the position of Dr. Camargo, old friend of the family, according to whom the Counsellor erred in putting emotion ahead of reason. It wasn't necessary for him to recognise Helena, or to leave her half of his estate; all that was needed was some token left to her in his will. Especially as the doctor intends to marry his daughter Eugênia to Dr. Estácio, the Counsellor's son. His 'objective' calculation of the material benefits and power relations makes Camargo the book's villain and, in a certain sense, a foreign body immigrated from another literary space.[54] Dr. Estácio, however, is almost perfect, needing only a bit more religion. 'Moved by a sense of equity or the impulses of nature', he accepts his sister, 'as she is, without regret or reservation'.[55] As opposed to his aunt's notion of family, his is not sclerotic: 'with respect to the social level to which Helena's mother belonged, he pays little attention to it, confident that they would be able to raise her to the level of the class she is entering'.[56] And, contrary to Camargo's example, pecuniary considerations do not concern him. In other words, his sense of family is an active one, not one enslaved to social class considerations, moral convention or money, which he brings into his sphere of influence, where they lose their narrow (which is different from unjust) character.

---

50   Machado de Assis 1959, vol. I, p. 189.
51   Machado de Assis 1959, vol. I, p. 189.
52   Machado de Assis 1959, vol. I, p. 189.
53   Machado de Assis 1959, vol. I, p. 189.
54   Machado de Assis 1959, vol. I, pp. 189–90.
55   Machado de Assis 1959, vol. I, p. 189.
56   Machado de Assis 1959, vol. I, p. 189.

The ideological convenience of this enlightened and conservative ideal is readily visible; in fact, Estácio often seems drawn from the pages of a manual of proper manners.[57] The virtues are ones that consider social compartmentalisation to be secondary and place sensibility as primary, which is the reason why only the hearts of the ruling class can practice them with largesse. If, however, the heart, insufficiently tempered by religion, weakens and balks a bit, differences in birth and fortune return to the fore and the equalisation of people by means of respect seems not the rule but rather a specific and idealised case within a situation of arbitrariness and humiliation. *A harsh turn of events, but one that is this novel's social nerve centre*. We shall see that the warm-hearted Estácio does not escape this eventuality, for he ends up playing every dirty trick imaginable on his new sister. The reader will have heard the note of self-righteousness in the passages reproduced above. In locating the most harmful of turns within the conduct of a character who is so pure, so socially exemplary – in which he may have been following a Christian and not a critical inspiration – Machado includes in his narrative an element of pessimism and social tension that does not become dominant but is the bearer of the realistic portion of the novel.

In the opposing camp, among the receivers of 'respect', it is only natural that the situation is conceived differently. And because Helena's ideology is the same as Estácio's, the differences contradict the reciprocity promised by paternalism. In that sense they are its internal refutation. Thence a certain climate of impotence particular to this book: two so-good people who are unable to respect one another.

Helena's passage into the Vale family takes place between two revelations. One, at the outset, that she is the Counsellor's daughter and another, at the end, that she is not. With the second, which changes everything, Machado pays tribute to the extravagantly-plotted Romantic novel. We learn retrospectively that Helena is not Estácio's sister and that she is in love with him, while his unconscious love for her, which the reader has intuited, ceases to loom as incestuous. For what interests us, plot details are dispensable. Suffice it that we know that Helena was not at fault in the mix-up, it was all a matter of *the fate of destiny*. Along with this outcome, which in outline assumes mythic proportions, Machado carries out a rational and profound analysis of paternalism. Once the Counsellor recognises her, Helena comes to her new home and endeavours to make herself acceptable. Her efforts provide us with the flip side of the coin.

---

57   Machado de Assis 1959, vol. I, p. 191.

'Helena possessed the skills needed to win the confidence and affection of the family'.[58] In addition to natural qualities, she had a 'magnificent contralto voice ... She was an accomplished pianist, she knew how to draw, she spoke fluent French and a bit of both Italian and English. She knew sewing and embroidery and the entire gamut of women's pursuits. She conversed with ease and read admirably'.[59] As one can see, the list of her talents is imposing, and it is dictated by the desire for social idealisation, which in this case goes side by side with analytical intent. The combination is odd, the patriotic purpose notwithstanding, for Brazil needed more demanding models as well as exacting self-analysis. Nevertheless, the Vale family and their friends give in, cautiously and parsimoniously. When Dona Ursula first lets escape from her mouth a positive word, she feels mortified and would have taken it back if she could. In another passage she tells her nephew that 'Helena is no fool; she wants to tie us up on every side, even on the score of compassion. I won't deny to you that I'm beginning to like her; she is dedicated, affectionate and intelligent; she has fine manners and no few social accomplishments'.[60] In sum, we witness a kind of struggle, not a negotiation, in which Helena has to please and provide proofs of her merit before the others will recognise her, a struggle to which she submits herself willingly and Christianly. 'By dint of her capabilities and a great deal of patience, art and resignation – not humble but dignified – she succeeds in smoothing ruffled feathers, winning over the indifferent and taming the hostile'.[61] And further along: 'Far from lowering herself or railing against the social feelings she encounters, she explains them and endeavours to turn them to her favour – a task in which she outdoes herself, overcoming the family obstacles: the rest came from what she herself is'.[62] The emphasis falls on Helena's strong will, which enables her to face the general reservation and soon win hearts without abdicating her dignity or complaining about the injustice of the situation. A strict line, for which the acceptable ends where servility, social recrimination and questions of propriety begin – for example, Helena does not want 'legal protection', that is, protection based on the Counsellor's will. That strength on her part is the inveterate constant of the book, occupying a central position within it, equivalent to 'honest calculation' in *A mão e a luva*.[63] Dependent upon it is whether or not social ascent is made without degradation

---

58   Machado de Assis 1959, vol. I, p. 196.
59   Machado de Assis 1959, vol. I, p. 197.
60   Machado de Assis 1959, vol. I, p. 203.
61   Machado de Assis 1959, vol. I, p. 210.
62   Machado de Assis 1959, vol. I, p. 197.
63   Machado de Assis 1959, vol. I, p. 197.

either of the person or of order, the pure outcome of mutual esteem within a family environment.[64] After a time of trial, spontaneous affection overcomes awkwardness and reciprocity of feeling covers over the differences of fortune without leaving a scar: the new situation is consecrated by recognition.[65] Nevertheless, it turns out that the unacceptable has reality on its side. Although the novel emphatically affirms the good norm, that norm falters, coming to exist in a state of extreme fragility – to which a certain realistic and disillusioned poetry that undeniably accompanies its moral is owing. See in that sense the episode in which Estácio, backed by his status as brother and head of the family, tries to force Helena to confess about her love life, 'to establish what is best'.[66] She rebels, and he, who 'possessed these two things, the ability to retract his error and the generosity of a pardon' (if the 'error' is his, why is the 'pardon' his too?),[67] admits that he gave in to a bad impulse. Helena: 'Thank you! If you hadn't told me that, you would have seen me go down that road for good and all, to the ends of the world or the end of my life ... Oh that isn't empty sensitivity, it is the very necessity of my position. You can look at it with benign eyes, but the truth is that the wings of favour are all that protect me ... All right, always be as generous as you have been here; don't try to violate the sanctuary of my soul'.[68] The redistribution of emphases is complete, the norm of respect held to be indispensable becoming, in crisis moments, a question of generosity. Where some see the benefit of protection, others see the spectre of subjugation and break into panic. Rather social limbo, or even death, than slide in the direction that paternalism tries to push to, a direction unacceptable to its own eyes. In the elevated terminology of Helena and of the novel, it is a matter of preserving the 'sanctuary of the soul'. In the language of the situation, it is a question of trying to escape more or less complete personal submission, at the extremes of which – never alluded to save in Estácio's euphemisms about 'that moral slavery that subjects man to other men'[69] – lie the figure of the *agregado* and the horror of being treated like a slave. Albeit in idealised form, the vividness of Helena's sensitivities reflects the weight of those more prosaic dimensions in which the asymmetry of paternalist relations is not disguised. Let us see additional examples before going further in our analysis. As is pointed out in various

---

64   Machado de Assis 1959, vol. I, p. 288.
65   Machado de Assis 1959, vol. I, p. 195.
66   Machado de Assis 1959, vol. I, p. 223.
67   Machado de Assis 1959, vol. I, p. 288.
68   Machado de Assis 1959, vol. I, p. 223.
69   Machado de Assis 1959, vol. I, p. 206.

passages, Helena's gratitude is limitless and eternal.[70] A sentiment that contradicts the ideology of reciprocity but corresponds to the enormity of the social differences that it is supposed to annul: 'the Counsellor's family was going to guarantee her a future, respect, prominence'.[71] Equally expansive is Helena's desire not to owe anything to anyone, which appears in other passages complementary to those above.[72] On the other hand, note that an infinite debt is not only a large debt but also one outside the market so to speak, one neither to be paid or collected, which in a certain sense restores the dignity of the debtor. Nonetheless, the truth of the gratitude in this case is a humbling of the debtor. Also in this sense, let us see the episode in which a poor but proud man appears.

A shack-dweller provides a service to Estácio and then refuses the help that the latter offers: 'I just did you a kindness, a simple neighbourly duty ... It would seem that you wish to pay me with a benefice. A benefice would be less spontaneous on your part and less agreeable for me. "Agreeable" does not perhaps express my whole idea, but you understand what I mean'.[73] Thus, more than gratitude, horror of gratitude expresses the trap of paternalism for the one in the position of disadvantage. In the episode in which Helena and Estácio face each other, the former's immediate response has kept the situation – which has not seemed degrading in itself – from degenerating. While in the shack-dweller episode, the disadvantaged's humiliation seems an inseparable part of the situation. In summary: favour is the norm, favour is intolerable, and outside of favour there exists only misery. In the words of another master in these ins and outs, living is all but impossible ...[74] Near the end, as the narrative arc is nearing completion, Helena is taken by a kind of purist delirium or aversion to anything in which there might be a debt or the hint of a hidden agenda, which leads her to push away family, inheritance, fiancé, the generosity or the complacency of friendly hearts. 'She prefers misery to shame',[75] or, in other terms, to realise paternalism's norm of dignity it seems best to her to run from it. The question is where to run, a question with which Machado will occupy himself in the next novel, in which paid labour appears on the horizon. For now, in *Helena*, peace within herself and with loved ones comes linked to the proximity of death but, before that, the refusal of all forms of favour between unequals, from which anxiety is inseparable. In place of material and social benefits, in

---

70 Machado de Assis 1959, vol. I, pp. 206 and 288.
71 Machado de Assis 1959, vol. I, pp. 195 and also 286.
72 Machado de Assis 1959, vol. I, pp. 288–289 and 291.
73 Machado de Assis 1959, vol. I, p. 264.
74 Guimarães Rosa.
75 Machado de Assis 1959, vol. I, p. 289.

place of the love, kindness and familiarity that her social ascent offers her, Helena ends up seeking – in her final exaltation – the generic sentiment of 'esteem' and the distanced position of an 'outsider', safe from all suspicion. The contradiction between the intensity of desire and the reduced and inhibitory character of her aims is glaring, and it determines a particular climate of great interest to Brazil. For the poor recipient of favour, personal independence is the indispensable minimum – at the same time that it is the unachievable maximum.[76]

Hence the personal aspect of paternalist debt linked to the conversion of favour into authority and obedience. Its material aspect, which is another stumbling-block in the ideology of *Helena*, still exists. Although rarefied and differently appreciated, its substratum is the same that we encounter in *A mão e a luva*: it is connected to the modern individualism that capital circulation produced, the European novel disseminated and we could neither adopt nor ignore. Just as the inequality within paternalist relations was not supposed to translate into the subjugation of the individual, the existing social and economic advantages were not supposed to lead to egoistic and self-interested behaviour in which considerations of wealth and position alienate natural – that is, familial and Christian – sentiment. Those are two types of behaviour that are taboo. Helena, then, struggles for the Vale family's esteem, not to pass

---

76 A delicate caveat: the reader may say, with justification, that I am fudging the argument and that Helena's resignation is linked to the error in the will and not to the humiliations of paternalism. That is the explanation that the novel gives on the plot level. The final revelation that Helena isn't the Counsellor's daughter transforms her into an involuntary and embarrassed usurper of an inheritance, and her instability comes to be explained as remorse rather than as susceptibility. Instead of the contradictions of paternalism, simple dishonesty. It so happens that this dislocation, connected to the rocambolesque plot, not only undermines the problems to which the book had been applying itself, but also, especially, doesn't fit with the narrative's analytical tenor. It represents, properly, a concession that allowed Machado to subordinate the work of observation and analysis, which is considerable, to a merely literary solution without any greater engagement. It is not the only point of incoherence in the book, as we shall yet see. Nevertheless, I believe that the humiliations deriving from paternalism are in fact the novel's basso-continuo, responsible for its strength and interest, to the occultation of which the scramble at the plot-level contributes. As the purpose of this study is to follow the formation of a thematic and formal complex that would be both observed and coherent, I have uncovered the line – one necessarily a bit broken – that is the most revealing in that sense. It is the same line, moreover, that Machado would choose for detailed exploration in *Iaiá Garcia*, his next novel. This complex is central to Brazilian literature and it deserves a separate study of its own. The development that we have seen is to be found in its pure state in *Fogo morto* [film title in English: 'The Last Plantation'] by José Lins do Rego, bolstered by monumental outbursts, imaginary and real, in which the character in question abuses others as much as he can.

from one social class to another, much less to become rich. For the same sort of reasons, when Estácio wishes to prevent his sister's marriage, he has only to recall that his fraternal friend Mendonça doesn't have money and could be suspected of marrying for interest. Mendonça backs out of the engagement immediately, motivated by his 'sense of dignity'.[77] After a night of reflection, he explains himself: 'If I go through with the marriage, they'll say I am manoeuvring for advantage; maybe the family already thinks as much; perhaps she herself does as well'.[78] Helena, who understands the risk, responds to the point: 'Oh, in the final analysis I would give up the inheritance'.[79] The same thing applies to her, for whom the worst insult of all would be the word 'adventuress',[80] which she herself realises. We have seen that the word does not apply to her, for she has no material ambitions. But how to avoid the fact that in the eyes of opinion the economic outcome might have contaminated the actual motive? An unanswerable – and therefore capital – question. On the one hand, the property owners and property (in mercantile form); on the other, the free men with neither property nor salary, who – labour being the task of the slaves – can share in social wealth only through favour. To these last, who have nothing 'objective' to contribute, it is understandable that the economic aspect of the relationship would seem a delicate issue. Such is the real constellation, to which the ideology of *Helena* must bring decorum and resolution. In response, liberal conceptualisations of property and of interest are condemned, since, as the poor have no commodity (labour) to exchange, the necessary reciprocity is blocked up. Even in their capacity of taboo, however, such conceptualisations are part of the problem: operating remotely, they break down the ideal paternalism that prohibits them (and, as we have seen in *A mão e a luva*, they also destroy the dignity of the paternalism that accepts them). Returning to our examples, we see that virtue is on the defensive and the difficulty in proving purity of motives is the dynamic element in the conflict. If the owners inevitably suspect the motives of the disadvantaged (Dona Úrsula commenting on Helena's suffering: 'But what hurt? what bitterness? ... The hurt of being legitimised? The bitterness of an inheritance?'),[81] then conversely the disadvantaged suspect the suspicion – and defend themselves by complete rejection of interested behaviour, which becomes their worst nightmare. Hence the poor people who respect property more than the wealthy do and the scrupulously

---

77   Machado de Assis 1959, vol. I, p. 256.
78   Machado de Assis 1959, vol. I, pp. 256 and also 259.
79   Machado de Assis 1959, vol. I, p. 259.
80   Machado de Assis 1959, vol. I, p. 292.
81   Machado de Assis 1959, vol. I, p. 210.

legitimistic natural daughter (which the modern reader will not find credible). In short, personal subjugation and economic interest pursue virtue, which only with supreme effort and at the cost of renunciation escapes not from the unacceptable, exactly, but from suspicion of the unacceptable, which in the situation seems as grave as the unacceptable itself. Speculating a bit, we can see in this sense the point to which virtue and fear of others' opinion, along with submission to that opinion, go hand in hand rather than separately: we are not on the ground of economic individualism and liberal guarantees in which others' opinion can seem secondary to moral autonomy, which proves itself precisely in this divergence. With us, he who didn't make himself respected and accepted would be abused and ignored ('Fear obscurity, Brás'),[82] and the greater or lesser respect of people of property was a real and efficient part of the material ground of life. Paternalist recognition, from which the moment of personal decision and the elements of appearance that might impress are inseparable, figures directly into the person's effective position, which is different from the highs and lows of bourgeois reputation and has nothing to do with the norms of the aristocracy. This objective and regular presence of subjective choice in the social process is transcribed in the conflicts we have been analysing. And perhaps we can say that later, when he reduces social life to the capricious movement of will, Machado was stylising, in a vein also pessimistic but by then comic as well, this same experience.

Looking at the totality up to here, we can say that *Helena* seeks to formulate for paternalism a route that both corrects the brutality of individual subjugation and the baseness of economic motivation. Those are our two dominant forms of social alienation aside from the relations around slavery, which is primary but is not addressed in the novel. From the point of view of our free men, it was a complete ideology: the Christian sense of family suppresses the inconvenient aspects of authoritarian paternalism as well as the degrading effects of capital so that neither of them becomes people's raison d'être. Estácio, for example, although renting out houses, likes to collect guns and study mathematics.[83] Examined more closely, the critique of the narrowness and the humiliation of paternalistic relationships represents, as in *A mão e a luva*, the interest of the more gifted and better-situated of the poor, candidates for co-optation. It represents as well a distant tribute to bourgeois individualism adapted to local conditions: it doesn't reach the extent of affirming rights, but it opines that subjugation is degrading. If its rules of respect

---

82 Machado de Assis, *Memórias póstumas*.
83 Machado de Assis 1959, vol. I, pp. 211–12.

were observed, they would create – so to speak – a thoroughly British distance between people, which would have been a way of keeping up with the times. And when disrespect affects an inferior who is well-turned-out and estimable but born 'below his merit', it wounds not a right but our sense of modernity and self-esteem, which amounts to almost the same thing. In their turn, modern wealth and merit gain much in terms of human legitimacy, or, rather, are cleansed of their exclusionary character, when subordinated to the recognition involved in favour. From the point of view of coherence, it is an impeccable ideology, which gives it a certain interest. From the point of view of accounting for real tendencies it could not be more contrary to nature: it asks power not to command, commercial wealth not to act on its self-interest, and above all else, asks economic motivation not to have influence in society. The foolishness is obvious, and it causes the book to have about it an air of empty rhetoric. Even so, we have seen in our examples that in this ideology Machado privileges the moment of impasse, which to some extent recuperates that ideology for realistic perspective, as an illusion, and confers firmness and interest upon its trajectory in the book. And it must be noted that the impasse establishes and clarifies the options of the subaltern, who are forced to face the unacceptable, and possibly to identify it as such, while the superior resolves its contradictions by simply overriding them.[84] In fact, non-authoritarian paternalism and disinterested commercial wealth, while being contradictions in and of themselves, are ideas that cater word-perfectly to the situation of the class of the dependents – oppressed and deprived – and in this restricted sense are distillations and negations of such impasses. The isolation, for the purposes of subtraction, of the elements of oppression and self-interest, while the general paternalistic arrangement is maintained, expresses as well the dependents' lack of any historical outlet. As ideology, their point of view is one from bottom up while advantage rests with those on top. The poor dependents can console them-

---

84 'From the reconstitution of the social category of free men without possessions it was concluded that, in the adjustments between the ruling and the subordinate groups, the two 'faces' constitutive of society were intertwined: on the one hand the area that tended to order itself according to ties of interest and, on the other hand, the sectors articulated by dint of moral associations. The presence of these opposed principles of organisation of social relations allowed the asymmetry of power to be carried to the extreme, with nothing limiting the arbitrariness of the stronger or strengthening the submission of the weaker ... Put into a crucial situation, the landowner always gave priority to his business dealings, even though in so doing he would cause harm to his tenants and thereby interrupt the chain of agreements upon which, to a great extent, his power rested. In the face of the necessity of expanding his enterprise, he would never hesitate to expel the tenants from his lands.' Carvalho Franco 1969, pp. 102–3.

selves with how things should be and with seeing their convictions recognised, which produces a non-antagonistic image of the relationship, one acceptable and consolatory for those on top as well, who are not bound to hold themselves to it; and it provides a mechanism through which the two parties can communicate. The price of that conciliation, in which social relations become imaginarily un-alienated, is, of course, denial of reality. Should it occur to any of the characters to transform it into an effective norm, we would see that it represents an alienation larger than any of the alienations that it is supposed to overcome. Under the circumstances, rejection of power and interest relations for moral reasons leads directly to disgrace. Avoiding reality as it does, it is a virtue that ceases to be humanly interesting. The signs of this inversion reveal themselves at every turn, and the inversion destabilises the book's very foundation; measured by the purist meter, the daily behaviour of the Brazilian would be a horror. That wasn't what Machado, alternately an observer and an ideologue, meant – or it was only in part. Thus Dr. Camargo is now a sinister villain, now a good, faithful friend of the Vale family, then a hard, egoistic man, and finally a refined citizen who lacks 'the gold coin of great affections';[85] Dona Úrsula detests natural children in a society in which there are no few of them, but she is a saintly lady; the deceased counsellor is a hypocrite in politics, dissolute as regards customs, a bad husband, a good, respectable man, a noble soul; the very machinations around inclusion in the will, inapplicable when it comes to the cases of Helena and Estácio, are given as normal in the cases of other families, etcetera. The same thing in the area of virtue: when the society is idealised Helena stands out a bit, but in general she conforms with the good norm; in other moments, to keep to simple decorum she turns to thoughts of martyrdom. The vacillations are similar with regard to Estácio, who prefers a withdrawn, strictly family-centred life to one involving the hardscrabble of politics, work, or the day-to-day. Is it a question of morality, since elections are fraudulent, work a farce, and social life an illusion, or is it a simple preference with no higher consideration? A virtue grounded in knowledge and thought, or a mode of life apart, one involving a somewhat misanthropic landowner? The purity meter has this advantage: it elevates the person above his circumstances without actually criticising those circumstances – although it does diminish the person a little bit. Hence an ongoing sense throughout the book that virtue is always on the run, trying to find a safe place for itself. Also, from the dramatic point of view, the purification of the alternatives with an eye to the moral dimension – the demand for a 'pure' paternalism – loses contact with

---

85   Machado de Assis 1959, vol. I, p. 236.

the reality dimension of the questions, which are outlined in the background. To judge by that outline, the country is one in which family has not become the rule, in which the labour of the free man is ridiculous ('are you thinking about a suspension bridge from Rio to Niterói, a road to the Mato Grosso or a shipping lane to China?'),[86] in which elections are decided in conversation among influential locals subject to agreement from the capital,[87] in which inheritances are major events, in which slaves participate in family life, in which marriage provides a good opportunity to make one's fortune and rise socially, in which the disadvantaged have the whole national territory in which to drop dead (see the wanderings of poor Salvador, Helena's secret father). For Christian spirituality, to which Helena and Estácio's moral exigencies adhere, the above are merely instances of the baseness to be risen above. A position that is not conformist, since it involves a certain distancing, but also is not critical, since it is not interested in the working of the real contradictions nor does it seek to interfere. From the formal point of view, as to the disposition of the materials it is natural that the conflicts of interest should occupy the margins and the moral conflict the centre. But in relation to the former, what relevance do Helena and Estácio's elevated sentiments have? Between their conflicts and the others there is a certain continuity connected with the ubiquity of favour, but the high moralistic formulation impedes poetic resonance. Thus, despite the radical exigencies, the central contradiction in *Helena* is contingent and peripheral whereas the real and necessary plane is spread out through the novel's fringes – in wait for a more mature novelist.[88] In sum, the dignity of the indi-

---

86   Machado de Assis 1959, vol. I, p. 211.
87   Machado de Assis 1959, vol. I, p. 241.
88   The reader may recall the analysis of *Senhora* previously undertaken, in which the central conflict also differed from the peripheral ones and in which as well the characters were seen in different perspectives, among which the author had not chosen. Comparison is useful to point out the path taken by Machado. In *Senhora*, the difference among perspectives was one of kind, and the conflicts of the central couple had nothing to do with the other characters. A formal fracture expressing the country's cultural subordination. In *Helena* the novelistic material is relatively unified, and the central conflict's relative lack of poetic resonance is owing 'only' to the moralism present in its formulation. In that sense, see its initial pages. The first paragraphs are admirable and with a little more resourcefulness could belong to the second phase of Machado's work. Counsellor Vale dies shortly after dining and napping. His friends are the judge, the priest and the doctor, a company of bigwigs come together by force of habit, by a liking for cards, by propinquity. All that is official, such as titles, professions, science, religion, public service, political parties, Paulista families [i.e., those from the state of São Paulo] and burial is relativised by the gentlest and most unsanctified of stock-taking by the family circle, its comfort, its appetites, vanities and customs, which themselves benefit to some small degree from the solemnity

vidual person floats above and beyond the inequalities of fortune. It proves itself in the detachment with which the owner gives and with which the poor man rejects. For the latter the unequal relationship is tolerable only if his disinterest in material things is recognised, which ensures his equality on another level. Hence susceptibility with regard to motives. If his detachment is questioned, he has to prove his independence, and even superiority, refusing once and for all, while arguing over money would be a diminution of his person. These are symbolic reparations difficult to countenance today. We are at the antipodes of modern economic behaviour, which in this scene would appear as the height of indignity – although the wealth of society was already in mercantile form. Helena's inheritance, for example, consists of two-hundred-and-some bonds, which, in the opinion of one secondary character, 'deserves a good tip of the hat'.[89] The reader will recall that *A mão e a luva* vindicated enlightened paternalism (something like a local echo of the new European utilitarian spirit) against the Romantic stylisation of the impasses of modern life. A solution that lay in a 'progressivist' harmony between the poor who had talent, who deserved to rise, and the elites who knew how to recognise such individuals, desirous as they were to improve our society morally and materially. That same alliance remains desirable in *Helena*, which, however, focuses on examination of its possible conflicts. Where *A mão e a luva* affirmed the difference of our society and freed it from the pessimism of Romantic literature – hence the specious 'positive' conclusion that with us wealth, appetite and intelligence could work together for the common good – *Helena* lingers inside that complex and arrives at a pessimistic outlook adjusted to local conditions: only through the strictest and most unlikely Christian rigour could capitalist paternalism cease to be degrading. Not even made subordinate to a sense of family could the liberal concepts of interest and of property be rendered acceptable.

To bring this analysis to a conclusion, let us look at the book's most audacious aspect, which lies in Estácio's oppressive concerns about his sister. In them a sense of authority combines with unconscious desire under the sign of paternalistic ascendency. Instead of the notorious version of arbitrariness, connected simply to disregard and to the right of the strongest, we shall see

---

taken from the other sphere. Then, like a cold shower, come the narrow moral considerations: was the Counsellor mistaken? does an illegitimate daughter have rights? what about family honour? Rising to this 'nobler' discourse, Machado in fact adopts a simpler, more ornamental and ideological outlook thereby descending to a level below that of the complexity and maturity of his initial discursive role as chronicler. Therefore, an unevenness from the outset, and a determining one; it will be repeated off and on throughout the work.

89   Machado de Assis 1959, vol. I, p. 240.

a version that is unaware of itself and exists within the staunchest virtue and respect. Between the sphere in which the desires operate on their own account, so to speak, and the sphere of accepted authority and the law, the transactions are always many; they are more palpable in a paternalistic regime, but the observation is true everywhere. With the figure of Estácio, Machado wades into modern waters. The personal power of choice, inseparable from paternalist relations, is indeed one of its distinguishing elements. Its presence can be understood in diverse ways. In *A mão e a luva* it provided an escape from the rigours of traditionalism, as well as from class antagonism. In *Iaiá Garcia* it will be looked on with horror as a permanent opportunity for abuse. In *Helena* we find ourselves halfway along the road: it requires purification through Christian and familial discipline. In this sense, the heroine is the book's exemplary character, albeit an uninteresting one. Helena knows that Estácio isn't her brother; that unconsciously he loves her; and that, in turn, she loves him 'a lot, a lot, a lot'.[90] Nevertheless, Christian sense teaches her that sacrifice is preferable to the scandal that would derive from a second revelation of paternity. Thus, in the interest of decorum, Helena insists that Estácio marry Eugênia and tries to arrange a marriage for herself with Mendonça. 'Possessing the secret of her birth and aware of loving without the taint of criminality, she nonetheless hurries Estácio's marriage and chooses for herself a husband who is at least esteemed'.[91] Estácio's conduct is different, for he is perfectly turned out and good, but he is a Christian only in a superficial sense. He lacks the firmness of his sister, who does not vacillate between family decorum and personal considerations. The poor young man, carried away by what seems to him the elevation and the magic of feelings, heads straight toward the sin of incest. As Father Melchior explains: 'temptation uses that serpentine and felonious tactic'.[92] Taking a detour characteristic of him, Machado puts on the shoes of religion and finds support in the tritest conflict in the novelistic repertoire in order to move into this new territory, namely the unconscious workings of desire. Herewith some examples: 'your heart is a great unconsciousness; it stirs, murmurs, rebels, roams in the manner of an ill-expressed or poorly-understood instinct. Evil pursues you, tempts you, ensnares you in its hidden golden bonds; you do not sense it, do not see it. You will horrify yourself when you confront it face-to-face. God, who reads you perfectly, knows well that there is a kind of thick veil between your heart and your conscience that keeps them apart, that prevents that pact

---

90 Machado de Assis 1959, vol. I, p. 221.
91 Machado de Assis 1959, vol. I, pp. 289–90.
92 Machado de Assis 1959, vol. I, p. 271.

between them that would lead to criminality'.⁹³ Thus Machado steps back from psychology and adopts the Christian terminology of struggle between good and evil, which too allows him to follow the psychic process more closely and, most importantly, without the presumptions of rational psychology. Hence the underground, independent life of the desires, the divided person in horror at himself. At another moment, after refusing consent to his sister's wished-for marriage and poisoning the spirit of the hopeful fiancé, his friend Mendonça, all under the honestly-felt cover of the best of intentions, Estácio senses that something strange is happening to him. 'He went out stunned, disconsolate, angry. In the street and in the house he kept thinking about the scene that had taken place in the last hour, and it seemed to him that he was reconstructing a dream. He didn't recognise himself, he tested his own intelligence, he invoked for his aid all the forces of reality'.⁹⁴ The reader should pause for a while and give full attention to those expressions. He will realise the extraordinary intimacy with the life of the psyche, the curiosity and the disposition to cold observation that Machado has involved himself in under the mantle of Christianity. Very surreptitiously and in an unusual context, they replicate the appetite for reality and knowledge, the scientific impartiality and sordid interest of the Realist literature of the nineteenth century.⁹⁵ In that episode seen as a whole, Estácio wanders as though walking in his sleep (the expression actually appears in those pages)⁹⁶ between reasonings and decisions, guided by his repressed urges. In explaining his opposition to his sister's marriage, he goes about tossing out seriatim his unconnected objections. Helena doesn't love Mendonça, Mendonça is inferior to Helena, Mendonça will be suspected of having base motives, Helena might meet another young man superior to Mendonça, and, last argument, it would be excessively sad if Helena abandoned the family in which they are all so happy.⁹⁷ Immediately afterward, such reasons all dismissed, Estácio is obliged to consent. To get Mendonça's agreement as soon as possible, Helena asks Estácio to take her note to him confirming the engage-

93   Machado de Assis 1959, vol. I, p. 271.
94   Machado de Assis 1959, vol. I, p. 257.
95   In a *crônica* ['chronicle', a short-fiction form widely practised in Brazil] of a bit later – which I ran across when this study was already complete – Machado comments on the case of a businessman who forged bills without needing to and having a great deal of credit in the market: 'It being thus, and there is no reason to doubt it, what he did was one of those unexplainable natural phenomena that a modern philosopher has explained with reference to the unconscious and which the Church explains by the temptation of evil.' Machado de Assis 1959, vol. III, p. 398.
96   Machado de Assis 1959, vol. I, p. 256.
97   Machado de Assis 1959, vol. I, pp. 254, 256 and 259.

ment. Estácio wants to wait until tomorrow. Father Melchior insists that it be today. 'Night had already fallen: Estácio went to dress himself. Not having sent Helena's note, he put it in his pocket so he could deliver it himself; then he took it out and re-read it; having done so, he made a motion as if to tear it up, got control of himself and ran over it again with his eyes. His hand, like an indiscreet moth, seemed attracted to the light; he resisted, resisted for some time; finally he moved the note over to the candle and burned it'.[98] Just as Estácio's objections don't hold together among themselves but rather are remote-controlled by an unconfessed goal (today we would identify them as rationalisations), his conscious decisions – to agree to the marriage, to deliver the note, not to tear it up, not to burn it – are all steps in the implementation of an opposite desire. To fully grasp the daring of the passage, note that it does not transform Estácio into an ignoble figure. We have seen the 'theological' justification: where there is no conscious awareness there is no crime.[99] From the literary point of view, however, the interesting conclusions run otherwise: the conscious motives could have been directed by other, unacceptable ones, and convictions of virtue do not prevent the practice of horrors – a conclusion that Machado would later explore with great liberty, in a satirical key. In sum, the passage introduces some new and difficult issues into which the writer delves prudently and which in themselves constitute a merit. But, picking back up the thread of our exposition, let us note especially that Machado's psychological reflections (the Christian cover will disappear in the ensuing novels) here complexify the representation of paternalism. Where we have heretofore spoken of arbitrariness, of the power to choose as pertaining to the despotic will of the strongest, we here have an analysis of will itself, which with the failing of Christian firmness is revealed to be a tangle of bondages. Now if paternalism itself is the lack of clear boundaries between social authority and personal will at the strong pole of the relationship, and if the will is itself a more or less contradictory set of unacceptable desires, from blindness to baseless justifications, then the situation of the weaker in the relationship takes on another dimension. His social integration is carried out through direct subordination to the superior's arbitrary demands and affective confusions – which are what make up authority, disrespect for which would constitute ingratitude. The reader will be recognising – I hope – some of the yet-unused clay of which Machado's mature work is made. Something perhaps of the nature of what today is the position of the household *empregada*.[100] But let's look at some examples. A voice inside

---

98   Machado de Assis 1959, vol. I, p. 258.
99   Machado de Assis 1959, vol. I, p. 271.
100 [Until recently the *empregada*, or live-in domestic, generally said to be one of the legacies

Estácio begins speaking to him, using Biblical language: 'sleepwalker, open your eyes, be conscious of your actions; your embrace is a hangman's noose, your scruples make you odious; your solicitude is worse than anger'.[101] In other words, Estácio's paternal concerns hide the most sinful of feelings, which he cannot know because those feelings are unconscious. After intervening harmfully on a number of occasions, Estácio himself senses that he has not acted well. 'My zeal may have been excessive; my intentions are good and pure. What could I desire other than to see my people happy?'[102] The question points to the character's unconscious, which Machado found it important to emphasise, but in the context he also expresses paternalist ideology, according to which the head of the family can have no other interest than the happiness of 'his people'. And as there is no authority higher than his – save religion – his decision has the force of law. Moreover, Helena herself respects it and seeks to avoid only what seems to her unacceptable. Even in that sense, see the disquieting and chaotic sequence of Estácio's decisions, always vested with due authority and decorum, that affect a relatively wide circle of people but are aimed only at assuaging his own affliction. Or recall the inquisitorial authority with which Estácio, dying of jealousy, throws himself into investigating Helena's secrets, for the purpose of defending family honour. Without cynicism or hypocrisy, because of the simple nature of things, law and desires formulated and unformulated get mixed together in one murky, unhappy and violent current. If we glance back, Estácio is the reiteration of Félix, the central figure of *Resurreição*. An indecisive character, besieged by cyclical bouts of jealousy, who because of infelicity of character – Machado himself says that the purpose of this first novel was 'to sketch out a situation and the contrast of two characters'[103] – is unable to convince himself of his social destiny, which is that of starting a family. It is a constellation in which the psychic dynamic and social dynamic are different in kind and have different goals. Neither can explain the other, nor can they exist separately. Hence *Resurreição*'s originality and promise of complex-

---

of slavery, has been a feature of Brazilian life. The *empregada* herself is usually a lower-class woman who lives in a small room within the house or apartment of an upper- or middle-class family, keeps the house, raises the children, cooks the meals, etcetera. In recent years, economic changes, including the building of smaller apartments, increased educational opportunities for women and other factors have curtailed both the demand for and the supply of *empregadas*, who in most instances now receive a wage and stipulated benefits.]

101 Machado de Assis 1959, vol. I, p. 256.
102 Machado de Assis 1959, vol. I, p. 257.
103 Machado de Assis 1959, vol. I, p. 32.

ity – qualities pointed out by the critics[104] – but also its disorganised character, since, although abundantly described, the social sphere does not present contradictions, the introduction of one more level complicates the book but does not help to organise it. In *A mão e a luva* the characters immediately adhere to social ends and the prior complexity disappears; what appears in compensation are the complexities of social contradiction and conciliation and around them the outline of a novelistic organisation. Finally, *Helena* is the synthesis of the two: Estácio has the flow of his psychic difficulties, which in turn impart a particular punctuation to the social contradiction and develop it in a particular way as well. As we have seen and shall continue to see, the confluence of unconscious motives and social ends forms a metabolism full of surprising aspects, with which a goodly part of modern literature connects. If we think about what is coming next, Estácio is a still-modest effort in that direction. For the time being, complexity notwithstanding, what is dealt with is the problem of just one character, and a somewhat isolated one. The generalisation of this 'clandestine' complexity to all characters and its transformation into normal life will be one of the accomplishments and one of the formal principles of the second-phase novels.

With all that established, *Helena* is a novel still more at loose ends conceptually than our analysis here would lead one to think – and than the tight plot evidences on first reading. With consummate mastery and without defining his position Machado circulates between ultra-Romantic intrigue, social analysis, deep psychology, Christian edification, and the repetition of very trite phraseology (e.g., Helena raises her eyes to the heavens in thanks for the favourable intervention of the *moleque* Vicente and then explains: 'I prayed to God ... because he had infused the lowly body of the slave with so noble a spirit of dedication').[105] The impression is akin to a person who dabbles in various languages. It is as if the writer had accumulated a great amount of material that at the time was exceptional but had done so to prove his competence in general and to become accepted, rather than trying to get to the bottom of the problems that the material sets forth. The instances of boldness that we have pointed out are instructive in that sense, for they always have some

---

104 See both Barreto Filho and Miguel-Pereira.
105 Machado de Assis 1959, vol. I, p. 276. [In slavery times, a *moleque* was an Afro-Brazilian slave boy too young for regular work; the word could also designate such a boy who had been chosen to play with the owners' children. The word comes from the Kimbundu language of West Africa. Today it means a 'scamp', an urchin, or someone who is clever – perhaps too clever – still usually young but not necessarily so; it can be pejorative or not according to social and/or verbal context. Except in metaphorical uses and derivative forms it still is applied only to males.]

ostensibly conformist cover and never have the last word. In our exposition we have sought to highlight the almost determinative position of the paternalist material as well as the contradictions linked to the well-meaning Christian framework within which it comes. Even so, the well-developed and exacting analysis of the relationships around favour – which does in fact exist – is merely one level among several, all done with similar care. It remains improperly integrated, however, as it will be later when Machado's novelistic universe becomes unified. Just like all the other books of the first phase, *Helena* is a transitional work. Thus it has various characteristics that don't fit on their own plane but that must be mentioned, since their presence is of considerable importance. The main of those is the highly marked stylistic diversity. The malicious Realist prose of the first paragraphs, close to Machado's mature prose, presupposes an unprejudiced, humorous view of Brazilian society. Then immediately after comes the emphatic and conventional prose of the moral profiles, of the sort to be found in breviaries of good conduct and whose presumptions are wholly distinct.[106] In the more novelistic-visionary passages connected to Helena's turbulent heart, the language is exalted, of the type to be found in a Romantic poem.[107] When Dr. Camargo appears, an ambitious man capable of anything, we enter the realm of Realism and social denunciation.[108] Then his daughter Engênia, an irritatingly sweet little thing after the manner of Alencar, which gives us pages of rosy romance novel.[109] If the primary issue is sin, or if Father Melchior is present, the language takes on Biblical tones ('suspicion is the teniasis of the spirit').[110] In other passages the prose is concise and attached to the essentials of the action in the manner of eighteenth-century narrative (the very 'logical' pace, especially of the final rush, may perhaps recall that of *Elective* Affinities)[111] and aspires to the stylised brevity of narrative verse, a strange combination of formal nobility and durability with the prosaic contingency of a nineteenth-century novel topic. Etcetera. What should be made of that diversity? Firstly, it is a demonstration of strength and of literary resources, the best comment on which, however, lies in the confusion it establishes within the work. The general conceptual precariousness leaps immediately to the eye, as

---

106   Machado de Assis 1959, vol. I, pp. 189–91.
107   Machado de Assis 1959, vol. I, ch. XXVIII.
108   Machado de Assis 1959, vol. I, pp. 231, 235–6.
109   Machado de Assis 1959, vol. I, p. 200.
110   Machado de Assis 1959, vol. I, pp. 256, 261, 271.
111   [*Elective Affinities* is one of the titles under which Goethe's *Die Wahlverwandtschaften* (1809) was translated into English. The same formulation, *Afinidades eletivas*, was used for the translation into Portuguese.]

does an eclecticism of the same order that permits Helena to shine, for her scrupulousness, in contradictory areas: the morality of the contract (the will), personal loyalty, filial obedience and Christian sentiment. Helena does not want to inherit in order not to prejudice third-party rights, but she agrees to inherit so as not to disrespect the dispositions of her adoptive father – and to obey her real father, who wants all the material advantages of life for her, to which she conforms only because of Christian moderation but to which, because of Christian elevation as well, she also does not form an attachment.[112] On the other side of the coin, carried much farther and treated in a humorous vein – something like a sentence-to-sentence imbalance – that same ideological and rhetorical diversity will be an essential ingredient in later Machadian prose, in which the peregrine and mercurial visiting of all styles ends up being our only authentic style, a literary find in which the intellectual salad of the country finds its immortal register.[113] The indiscriminate coexistence of ways of writing, all equally valued as long as they are done competently, is the fate of dependent cultures like ours, which possess no internal criteria but want to keep up. For this issue see the beautiful study of João Caetano by Décio de A. Prado.[114] In Caetano's repertoire are to be found Neoclassical and Romantic plays as well as melodramas; what are not there are Realist pieces – because João Caetano is too old to change. That desire to keep up with the times and omit what in Europe separates those times from each other exists as well in *Helena*, the inclination of which to stylistic assimilation is of a similar sort. It is clear as well that the four styles mentioned above are within its basic registers. Hence Machado's well-known reputation for critical impartiality – namely that he sought to take from every school what was best – appears in a new light. It really was a question of the eclecticism to which we were condemned, which Machado practised with exceptional appetite and skill and which only somewhat later, when it was recuperated in a derisive key, ceased to be a literary defect. One can make analogous observations about *Helena*'s composition. Its frame, within which is a core composed of paternalism and incest, is made up by the three kisses that the frivolous Eugênia receives from her pernicious father, whose tenderness is inspired only by ambition. The first kiss, when the death of the Counsellor transforms Estácio into a rich man. The second when Estácio requests Eugênia's hand in marriage, pushed by Helena, who is being blackmailed by Camargo. And the third, when Helena's death eliminates the final obstacle. In style and in the represented motivations the frame belongs to European Realism, which,

---

112   See the explanations given by Helena's father. Machado de Assis 1959, vol. I, p. 286.
113   On the 'carnivalisation' of the rhetorical element in Machadian prose, see Merquior 1972.
114   See Almeida Prado 1972.

in the figure of Dr. Camargo, will get the last word, as opposed to the virtues of Christian paternalism incarnated in Helena. There is in the composition a vague purpose of suggesting the stages of an historical inevitability, according to which we are entering into materialist time. Nevertheless, as we have seen, before being blackmailed Helena was already pushing Estácio to marry Eugênia, and at other moments Dr. Camargo seems to be an average man and friend worthy of confiding in. On the other hand, Estácio is much wealthier than he, Camargo, is, effectively living off his rents, not to mention that the origin of all the dramas lies in the immoral life of the deceased Counsellor. Hence the suggestion of a decay in customs – and in this sense the book's frame does not resist its own material. We were not coming from a Christian world in which money did not count; neither was a purely bourgeois Brazil present on the doorstep. The contradiction existed, but this was not the organisation that best suited it. To conclude, let us look finally at the novel's turbulent and melodramatic plot, carried out through contradictory revelations of paternity, irregularities of birth, the danger of incest, blackmail, clandestine visits to a mysterious shack, terrible suspicions and crises, a young woman delirious with fever out in a storm, and the final confession of love taken from moribund eyes. From the point of view of literary coherence, the inappropriateness is complete. The second revelation regarding paternity removes the foundation for the initial conflict, which rested on the question of recognition of an illegitimate child and was both interesting and well-developed. Whereas the situation of incest relegates to a status of exceptionality the irrational aspects of the paternalistic relationship – aspects that are the book's major find. Thus the ultra-Romantic plot-line strongly organises the narrative – in a direction that does not impart continuity to its material. *Ressurreição* and *A mão e a luva* are books almost without plot, and even *Iaiá Garcia* is substantially unformed. Those were deficiencies that for Machado's evolution were virtues, for they left in suspense the question of the appropriate form for his material, a question that would find solution only with *Brás Cubas*. *Helena*, however, is a false solution, and moreover the application of a form found ready-made. With those aspects – which are the essential ones – admitted, what remains is to recognise in *Helena*'s plot a surprising, and Brazilian, poetry – perhaps born in the conjunction of the Romantic form and paternalist conflict. From their first encounters, the bond between Helena and Estácio is formed – an unconscious one on the part of the young man, given the taboo, and a conscious but impossible one for the young woman. From then on all the novel's episodes bathe in that attraction, which forms something like a never-fully-restrained current. Thus decent, family ideology, friend of sacrifices and stranger to all Romanticism, runs parallel to an underground nostalgia for complete individual satisfaction beyond limitation – without explicitly invoking the absolutes of Romanticism. While it is neither denied nor questioned, in this company paternalist decorum acquires a noticeable component of renunciation. To the Christianly-positive idea of sacrifice are added negative connotations of individual suffocation and frustration in which Romantic individualism is present, but in a recast form, giving expression to the local conflict.[115]

4   *Iaiá Garcia*

Who was she to dismiss him like that?[116]

... do not give in to the novelesque, the novelesque is perfidious.[117]

With *Iaiá Garcia* we arrive at the end of Machado's first phase – and the end of this chapter. After the ingenuous cynicism of *A mão e a luva* and the purism of *Helena*, we shall see an attitude that, while never falling into disrespect, is one of total disillusionment. A circumspect position – grown-up, so to speak – that does not renounce analysis or disabused feelings, nor the support of the established order. A compromise between Helena's moral exigency and Guiomar's realism. That attitude is responsible for the somewhat nondescript and at the same time powerful climate that pervades this humourless book. Better, points of view that bespeak an often-exceptional audacity remain on the margins, with no effect other than that they exist. The novel's pessimism reaches to neither the extent of dispassion nor that of vigorous critical commentary and has about it an aspect of the unredeemed, which is in some way contrary to literary beauty.

Such being understood, we shall see that even this disbelief is an idealisation, imagined by Machado for the purpose of making the basic facts of Brazilian life acceptable. In the case of this novel the idealisation is minimal but sufficient for its purposes: to protect people against the illusions with which paternalism deceives and diminishes them. *The disillusionment protects their*

---

115   It would be interesting to examine from this point of view the strange 'Ainda uma vez, adeus' [One More Time, Good-bye] by Gonçalves Dias [Antônio Gonçalves Dias (1823–1864), a prominent Romantic writer sometimes referred to as Brazil's national poet], so Romantic in expression and so faithful to the civil contingencies placed upon the existence of the lovers. A comparable development is to be found in Alencar, for example in the figure of Mário, the prideful and wronged young man in *O tronco do ipê*.
116   Machado de Assis 1959, vol. I, p. 316.
117   Machado de Assis 1959, vol. I, p. 380.

human dignity, and in that same unexpected way it safeguards the dignity of paternalism as well. Thus, while being incomparably more serious and more realistic than the prior novels, *Iaiá Garcia* joins with them in the intent to justify, which represents the true upper limit of Machado's first phase.

As regards the interests of literary Realism, it must be noted that this idealisation is in the line of 'the lesser evil', and that its terrain – the terrain of disbelief – is real paternalism in all its variety. Such was not the case with the cynical optimism of *A Mão e a Luva* or the purism of *Helena*, which did have their grounding in our social process but dealt with it from very limited points of view that correlated with concentration on simplistic alternatives (for example: interpersonal respect or disrespect, elevation or baseness of motives, being a weak person or a strong one), the slightest development of which would easily lead to its invalidation. From the first pages of *Iaiá Garcia* the reader can perceive a more robust, less schematic and, even so, more unified reality. As was to be expected, that realistic appreciation of social relations is propitious for literary Realism as well, and though it does not establish a position of radical critique since it can be linked to a conformist attitude, it secures a propriety and a latitude for the incorporation of empirical detail. If the prior novels' narrowness of point of view ends up distancing literary paternalism from the paternalism of real practice, now Machado sets out a position that brings them closer together and allows freer circulation between the spaces of novel and those of reality. In place of the somewhat generic questions posed in the prior books, we shall see the spectrum of period positions and relationships, accompanied by their proper vocabulary.

It is thus that they enter literature as problematic material of the first order – that is, material in which the meaning and value of contemporary life are in play, which is the opposite of localist use of them. A large set of expressions and notions related to the practice of paternalism comes to the fore, which was new. Examples more or less at random: your father was a friend of my father's, I was a friend of your family, I owe you significant acts of favour;[118] who was she to dismiss him like that?;[119] relations were never either assiduous or close but they always held him in good regard and treated him endearingly;[120] his wife was brought up by my mother;[121] he has great respect for him – 'respect' isn't really the proper word, 'caterage' might fit better, it would express the real

---

118   Machado de Assis 1959, vol. I, p. 345. (The following references are paraphrased to facilitate the exposition.)
119   Machado de Assis 1959, vol. I, p. 316.
120   Machado de Assis 1959, vol. I, p. 304.
121   Machado de Assis 1959, vol. I, p. 343.

nature of the relationship between the two;[122] he obliged without enthusiasm but effectively, and had the peculiarity of forgetting the favour before the recipient did;[123] they always merited our consideration, not going to anybody else;[124] it was the first time she was having recourse to his help with such solemnity;[125] that didn't discourage his fondness for servicing;[126] the benevolent friendship I have always found in this house;[127] the caution with which he proceeded without either claiming intimacy or falling into gestures of servility;[128] a lady has favoured you;[129] etcetera.

In more general terms, many trivial, even sordid things are called by their proper names. Despite Machado's anti-Realist declarations, which we have seen, the emphasis on paternalism does not run contrary to the Realist impulse. Thus Luís Garcia is a civil servant, has an account at the savings bank, the straw in his waiting room chairs is grimy, when the service day is over he takes work home with him to bolster his income;[130] the war against Paraguay is a patriotic one but also an opportunity for business favours and inside deals that enable a supplier of the army to triple his investment in little time;[131] the widow Gomes goes to examine a house she has in Tijuca and gets irritated at the damage left behind by the renters; the builder who goes with her has awful pronunciation.[132] Etcetera, etcetera. These are aspects that do not have to do with the main conflicts but at the same time don't run counter either to them or to external verisimilitude – a deployment at one and the same time loose and unified, contingent and necessary, in which are expressed the coherence, the breadth of spectrum, and the experienced view of things upon which the poetics of the Realist novel depends and which in this sense numbers among its formal elements. In this same line, there is the occasional – and one might even say fluid – incorporation of a great episode in national history into the fictional plot, an opportunity in which literary form openly presumes itself to be the form of reality.[133]

---

122   Machado de Assis 1959, vol. I, p. 306.
123   Machado de Assis 1959, vol. I, p. 300.
124   Machado de Assis 1959, vol. I, p. 305.
125   Machado de Assis 1959, vol. I, p. 304.
126   Machado de Assis 1959, vol. I, p. 299.
127   Machado de Assis 1959, vol. I, p. 306.
128   Machado de Assis 1959, vol. I, p. 334.
129   Machado de Assis 1959, vol. I, p. 329.
130   Machado de Assis 1959, vol. I, see the first chapter.
131   Machado de Assis 1959, vol. I, p. 339.
132   Machado de Assis 1959, vol. I, p. 315.
133   See in this regard the good explanations by Lukács, in the first part of Lukács 1965b.

The episode of the Paraguayan War is an effort in that direction. If we look closely, we shall see that even though the very official-sounding prose spoils it for reading, the chapter is daring. Patriotism, when it appears, is quickly retracted, and the motivation that dominates is one consonant with the book's private, paternalistic climate. Thus Valéria Gomes gives patriotic reasons but in truth she sends her son off to the war to separate him from an *agregada* of the house with whom he is in love. Luís Garcia advises the young man to obey but does so with regret, pressured by Valéria, whom he owes family obligations. Jorge (the son) joins up, more to burnish his image in the eyes of his beloved, who wants nothing to do with him and whom he, a rich boy, had somewhat brutalised in the past. Later Jorge will fight with uncommon heroism, like someone who wants to die – after learning by letter that his mother had availed herself of his absence to marry off the *agregada*. As a result the young man earns the rank of major, while the colonel is telling himself that all that the young men are after is promotion. The war over, three months after returning to Rio the climate isn't one of triumph for Jorge. Although covered with laurels, he has seen in the war 'alongside just glory for his country, the irremediable conflict in human affairs'.[134] That expression exemplifies the limited Realism that is particular to our book, in which the 'conflict in human affairs' is amply developed, but the 'just glory for his country' is not eliminated from the prose. But let us abstract from that limit, to which we shall return on several occasions. We must note that Machado makes three factors commensurate there: literary fiction, daily life and a crucial episode in national history, a result that is appreciable and represents a truly judicious adaptation of one of literary Realism's great commonplaces to Brazilian reality. If, however, it is clear that the dissolution of the patriotic war into private motives integrates it coherently into the novel's texture, it is also true that the chapter does not have the fundamental effect that its European fellows do, even the bad ones, which is that of providing the novel its historical dimension. *Iaiá Garcia* lacks a clear conceptualisation of what the Paraguayan War was, and its inclusion by means of private motives is clever but devoid of precisely that dimension. This was not an individual failing on Machado's part, for yet today the meaning of that war is poorly understood. It is a difficulty that a Brazilian writer could not escape. While the French novelists, good or bad, progressive or reactionary, benefitted from the clarity provided by their social classes and their historians as regards the 1789 Revolution, the Napoleonic Wars, the Restoration, etcetera,[135] our novelists remained without support, were obliged to make ideology, historiography and fiction all at the

---

134   Machado de Assis 1959, vol. I, pp. 327, 335.
135   The *Revue des Deux Mondes* is an impressive read on this issue for the constancy and frank-

same time, thus one way or another paying their fine to the poorly-endowed national culture. It is a case of unforeseen social presuppositions that literary borrowings can have – such as greater maturity of class consciousness or the degree of the social division of intellectual labour. Something comparable can be observed today in our Marxism, the general lines of which presuppose historiographical work that has not been done. To illustrate that thesis, better than Stendhal or Balzac let us have recourse to a weak novel by George Sand, the *Marquis de Villemer* [Marquis of Villemer], which, according to Pujol, may have inspired *Helena* and *Iaiá Garcia* – which is a plausible idea.[136] Scholarly and modest, the marquis in question is preparing a historical study of the *ancien régime* through which, despite his illustrious name, he plans to demonstrate that aristocratic titles are nothing more than usurpations. It so happens that Villemer is madly in love with the young woman who serves as a companion for his aged mother, whom he also loves wholeheartedly, even though she is shallow and protective of her genealogy (the young woman's name is Carolina de St. Geneix, and, with the differences of which we shall speak, she can be compared with the *agregada* of *Iaiá Garcia*). Everything works out in the end, but what interests us is that the lovers find an ideological justification for what they feel in the hero's intellectual convictions as well as in an overall vision of the history of France, and, by extension, of Europe – in addition to transforming themselves into figures existing within that same process, which amounts to historicising themselves. In sum, a powerful effect linked to a degree of historical consciousness by no means exceptional that nonetheless was inaccessible in relation to his own country to the cultured, reflective and daring writer that then was Machado de Assis. As regards importance within the respective literatures, when it comes to a disposition to innovate, to see and say things as they in fact are, there obviously is no comparison between the *Marquis de Villemer* and *Iaiá Garcia*. Nevertheless, from a limited viewpoint (but not therefore a less real one) relating to the novel's shape, in which the social order is transposed with ease, it is the former work that gets the better of the comparison.[137]

---

ness of its commentary on class struggle, for the simplicity of its periodisation and in its concise analysis of each revolution's objectives: 1789, 1830, 1848, 1871. The Europe-wide generalisation of historical consciousness from the Napoleonic Wars on is, according to Lukács, a social presupposition for the historical novel. See the already-cited first part of Lukács 1965b.

136   Pujol 1934.
137   The problem is a Brazilian one, not one particular to Machado. So much so that we were able to make the same observation about Alencar in comparing *Senhora* to Feuillet's *Le Roman d'un jeune homme pauvre*. Indeed, the lack of a historical dimension itself has a historical basis – in the immense distance between the life of the people and the history

But let us return to our topic, namely the progress that *Iaiá Garcia* brings to the elaboration of social order, and let us look at the cast of characters. On the side of the dependents the gallery describes something like a ladder that begins at the bottom with total, innocent submission, akin to slavery or religious devotion, moves up to the abject submission of the opportunist, reaches the grudging submission of the people who have self-respect and ends up at the rupture of the very ties of dependency via compensated employment. A whole gamut by means of which the variability of the social process is configured, with the characters as types.[138] Thus Raimundo is a 'dedicated and submissive' servant, a freed slave who plays the marimba and sings 'African sounds' and whose attention is riveted on his present 'senhor' and former owner like 'a protective spell', while none of that keeps him from being as punctual and impeccable as an English majordomo.[139] Maria das Dores is a poor wet nurse from Santa Catarina 'for whom there are only two devotions that can take a soul to heaven: Our Lady and the daughter of Luís Garcia'; the poor old woman can't rest until she can rent a little cottage in Santa Teresa to be closer to this one of 'her children'.[140] Antunes is a clerk, *agregado* and factotum of the departed Justice Gomes; an inveterate flatterer, partaker of lunches and cigars, the judge's right hand in the office, in electoral communications, love affairs and domestic purchases; he has illusions of grandeur and the secret hope of marrying his daughter Estela to Jorge, the judge's son.[141] It so happens that Estela has a very different outlook from her father's. She is one of the proud *agregados* and doesn't succumb to the siege to which Jorge in fact subjects her. He pursues her first with his eyes, then with brute force and finally, very respectfully, from afar; 'who was she to dismiss him like that?' he asks himself, with which question he brings paternalism into the love relationship – and into the book's dramatic centre.[142] Later, Estela will engage in a loveless marriage, but one of her own making, without undergoing social humiliation, and when her husband dies

---

that our elites fashion. As an example, it is useful to recall Aristides Lobo's remark that the people attended the proclamation of the Republic 'dumbfounded.' Later, in *Esaú e Jacó*, Machado would go in that same direction, in the famous chapter of the tablets in which the proclamation of the Republic sickens the proprietor of the 'Empire Sweetshop.' If the historical dimension is absent in *Iaiá Garcia*, in *Esaú e Jacó* that absence is the point of humour. In this perspective, 1964 may have been a watershed moment, since generally speaking the participants were cognisant of what was at stake.

138   On the formal importance of the gallery of types, see Lukács 1965a.
139   Machado de Assis 1959, vol. I, pp. 300–1.
140   Machado de Assis 1959, vol. I, pp. 303–4.
141   Machado de Assis 1959, vol. I, pp. 303–4.
142   Machado de Assis 1959, vol. I, p. 316.

she becomes a teacher in a boys' school in the north of São Paulo, having finally escaped the web of family obligations. As her disappointed father will say to her, 'you are a tigress'.[143] Estela's husband, Luís Garcia, is a hardworking, standoffish public servant who above all else prizes his independence, although it is linked – often to his displeasure – to favours received from the judge's family; his ideological point of view more or less converges with the book's ideological climate, and we shall return to him in more detail. Finally, Iaiá Garcia, daughter from Luís Garcia's first marriage, is a milder version of Guiomar: she has a liking for luxury, and despite her modest origins she will marry Jorge and make a life for herself in high society. Overall, we see that the ladder is complex, since dependency is not always disgraceful and independence is not always happy. Now let us take a look at the socially-powerful characters. They too are different from each other. If we compare them to the prior group, we see that among them virtue is almost absent, which is decisive ideologically. Some, though, feign more than others. Valéria Gomes, widow of the wealthy judge, likes those who depend on her, and because she is warm toward them does not hesitate to deal with them according to her own inclinations. Her son Jorge is a good person as well, respectful of decorum and serious in his attitudes. That does not keep him from being irresponsible, inconsistent and somewhat useless, however – the kind of estimable upper-class man that Machado studied and still doesn't dare name. Later, in the *Memórias póstumas de Brás Cubas* the narrator will call that figure 'a compendium of triviality and presumptuousness'.[144] His every step is taken under the cover of family relations. The gallery is filled out by Procópio Dias, the book's villain, who will stop at nothing. His crimes stretch from under-the-table dealings during war time to calumnies and gluttony for good food and the opposite sex. Even worse, being in his fifties, he wants to marry Iaiá, who is seventeen. A spectrum that the notion of materialism ('for him, physical life was the whole destiny of the human species')[145] and brushstrokes taken from Realist literature hold together in very self-righteous tones. He too, however, belongs to the universe of paternalism: his business is carried out through personal influence, and his love for a poor young woman to whom marriage would give everything is motivated by the eternal obligation to him in which she would remain. We shall presently see that this figure, so different from the others, lives very easily amongst them and that social process is continually unifying what ideology and literary style keep separate. Moreover, the relative normalisation of relations between paternalism and

---

143   Machado de Assis 1959, vol. I, p. 406.
144   Machado de Assis 1959, vol. I.
145   Machado de Assis 1959, vol. I, p. 339.

material interest is one of the signs of this novel's maturity. It is an issue we can follow as we observe the discernment with which Machado was evolving: in considering material advantages he takes up again that naturalness that was the strength of *A mão e a luva*, this time leaving out the ostensible and forced satisfaction, while from *Helena*'s sensitivities there remains the sensitivity to oppression, which is its critical component, and the moralising disappears. Thus the disappointment without revolt that rules in *Iaiá Garcia* is a precise and reflective synthesis of what was active in the preceding experiments – not to say that Machado thus freed himself of all of their dead weight.[146]

In their general lines, the observations we have made show that the material of the prior novels is broadened, more unified and mature. Paternalism is present everywhere and in various ways, at the centre of the conflicts and in the peripheral characters, as terminology, material drawn from observation of trivia, more sustained issues developed by reflection, as climate, ideology, element of characterisation, and as we shall also see, as deep motive behind the plot and for the novel's formal organisation. The reader who is following this analysis knows that this unity, to which verisimilitude lends naturalness (or, better, would lend it, for we shall soon see how precarious *Iaiá Garcia*'s unity is) is an arrival point, not a point of departure. It evidences a considerable work of appropriation and critique of reality and of literature.[147] Thus, contrary to appearances, the growth that we observe in social, historical, even geographical space is not primarily quantitative, to do with the inclusion of new elements, but rather depends on an effort of internal differentiation and critique, on various planes, of ideological and formal elaboration of which the literary effect is constituted. At least in part the quality of the observation, its quantity and especially its reality effect, depend on those elaborations and the novel's empirical details are the result of a lot of reflection and construction. One example of this influence of critique upon what seem to be elementary data of observation: we have previously noted that *Iaiá Garcia*'s ideology outstrips the limits in the previous novels. A kind of negative version of improvement, as absence of prior defects. But in the absence of those limits new aspects of the material assume formal functionality, and the result is reality better 'observed', that is, better re-created. Thus the climate of disappointment in *Iaiá* permits a more far-ranging

---

146   Machado de Assis 1959, vol. I, p. 362.
147   See Marx's methodological observations, according to which the concrete in the work of social critique is an *outcome*, and it comes at the end, a synthesis of abstract determinations. What I endeavour to indicate here, in relation to the novelist's work, is analogous. See Marx 1953, p. 21. For an excellent Brazilian commentary on the issue, see Giannotti 1968.

consideration of the movement of favours and dependencies, through which a different social – and literary – unity is constructed, though not, properly speaking, affirmed. Paternalism is no longer treated and contained within the modest confines of a single family, and the total of people the book follows has been slightly adjusted in the direction of what is to be seen in reality. In place of the narrow family united by blood and upset by contact with outsiders, we shall see one of those somewhat free and contingent molecules that can be called an 'extended family' in which arrangements deriving from convenience and circumstance coexist with blood ties, godparenthood and the exchange of favours.[148]

We have been saying that in *Iaiá Garcia* relations between paternalism and material interests are normalised, which makes the book more of a whole and is a sign of maturity. But at other moments in this study we have insisted on the importance played in our ideological life by that contradiction, which was, given the circumstances, irresolvable. Where does the matter now stand? To recapitulate: in *Helena*, paternalism and considerations of wealth are like oil and water – a naïve perspective. In *A mão e a luva*, they cohabit scandalously, and the ingenuousness lay in supposing that this arrangement was beneficial. Now in *Iaiá Garcia* the problem apparently doesn't exist, which in a certain sense fits better with reality but in another sense does not. Generally speaking, historians agree that starting in 1850 Rio de Janeiro entered a new phase, with urban improvements, available money, shops, luxuries, the founding of banks, financial speculation, bankruptcies, etcetera. As regards our interests here, the issue is the entry into daily life of the commodity form and its ideological entailment, namely fetishism – which consists in seeing in the commodity not the effect but the logic of the social relations, which is contrary to paternalistic relations, for the latter naturally see themselves as foremost.[149] It was an entry

---

148   'A colonel was also, in general, the head of the extended family, of which he constituted the pinnacle, so to speak. The family was composed of a large array of individuals related by blood, choice (godparenthood) or family alliance (marital unions). A large portion of the individuals in one group came from the same tree, legally, or by illegitimacy. The alliances by marriage established ties among families almost as highly prized as those by blood; finally, the connexions by godparenthood allied not only godparents to godchildren but parents and godparents among themselves in as close a way as did blood relationship.' The prestige position of colonels 'accrues to them from their ability to do favours.' Pereira de Queiroz, in Fausto n.d., pp. 164–5 and 171. In Rio de Janeiro the practice persisted as well, but in a slightly different way – which is precisely the subject matter of *Iaiá Garcia*.
149   'The fetishism of the commodity', in Marx 1972, ch. I, art. 4. See in this regard the beautiful study by Pierre Villar on the literary presence of the fetishism of money in Cervantes' Spain. *New Left Review*, London, no. 68. Machado registers the phenomenon frequently, with Procópio, with Cristiano Palha, with Batista, etcetera.

accomplished without transformation of the base of the economy, namely slavery. It is clear, however, that paternalism did not keep the wealthy from following their consumerist bent; moreover, it would have seemed to them the natural and modern complement to their power, the basis of which had always been capital. But it is clear too that the ideology secreted by the introduction of the commodity into daily life is contrary to paternalist relations. Thus, perhaps it is possible to say that there was a contradiction but it did not express a class-based antagonism, or rather that it expressed two forms of one and the same power, which, gradually and always in concert with convenience, moved from one form to the other – without the dissolution of the traditional ties taking on a subversive character. The historical (local!) inanity of this contradiction – which from the moral point of view is totally blatant, besides being assimilated to the contradiction between feudal and capitalist relations that catalysed the whole of European ideology of the age – provides the basis for the cynicism of *A mão e a luva*, which, if we ignore its optimism, is exactly the same as in second-phase Machado: money and paternalism are ostentatiously located together. In *Iaiá Garcia* that contradiction is hardly noticed. Procópio Dias is a wheeler-dealer and an authentic representative of soulless money, but it is not in that quality that he participates in the novel's conflicts. Jorge is, at the outset, a dandy of Ouvidor Street, though matters of mundane luxury are unrelated to the conflicts of which he will be part. In other words, the separation between social tradition and the power of money, which gives the latter its diabolical literary *frisson*, has a merely picturesque role in the novel. Now Valéria, whose fortune does indeed have an influence on the course of the conflicts, disposes of her possessions in a traditional way – and naturally in conformity with family design – providing the two poor girls who frequent her house, Estela and Iaiá, with dowries. Thus in this novel money doesn't have an autonomous existence but rather appears directly and 'naturally' connected to paternalistic power, of which it is a non-contradictory appendage. A solution that, as we have seen, possesses a relative truth and which is advantageous from the point of view of literary unity, but at the price of retreating from contemporary society, which is much more present in *A mão e a luva* – which is, in turn, so much poorer in other respects. No matter the rigour of the analysis of paternalist relations, the exclusion of the sphere of autonomous money has an idealising effect and imparts an antique dignity to the conflicts in the book which the others, more pervaded by money, do not have. On the other hand, the idealisation does not seem forced, and we could perhaps say that it consists merely of a slightly outmoded way of looking at contemporary society, in terms proper to the prior phase when the presence of money and the commodity in personal relationships was less – a way of seeing that certainly continued on, although it was no longer relevant, thus marking an intellectual retreat. Be that as it may, pushed out through the front door, reality returns through the back. The matter of the dependency or independence of Estela and Luís Garcia, to the analysis of which Machado commits his entire sense of writerly dignity, will make those same contradictions reappear – on another plane and not always voluntarily – and with them modernity. Let's see.

The climate of the book's first episodes is one of constraint. Beginning with the first pages we learn that nothing is as dear to Luís Garcia as independence – and distance. Nonetheless he sees quickly to the note from Valéria Gomes, which, as is abundantly clear, has disturbed his work schedule; and after putting up a little resistance against the widow, he consents to do the favour that she asks, even though it runs contrary to his convictions. Why does he give in? The answer remains unknown. Instead, the silence on his part allows us to situate him and, to some degree, the novel. We are dealing with a character who does not allow personal dependency and who will not order his own behaviour by means of it. As far as his taste and reasoning go, Luís Garcia doesn't owe anything to anyone. Nevertheless, in practice, albeit against his will ... Thinking ahead to consequences, let us note that in this picture the motivations and compensations for real behaviour cannot be expressed, since they are considered indecorous, while the expressed motivations are forever being frustrated – which is a recipe for a stifling novel.

The initial portrait of Luís Garcia is made up of an accumulation of negatives. He is a taciturn, retiring widower, a civil servant who lives in a very plain, isolated house. Methodical and hard-working, even his least unfriendly qualities are not spontaneous; he is inoffensive, and his modest, courteous manners are cold. There are traces too of antipathy: he doesn't return affection, evidences hints of disdain and a sardonic wrinkle in his heart. Nevertheless, surprising though it may be to the reader, despite all else 'he is not therefore the less accustomed to be helpful. Luís Garcia loved the species and hated the individual. If someone came to him for a service it was rare that he wouldn't receive it. He obliged without enthusiasm but effectively and had the peculiarity of forgetting the favour before the recipient did'.[150] Apparently a kind of misanthropy that is not counter to paternalistic relations, even favours them, contrary to what might seem logical. It should be noted that Luís Garcia *has chosen* the isolated house and *wanted* the solitude, which adds the feature of volition to his profile, which on this point is compared to that of the monks who lived

---

150   Machado de Assis 1959, vol. I, pp. 299–300.

on the hill in front, where they too sought refuge against civil drudgery.[151] Further along, he thinks of his daughter, who dreams of becoming a piano teacher: 'Moreover, what more could he desire for her than something that would make her independent and provide her with the means of living without favour?'[152] Withdrawal, disposition to oblige, aversion to receiving, esteem for independence are dissimilar – and in part incompatible. To appreciate the implications of this picture, which is less negative than it might appear and which in a certain sense might in fact seem an ideal – a turnabout of the sort we have seen with regard to Guiomar, whose defects also showed themselves to be virtues in the light of practical context – we must accompany the character on his visit with the widow Gomes.

Valéria wants to send her son Jorge to Paraguay as a 'volunteer' in order to create distance between him and Estela. When she summons Luís Garcia, it is for the purpose of having him put pressure on the boy. The reasons she gives are patriotic, but Luís Garcia doesn't believe them and tries to wriggle out: 'he didn't have any liking for the charge but didn't want to refuse it openly; he looked for a way out of giving an answer'.[153] Valéria, however, brings to bear every means at her disposal. Indeed, her message already had the sense of an appeal about it, which was quite unusual, for it spoke of 'advice',[154] which served to give a good deal of 'solemnity'[155] to relations between a wealthy widow and a modest functionary whom on occasion the family was wont to ask for services.[156]

In and of itself the patriotic motive is unassailable, but its principal benefit in the circumstances is to involve the lady and the civil servant in a common goal. As Luís Garcia shows little enthusiasm, Valéria talks up the respect that Jorge has for him – which is also untrue, since, as the narrator states, the relationship between the two has not been one of that sort,[157] and then immediately afterward the younger man will smile twice at Garcia's advice, one smile of disdain, the other of affability.[158] In the face of further avoidances by the civil servant, Valéria bites her lip and makes a gesture of spite but persists, now in the name of the consideration that the family and she deserve, which for all practical purposes inverts the hierarchy that exists between the two.[159] Cornered, Luís

---

151   Machado de Assis 1959, vol. I, p. 299.
152   Machado de Assis 1959, vol. I, p. 303.
153   Machado de Assis 1959, vol. I, pp. 305–6.
154   Machado de Assis 1959, vol. I, p. 299.
155   Machado de Assis 1959, vol. I, p. 304.
156   Machado de Assis 1959, vol. I, p. 307.
157   Machado de Assis 1959, vol. I, p. 306.
158   Machado de Assis 1959, vol. I, p. 309.
159   Machado de Assis 1959, vol. I, p. 306.

Garcia gives in 'weakly',[160] only to step back once again, when Jorge, without revealing the young woman's identity, explains what Valéria's real motive is.[161] New attack by the widow, who remains at the doorway complaining about the loneliness she faces. Taking Luís Garcia's hand, she lies to him in a hushed voice, saying that the woman Jorge is involved with is married and that is the real reason for getting him out of Rio.[162] The same so-to-speak 'staged' insinuation has been made before, albeit less obviously, at the outset of the chapter, when Valéria gives Luís Garcia her hand and is looked on by the narrator from the point of view of her attractiveness: 'Valéria received him affectionately, reaching her hand, still youthful despite her forty-eight-plus years, out to him'.[163] In the book's remaining pages no further word about this issue, which disappears like a bad thought (not even in the two aforementioned brief instances when something hangs in the air, does it get named, which is one example of the tacit presences characteristic of this book). On the other hand, the adultery argument leaves Luís Garcia without recourse, and he finally falls in line with the widow's plans and agrees to help her.[164] 'It was night when Luís Garcia left Valéria's house. He quitted it upset about everything – the mother, the son, his relationship there, the position he found himself in'.[165]

In other words, at the same time that Valéria asks Luís Garcia for a favour that he doesn't want to provide and thinks he ought not to, she offers him all kinds of imaginary compensations, each implying suppression of the social difference that separates them. His advice will be listened to, he will be highly esteemed by the High Court Justice's family, and she, Valéria, will be so alone that even a love affair between the two of them is a possibility. All the while we know that she is really not interested in advice, that the story about respect is an invention, that she would force Luis Garcia if she could, and that soon afterwards, in order to make things complete, she would arrange his marriage to Estela, who is not a wealthy lady but rather a poor young woman. Valéria wants to prevent entry into her family of that same young woman, who nonetheless, in the opinion of the widow herself, is highly estimable and deserves an excellent husband. In sum, in terms of gall the widow is willing to go far, improvising according to the needs of the moment and not fearing any sudden reversals, in which precisely the arbitrary aspect and the tranquil sense of impunity deriving from pater-

---

160 Machado de Assis 1959, vol. I, p. 306.
161 Machado de Assis 1959, vol. I, p. 308.
162 Machado de Assis 1959, vol. I, p. 310.
163 Machado de Assis 1959, vol. I, p. 304.
164 Machado de Assis 1959, vol. I, p. 310.
165 Machado de Assis 1959, vol. I, p. 310.

nalist authority are on display – in this case endowed with the supplementary cover of 'femininity'. As regards Luís Garcia, he forms his judgment independently, does not believe the widow's words, feels 'upset' at the promises and the pressures she produces, but doesn't go so far as to 'absolutely refuse'. He agrees 'weakly', which is the manner that social relations take on in this book: namely, with a thousand reservations. On the other side of the coin, when matters are seen as a whole Luís Garcia comes out very well, for in the future Valéria will give a dowry to Iaiá, daughter of Luís' first marriage, and another to Estela, with whom he will make his second marriage, one which improves his life considerably.

To summarise: a dynamic in which, from inferior to superior, services are exchanged for personal esteem while, in the inverse direction but without the connection between the two moments being made explicit, that esteem translates into material benefits. An obligatory and crucial point of passage in this deferred exchange is the arbitrariness of the people of means, whose benevolence is never out of the question and who even have it in their power to annul the difference between the parties, by co-optation – never leaving aside the other pole of arbitrariness, namely despotism – so that the dependent party can always nurse fantasies that the dominant party may abuse as they see fit. The social presuppositions are the same as in the previous books, but the dynamic here is more complicated, and, above all else, it comes in terms that, well into the bourgeois age, are difficult to dignify. In the light of this example, the cases of Helena and Guiomar seem simple-minded.

Such is the context in which to understand what Luís Garcia represents. His systematic aloofness defends him against the illusions that the component of capriciousness, inseparable as it is from paternalist relationships, in effect authorises. Those well-grounded illusions constitute, according to Luís Garcia, the true evil. It is in response to them that his negative traits become virtues and his figure, intentionally dulled down and unattractive, is transformed, to some degree, into an *ideal* – a reversal, let it be said within parentheses, in which the desire to idealise and perfect is allied with an uncommon degree of scepticism. Given that fortune and social distinction exist in dependence on favour and therefore on the chimeras of the wealthy, the best thing to do is to minimise hopes and ambitions. They inevitably deliver over the dependent party bound hand and foot like a puppet. *Now nothing is as detestable and unworthy as to give over your inmost desires to be made into a spectacle for someone else's vagaries.* The humiliation of all humiliations as seen in this book lies not in relations of dependency as a fact but in the illusions that come with them. There exists a kind of licentiousness in paternalism – touched on obliquely in *Helena* – that at this moment Machado finds horrible but that he will nevertheless take infinite pleasure in exploring in the second-phase novels – two years later! – in which it will become subject matter par excellence. Thus, rejecting the imaginary constructs that Valéria insinuates, Luís Garcia pays no heed to social difference, which then remains reduced to its simplest – and therefore least justifiable – expression (though it is never criticised). A harsh judgment: a regimen that renders its people vulnerable because of their best qualities, because of the natural desire for recognition and distinction, while only complete disillusionment can defend their dignity against the indecencies of social illusion. Under these circumstances the greatest homage a man can pay to his own humanity is to not allow it to blossom forth. Along these same lines, the book steels itself against everything that is imaginary and spontaneous. It values marriage that is loveless but also illusion-less,[166] takes the side of the adult against the childish,[167] of the durable against the transitory,[168] it sees patriotism as relative, just as it does with any other enthusiasm, and in the passage we are citing here, in which Iaiá's piano studies are looked upon as a possible guarantee of economic independence for her, the narrator hastens to make it clear that she has no talent: 'What does it matter? To teach the grammar of an art form, all one needs is to know it'.[169] It is as though a little bit of enjoyment were deadly because it lays open to the world a piece of our inner life, which is where the stream of illusions can catch us up and swallow us whole. In fine, a sad asceticism, one which relates to no absolute whatsoever. The collection of privations does not lead to heaven, nor does it teach spirituality; it is not even linked to the valorisation of labour. It exists merely as an avoidance of the humiliation that comes with being deceived.

Nevertheless, that does not mean that Luís Garcia evades the practice of favour. We have already seen that 'he is not therefore the less accustomed to oblige ... If someone came to him for help it was rare that he wouldn't receive it ... he obliged without enthusiasm but effectively, and had the peculiarity of forgetting the favour before the recipient did'.[170] The key expression is 'without enthusiasm but effectively'. In its first half we find our now-familiar disillusionment. Luís Garcia gives out his favours coldly, with no great personal involvement, to the point of soon forgetting them – which preserves him from the wheeling and dealing that come with the imaginary dimensions in paternalistic giving. In this sense what is at stake is cleansing the exchange of favours

---

166 Machado de Assis 1959, vol. I, p. 335.
167 Machado de Assis 1959, vol. I, pp. 303, 320, 330.
168 Machado de Assis 1959, vol. I, p. 402.
169 Machado de Assis 1959, vol. I, p. 303.
170 Machado de Assis 1959, vol. I, pp. 299–300.

of its warm, disgraceful aspect linked to the dependency relations for which Machado had so harsh an analysis. Conversely, that cleansing also has about it the character of a rationalisation. It is as if, in the absence of personal investment, the flow of favours would run fuller and more effectively. The giving would be made to it didn't matter whom and without any subjective motive, which has it seem to be a service being provided to society and separates it from the personification of power, which would be not only degrading but also contrary to effectiveness. This is the character's ideology, which very consciously represents a critique of our ills, and a cure, as has previously occurred with Helena and Guiomar.[171]

Before we go into greater detail, we must note that this idea of the impersonal favour is itself a contradiction. It maintains the form of the social relationship and ignores its reasons (namely, the satisfactions and advantages linked to favour's obligations), which it considers unacceptable. Something analogous pertains to our present-day military, who defend capitalism but do not like the profit motive. This understood, from the ideological point of view it is a fine solution, reconciling as it does the interests of the dependents, the owners and the inspiration of modernity. In fact, the impersonality removes the moral drawbacks of dependency, though not its grounding, and at the same time represents the appropriation of the spirit of the age without a contextual rupture: favours, assimilated as much as possible, through their stylisation, to the exchange of impersonal services, are perfected, and the dependent is conceived of as a functionary for their flow. Add to that the fact that the criteria for impersonality and for efficacy themselves constitute a tribute to classic bourgeois ideology, albeit in its utilitarian dimension, which seemed to be more real for Machado than the liberal dimension. Also in this same direction, Luís Garcia's regular and methodical habits, his moderation, seriousness, etcetera, which are part of the climate of sadness that surrounds him, can also be viewed as aspects of the work ethic and of personal autonomy. And, to complete this list of accommodations to modernity, there is Raimundo the servant, in whom traces of slavery, of Africa, of fetishism, and of the English major-

---

171 For a practical commentary on this impersonalisation of favour, see Machado's correspondence with Nabuco. 'I suppose you still use the same sign to indicate that the matter is not unavoidable, just a bit pressured. That is what I understood and showed to Graça Aranha' reads a reply from Nabuco. [to Machado]. It would seem that Machado did not refrain from transmitting solicitations to his eminent friend, but he would discreetly indicate the cases to which he was not himself fully committed. In this case he had communicated in that way the desire on the part of Luís Guimarães, Jr. that he be appointed to fill a vacancy in the mission that Nabuco was leading in Europe. See Machado de Assis 1955, pp. 45–7.

domo combine. From the practical point of view, it is an ideology fashioned more to civilise the dominant order than to change it. Yet another variant of enlightened paternalism. From the literary point of view, though, it is interesting to see the oblique manner through which Machado was inspired by the contemporary world at large, of whose ways he was well aware but kept from replacing his sense of local reality, to which, good or bad, they were subordinated in the process of intellectual elaboration. A non-fanatical conviction of the priority of experience, both his own and that of the country, which would have been difficult to sustain since it meant confronting the enormous intellectual superiority on the part of the so-called civilised world without giving in and also without shutting himself off from it. The phenomenon is a rare one, which is indicated too by the sense of miraculousness that Machado will elicit later, when he is clearer in this aspect. On the other hand, this is a reason, albeit a secondary one, for this book's relative lack of brilliance: the issues that it deals with are indeed weighty, but in this version they are not eyebrow-raising.

Nevertheless, there are also planes on which the synthesis isn't complete. The tension between paternalism and the bourgeois sense of things is not only a conflict internal to the characters. It is a technical hesitation on the part of the narrator. For example, in the book's first pages where Luís Garcia's cold, aloof manners allow us to suppose that he bears a history of suffering and disappointment that explains those manners. But such is not forthcoming. The fact is that Machado has presented current modes of paternalism, which do not require biographical explanation, as being strange and particular traits, which, within bourgeois coordinates, they certainly are. As a consequence, our public servant begins as a mysterious oddity and ends up as the most normal of men. The matter can also be seen through the lens of literary borrowing: the enigmatic countenance, for an understanding of which past events and peculiar aspects of contemporary society provide the key, is a classic beginning of the Realist novel. But it doesn't serve well the novel that is completely contrary to the surprising and the exceptional, which is what Machado sought to write.[172]

---

[172] Walter Benjamin relates the nineteenth-century vogue of physiognomical analysis (the 'physiologies') to the anonymity of the city and the universalisation of competitive relationships. The myth of the readable face would have served as a sedative for the disquietude that came with life amid hostility and competitiveness. See Benjamin, 'Der Flâneur' [The Flâneur], *Charles Baudelaire*. For an example via caricature, see the opening pages of Balzac's *Cousin Pons* [Cousin Pons]. Needless to say, the context of *Iaiá Garcia* differs from this.

In a more profound way the same problem appears in the back-and-forth between Valéria and Luís Garcia, in which the list of reasons for discontent on the part of each, but especially on Luís's part, keeps growing. Given his independent character, the reader can well imagine that the accumulation is going to culminate in confrontation, which too is not forthcoming. The fact is that, despite what might be supposed, Valéria's many manoeuvres are not chalked up as infractions against someone else's liberty but rather as manifestations of her position and her will, which the dependent can evade a bit but which he neither challenges nor judges, and above all else the legitimacy of which factors lies not in reasons given but in benefits performed. Now these are aspects that given Luís's ideology – and the book's – seem indecorous and consequently are left in the dark. Therefore the conflicts that the characters' moral physiognomy makes us expect do not come to fruition, and the various accommodations linked to the real complementarity of interests are neither commented on nor made explicit. Such is the omnipresent and most important formal aspect of the book – a defect, but only in part. We shall return to it in detail. For now, let us retain just its frustrating effect of loss of tension owing to the hesitant way of presenting the character, first as a gentleman in the style of the second half of the nineteenth century, and then as a dependent man in a paternalistic context. In the very episode of Luís Garcia's visit this vacillation can be easily followed. As we have seen, Machado tries to conceive of a discreet and impersonal comportment – enlightened, so to speak – that would free dependency of its indignities. What happens is that, to impart more convincing dignity to his creation, Machado ends up lending it traces of elegance, along with a moral tone, the presuppositions of which are quite different. The character comes out lame in one leg because the central nerve of his behaviour, which is precisely what links him to his precarious social position, has disappeared. So Luís Garcia is interesting when he is on the defensive, when he neither accepts nor rejects but dodges,[173] when he does not dare to formulate his doubts,[174] when he tries to reconcile Valéria's desires with his own neutrality,[175] when he adopts a halfway measure,[176] when he meekly agrees,[177] when he refuses but can't resist the widow's repeated insistence,[178] when he stealthily examines the expression in

---

173   Machado de Assis 1959, vol. I, p. 306.
174   Machado de Assis 1959, vol. I, p. 305.
175   Machado de Assis 1959, vol. I, p. 306.
176   Machado de Assis 1959, vol. I, p. 306.
177   Machado de Assis 1959, vol. I, p. 305.
178   Machado de Assis 1959, vol. I, p. 307.

Jorge's eyes,[179] when he tries to escape after the dinner without speaking to the young man,[180] when he confirms with silence a white lie by Valéria,[181] when he can't summon the courage to ask,[182] and especially when he returns home upset about everything – the mother, the son, his relationship there, the position he finds himself in.[183] The other line, however, in which the tension is lost, is equally present. In it Luís Garcia is the obsequious gentleman but not an obligated one[184] – who deals with Valeria on equal terms,[185] who makes just observations to her about the disproportion involved with what she is asking,[186] who does epigrams, who, in a mode of superiority, does not believe in premonitions, who is called a sceptic but not a hardened one,[187] all of which gives his behaviour a basis of compassion rather than of social dependency, who draws cold conclusions about Valéria's arguments,[188] who sees it as wrongheaded to resolve through war a problem with which a priest would be better placed to deal,[189] who finds irritating the request for discretion that Jorge makes of him, since between gentlemen these things are self-evident,[190] who speaks to the widow frankly,[191] etcetera. Although he has thoroughly identified the predicament the inferiors face and their reasons for resisting and wishes to enhance them, Machado seeks out terms that will make them look good – the very terms of the enhancement – in the ways of the wealthy people.

Stronger yet, Estela is a female version of Luís Garcia. The two present parallel figures and situations, independent of each other at the start, which generalises to the society the problems they face and their reactions to them. Like her parallel figure, Estela is characterised by renunciation, defensive in nature rather than ascetic.[192] To understand her rigidity we must go through Valéria's son, just as we went through Valéria to comprehend Luís' aloofness.

After weeks of resistance, Jorge agrees to go off to the war. Not to obey his mother and not after hearing out Luís Garcia but to seek the esteem of Estela,

---

179 Machado de Assis 1959, vol. I, p. 307.
180 Machado de Assis 1959, vol. I, p. 307.
181 Machado de Assis 1959, vol. I, p. 308.
182 Machado de Assis 1959, vol. I, p. 308.
183 Machado de Assis 1959, vol. I, p. 310.
184 Machado de Assis 1959, vol. I, p. 310.
185 Machado de Assis 1959, vol. I, p. 306.
186 Machado de Assis 1959, vol. I, p. 306.
187 Machado de Assis 1959, vol. I, p. 306.
188 Machado de Assis 1959, vol. I, p. 308.
189 Machado de Assis 1959, vol. I, p. 309.
190 Machado de Assis 1959, vol. I, p. 309.
191 Machado de Assis 1959, vol. I, p. 310.
192 Machado de Assis 1959, vol. I, p. 313.

who had not asked anything of the sort from him. This kind of mismatch of motives, let us observe in passing, is constant in *Iaiá Garcia*, and we shall see that it is in fact a formal principle. At the moment what we shall merely observe is that this is not, and will not always be, Jorge's attitude, which is itself inconstant. At the start, when Valéria brings the young woman to the house, she elicits 'a strong impression'[193] from Jorge. He seeks her out with his eyes, a 'language that she doesn't understand – or pretends not to'.[194] Who was she to dismiss him like that? the young man asks himself, meaning that an *agregada* doesn't say 'no'. As she continues to flee from him, the 'sensual fantasy of that first instant'[195] is transformed, and by the end of a month 'the nature of his sentiment ... [is] purer'.[196] Estela continues to avoid him, which represents 'yet another sting',[197] and provokes the same question for a second time: 'Who was she to dismiss him like that?'[198] The classist reaction is harsher this time: 'Know that I could come to hate you; maybe I already have. Know too that I can get revenge for your deprecations, and, if it proves necessary, I will be cruel'.[199] Estela doesn't answer; she turns her back to him and kisses the doves that she has in her hand at the time. Jorge: 'Why are you wasting on animals those kisses that could be better employed elsewhere?'[200] Then, as a continuation, 'he pulls her to him before she can get away or scream and covers her mouth with kisses'.[201] This is the dramatic apex of the book. 'From here on the young man, wounded by remorse, seeks to rehabilitate himself in the *agregada*'s eyes and becomes respectful ... a part of the influence for which is owed to Estela's severity of character, which finally succeeds in instilling in Jorge's spirit a different idea about her than he previously had'.[202] To such an extent that for four months 'Jorge strives to erase the memory of that episode, behaving with the respect and consideration that seem to him sufficient to redeem the lost esteem'.[203] Only when he loses hope of 'winning her over by the ordinary means'[204] does he accept the proposition of enlisting in the army. On the eve of

---

193   Machado de Assis 1959, vol. I, p. 313.
194   Machado de Assis 1959, vol. I, p. 313.
195   Machado de Assis 1959, vol. I, p. 314.
196   Machado de Assis 1959, vol. I, p. 314.
197   Machado de Assis 1959, vol. I, p. 313.
198   Machado de Assis 1959, vol. I, p. 316.
199   Machado de Assis 1959, vol. I, p. 317.
200   Machado de Assis 1959, vol. I, p. 317.
201   Machado de Assis 1959, vol. I, p. 317.
202   Machado de Assis 1959, vol. I, p. 318.
203   Machado de Assis 1959, vol. I, p. 319.
204   Machado de Assis 1959, vol. I, p. 319.

his departure this phase of his penitence culminates in a properly formed declaration of love, which amounts to a proposal of marriage. Estela's pride doesn't allow her to settle for the reparation, and she responds with 'this bad and disdainful word: You, sir, are a fool'.[205] Jorge leaves, and on the fields of Paraguay his love will be transformed into 'a religious faith'.[206] When he returns to Rio four years later, he will find Estela and Luís Garcia married. For a period of time he avoids their house, and after that he frequents it with confused emotions, which will later become clear when a doctor tells him that Luís is suffering from a heart ailment and has only a few months to live. (Parenthetically: this is one of the elements responsible for the book's adult climate, noteworthy in that regard within the early stages of our literature: Machado does not limit himself to young love, dealing as well, in detail, with the ambiguities of love among married people.) 'He frequently thought about the consequences of being soon to inherit Luís Garcia's wife, a resolution that seemed to him a necessary one; that is what he said to himself. And that marriage would have two outcomes: it would be a reparation of the bad things he had done to her and a just comeuppance for the way she had treated him'.[207] Not too long afterward Jorge loses interest in Estela – 'between two cups of tea',[208] as the latter puts it – and gets married to her stepdaughter Iaiá, child of Luís Garcia's first marriage.

In the light of this résumé, the reader will gain an idea of the non-Naturalist rawness that Machado and the book are aiming to achieve, linked to the goal of investigating the humiliations inherent in paternalism. The reader will get an idea as well of the level of arbitrariness to which the dependent sees him- or herself subject, especially if she happens to be a woman. Thus what from Jorge's viewpoint is an evolution of his emotions, from the viewpoint of the *agregada* is the gamut of the vicissitudes that the love of a wealthy boy holds for her – from the great prize of an improbable marriage to brutalisation, 'fall' and abandonment. In this context of extreme inequality in which the fancies of one are almost the fate of the other, Estela's conduct is explicable and admirable, a singular mixture of obedience, desire to avoid confrontation and resistance without concession. Loving and being loved, Estela 'pretends – and 'strangles' her own feeling: 'Never!' she swears to herself'.[209] Anti-romantically, social distance prevails over love, but on the basis of self-worth, not traditionalism. So Estela's very decisive rejections have some Romantic reverberations about

---

205 Machado de Assis 1959, vol. I, p. 321.
206 Machado de Assis 1959, vol. I, p. 325.
207 Machado de Assis 1959, vol. I, pp. 348–9.
208 Machado de Assis 1959, vol. I, pp. 402.
209 Machado de Assis 1959, vol. I, pp. 315.

them, for the flight from an unequal relationship echoes refusal of inequality itself, in addition to implying a more demanding concept of love, of which the situation of dependency is unworthy.

Estela looks at dependency and the favours that come with it through the same eyes as Luís Garcia, but, being a woman, the margin she has to work with is smaller. She lives in the house of her protectress, who deposits her 'ideas and headaches'[210] in her and to whom Estela is 'obedient and grateful'.[211] It is a part of the book's realist spirit that the *agregada*, despite her proud character, should accept in a natural way the favours necessary for her life and that she should do everything necessary to deserve those favours. Valéria says with appreciation: 'she has never failed to listen to me and never tried to win me over with flattery'.[212] There comes the time when Valéria offers her the dowry. The young woman's first reaction is not to accept, since it would come from money that the mother shares with the son, but she soon returns to 'the reality of the situation'[213] and agrees. Within the narrow and oppressive terrain that is hers, she seeks a kind of obedience without abasement that correlates with the coldness of Luís Garcia's performance of favours. What makes her uncomfortable, however, is Jorge's courtship. Luís Garcia puts a chill on the exchange of favours in order to erect a dike against the effronteries of the imagination, ever eager for social greatness and therefore ever open to humiliation. It is in that same spirit that Estela is a decided opponent of the novelesque. The love of a rich man could erase social distances, which, in the eyes of the *agregada*, does not recommend it. On the contrary, it underscores the helplessness of some and the unpunished caprice of others, as well as nourishing disgraceful hopes that must be rejected. Thus Estela's dignity and Luís Garcia's are constructed as responses to their protectors' arbitrariness, especially in its most whimsical aspect, which is where the most personal and degrading character of the subordination is concentrated.

'Mere *agregada* or *protegida*,[214] she didn't think she had any business dreaming about a better, more independent position for herself; and, assuming she could somehow come into such a position, it is reasonable to assume she'd turn it down anyhow, because to her eyes it would be a favour – and her cup of

---

210   Machado de Assis 1959, vol. I, pp. 330.
211   Machado de Assis 1959, vol. I, pp. 318.
212   Machado de Assis 1959, vol. I, pp. 314.
213   Machado de Assis 1959, vol. I, pp. 329.
214   [In Portuguese the word *'protegido'* – in Estela's case, in the feminine *'protegida'* – is a form of the verb *'proteger*,' which means 'to protect' (obviously a transparent cognate with English). But the logical translations, 'the protected one (f.),' 'the protectee,' don't work in colloquial English. At the same time, Roberto's text uses several other forms of *'proteger*',

gratitude was full up'.²¹⁵ As the reader can see, the first part of the sentence is modest and compliant while the second is brash and prideful. In the latter her social inferiority seems to have transformed itself into superiority. Be that as it may, the duality reproduces the synthesis of submission and dignity that Estela seeks. If we look more closely, we can see that the refusal is an exasperated one – the cup that is full up – and that the cause for the exasperation lies in the repugnance accorded to favour. This movement will find its completion at the book's end, when Estela abandons the sphere of family for that of work and asks her father to come with her to end 'the life of dependence and servility that had been theirs up to now'.²¹⁶ In other words, the rigour with which Estela clings to her subaltern condition is an expression of her sense of equality and serves to keep her safe from her protectors and to impede them from exceeding their proper bounds. Hence, for example, the scene in which she puts Jorge in his place as a wealthy man – 'You, sir, are a fool' – precisely the categorisation from which he is trying to escape. These are interesting intricacies in the appropriation of the egalitarian outlook inside the context of paternalism. In that same passage – at the risk of overplaying my hand a little – let me observe that the 'right' to which Estela does not aspire in the above passage does not refer directly to the 'better, more independent position' for herself but rather the right to 'dream about' such a position. Like Luís Garcia, Estela has a horror of that kind of dream, in which the subordinate lets down their guard and allows him- or herself to be seduced, in addition to recognising as such their own subaltern status.²¹⁷ Later, in justifying her marriage to Luís Garcia, in which there existed

---

      with which the usage in this passage combines very meaningfully – echoing back and forth with them, so to speak. I have chosen, rather than use an echo-less synonym in English, to keep the echo by simply leaving the word(s) In Portuguese.]
215 Machado de Assis 1959, vol. I, p. 315.
216 Machado de Assis 1959, vol. I, p. 406.
217 The price the dependent pays for the novelistic illusion is also the subject matter of 'Sabina', a narrative poem from the *Americanas* (1875) in which Machado seeks to combine Neoclassical diction and the social sphere of the plantation. The female house slave, Sabina, moons for the son of the owner, who one morning surprises her at her bath in the river:
      'Flower of the plantation born beside the river',
      Began Octavio, 'perhaps more beautiful
      Than those cultured beauties of the city
      So covered with jewels and silk,
      Oh don't deny me your soft aroma!
      Your birth made you a captive; the law only
      Put shackles on you; in the free breast
      Of your masters you have freedom,

only esteem: 'I didn't see any door open as a favour, no hand has grabbed mine in simple condescension. I didn't meet with humiliating politeness or affability without real warmth. My name did not serve as fodder for the natural curiosity of my husband's friends. Who is she? where did she come from? ... there was no need either to move upwards or downwards'.[218] Thus, favour, condescension, affability and curiosity on the part of the wealthy are humiliations that Estela escapes by staying where she is – besides being so many pleasures that she deprives the fine people of. In other words, co-optation is always degrading, and, in contrast to the prior novels, love is not cleansing enough. On the contrary, being the more visceral illusion, it is the cause of even deeper humiliations. That is a reason not to believe in it – which nonetheless produces the paradoxical outcome of preserving it. Estela's solution consists of dividing herself in two. She gives to paternalism what is paternalism's but she refuses to give it love. A compliant and strict *agregada* who is not foolish, bolstered by an unconditional but suppressed soul. The impulses are both opposed and combined. One of resistance and personal fortitude in the face of arbitrariness, the other Bovaristic. Thus Estela's practical anti-Romanticism has a Romantic and egalitarian connotation, a constellation parallel to what we see in Luís Garcia, whose favours have the connotation of a modernist impersonality.[219]

So the surprising outcome of so much moral sensitivity is immobility. In fact, it's best for all the characters to stay where they are and maintain awareness of their condition. Not because social differentiation is just or because social tradition justifies it, but because the mediators of movement – favour, along with the desire to rise socially – are even more degrading. That defines the conservative side of these figures whose awareness of the situation is acute without becoming class-conscious. More precisely, in the generalisation that

---

> The greater freedom, pure affection
> That has chosen you from among the captives
> And covers you with caresses! Flower of the countryside,
> Lusher far than those other flowers
> Grown in greenhouses and in drawing rooms,
> Wild rose born beside the river,
> Oh don't deny me your soft aroma!'
>
> Sabina, who isn't Estela, yields. The moral is not long in coming: while the slave awaits a child ... 'the young man's heart, as voluble as the passing breeze or the waves,' moves on to a young woman from his own class whom he has met 'in one of the court festivities' and with whom he returns to the plantation to tie 'the conjugal bonds.' Machado, in introducing a slave woman, gives us his thought with little niggling: novelistic expectations are specious. They serve the whims of the master and do not serve the dependent. See Machado de Assis 1959, vol. III, pp. 140–5.

218 Machado de Assis 1959, vol. I, pp. 402–3.
219 Machado de Assis 1959, vol. I, pp. 402–3.

they embody and in their rejection of a personal solution, their analysis does indeed involve class. Its collective dimension, however, has no follow-up route, and its outcomes are seen through the lens of decorum and the dignity of the individual, which recuperates them for the sphere of paternalism. Thus co-optation is repugnant not because it is the result of individual solution – which leaves all the other dependents right where they are – but because it is a favour, so great a favour that there is no way to repay it. Along this line, the debt of gratitude seems to weigh more than the social inferiority, the sense of being even is compatible with the situation of dependency, and independence can be a state of indebtedness. In other words, the accountancy of favours prevails completely, and Estela and Luís Garcia are purists with regard to personal debt, much more so than the people of means, who beyond that mode of accounting have another – the one involving objective wealth. These aspects exist, and in them is revealed the lack of an historical way out for dependent social levels.

Such is the case with regard to Estela's convictions, which have interest for our argument although within the body of the novel they don't carry much sway. The literary and realistic merits of her character do exist, however, and are found in other, less ideological passages. Here and there the complex of the young woman's motives creates flights of an unexpected and very particular poetry. See for example her relief when her lover departs for the war, breaking off his irritating pursuit.[220] Or the episode of the forced kiss, in which Estela has to smother a whimper, doesn't scream, doesn't flee, and tries to get out of the situation without affronting Jorge or referring to any right. Her behaviour has something canine and moving about it that wants neither to be mistreated nor to bite – or even to leave the master's side. In the background, the necessity of not breaking with the family that protects her and the decision not to give in.[221] In the same sense, note the way Estela has of sticking with Valéria in order not to find herself alone with Jorge.

In recapitulation, the ideology of Estela and Luís Garcia represents an attempt at rationality. Its strength lies in disbelief and renunciation, which elevate them above the other characters. A rationality, in the first place, from the point of view of dependents, who learn not to invest their hopes in their protectors' fantasies – or in their own. Disillusionment provides them with clarity, eliminating internal dependency, which is the relationship's subjective glue. They don't get free of domination and caprice, which under the circumstances would be impossible, but they are no longer deceived and have the distance

---

220   Machado de Assis 1959, vol. I, p. 319.
221   Machado de Assis 1959, vol. I, pp. 316–17.

necessary for self-dignity and the principle of the lesser evil. Looked at through its actions, social authority does not correlate with the paternalistic arguments that would seek to justify it – and its myth is destroyed. Seen on another level, however, this critique of arbitrariness benefits from aspects of the very prestige it is struggling against. Its convergence with bourgeois rationalisation lends it a modernist connotation and makes it a welcome ideology. The ideal of distanced conduct that Machado sets out brings a sense of modernity to the two parties and does not eliminate paternalism. Against the naysayers, the dependents swear that their protectors are not barbarians, the latter abstain from abusing them and even treat them like competent, independent people. In other words, critique, functional behaviour and the Rights of Man are appropriated by velleity – on the outside only, so to speak, in order to keep up with the times. Having renounced the straight course, Machado tries another route: appeal to the vanity of people of good will … But let us return to the rational dimension of this ideology – which is the more striking of the two – to emphasise its classist position. It in fact consists of the collection, exploration, summarising and critique of dependent experience, and its literary importance depends on a full and hard-hitting presentation of the arbitrariness of the wealthy. In addition to which, disbelief and renunciation are not merely intellectual outcomes; they also constitute proof of human value, for they represent the capacity to combine thought and practice, even with sacrifice. Now it is clear that the powerful in *Iaiá Garcia* have none of those qualities. Even in the sacrifices they make Valéria and Jorge are arbitrary. In this book, then, as regards ideology, the area of intellectual and moral merit amounts to a monopoly on the side of the dependents. It is worthwhile to underscore this opposition, for it determines the novel's initial part and has us expecting a confrontation – that doesn't take place. Pages ago we remarked that this repetition of non-consequentiality amounts to a construction defect. Now, however, we shall see that this defect is also the most profound and original aspect of *Iaiá Garcia*, upon which depend decisive formal innovations that bring us close to the mature novels. As our main thread, one impression can serve as our guide: the second part of the narrative does not correspond with the first.

The initial movement, which we might call 'exposition', in which the conflicts and problems are set up, closes with Jorge's departure. The tensions that we were following remain without immediate continuation, suspended, and it seems like the time for a first summing-up has arrived. Luís Garcia's independence has suffered under Valéria's arbitrary acts, Estela has suffered under Jorge's disrespect, and Jorge has suffered as well, under the pressures exerted by both his mother and Luís Garcia serving as intermediary for the widow. In all those oppositions, one of the poles is paternalistic arbitrariness while the other varies, even to the point of inclusion of a reference to individual rights. The ideological contradiction is clearly traced and appears to be central. The fact is, however, that the novel's subsequent development bypasses and, figuratively, forgets it. In this regard see the odd Chapter VI, in which, shortly after the separation, Valéria offers Estela a dowry and tries to marry her off to Luís Garcia in order to carry out her plan. Surprise: neither the *agregada* nor the functionary harbours ill will toward her, they don't stop frequenting her house, and the marriage works out for both. Even Jorge does not harbour rancour against his mother, whom he 'adores'.[222] Thus, belying expectations, the series of contrarieties that Valéria has created remain without effect upon the course of the narrative. The prime motivation for events lies in the rich widow's authority, not in the ideological antagonisms or the question of right. The dependents' firmness is stronger than that of their protectors, but that doesn't seem to move people to confrontation, and *for all practical purposes the contradiction just disappears*. That fact is all the more noteworthy given that the salient note in Valéria's authority is always capriciousness, as the narrator insistently points out, that same capriciousness that the book finds horrible. Operating with candour and method, the widow sees her wishes as objective and sufficient reasons – in which behaviour she is a precursor of the heroines of the second-phase novels. Why would it be desirable that Jorge remain in Rio? Answer: 'Because separation would be hard on me too'.[223] When the son (trying to avoid complications) tells her that it isn't a good idea to have Estela in the house since she is an outsider: 'What does that matter if I get along well with her?'[224] In thanking her, Antunes says that his daughter is coming to be like her mother, who was a saintly soul. Valéria: 'Estela is nothing less than that. She is pretty!'[225] This last rejoinder involves a 'quality dear to the widow, who had been one of the beauties of her time'.[226]

The observations to be made are various. We saw that the ideological dimension reflects and validates the dependents' point of view. We shall now see that the plot dimension is ruled by their protectors' arbitrariness. Let us say that, in order to become formulated, both problem and conflict are sustained by a vague appropriation of bourgeois egalitarianism, while their 'real' evolution – that is, the evolution that the plot imprints them with – runs along the track of personal dependency, which holds out altogether other alternatives. Hence the

---

222 Machado de Assis 1959, vol. I, p. 327.
223 Machado de Assis 1959, vol. I, p. 305.
224 Machado de Assis 1959, vol. I, p. 328.
225 Machado de Assis 1959, vol. I, p. 328.
226 Machado de Assis 1959, vol. I, p. 330.

discontinuity and loss of tension that we have pointed to, *a disharmony that, however, is itself a form*, the formal transcription of real relations, in this case the permanent frustration of the aspirations of independence in a dependent class. In the perspective of our study, this form should be saluted as the first considerable accomplishment of the Brazilian novel – something of which further along I shall be attempting to persuade the reader. A form much better than new – original in the strong sense of the word, in which the originality of the national process becomes the premise of the novelistic fantasy, which is coming into focus. Before we go into the detail of that interpretation, however, let those of you interested in Marxism note that the truth of this form does not seem to be reducible to the classist points of view that it brings up. It is clear that the form comes together because Machado takes on and validates the dependents' outlook, but it seems to me clear as well that the form's most vibrant effects are not fully contained within that outlook, just as they are not within the opposing outlook, but rather that they are attached to the gravitation of the whole set, in which the intention of the parties is lost and becomes difficult to attribute to one or the other.

Taking up our thread once again, let us remark that the initial contradictions soon lose their tension and become mere contrarieties. At no time will Estela, Luís Garcia or Jorge confront Valéria, whose authority is *a given – the* unquestionable given of the book. All the disbelief and critical insight piled up by Machado and by the characters is designed to escape from the illusions of paternalism, but not to question paternalism itself, for that would represent a lack of respect and gratitude. Valéria's right is a taboo area. Note, though, that that critical restraint – the most glaring unilaterality in the book and its visible ideological limit – does not conceal Valéria's negative aspects. Therefore, its strategic effect must lie elsewhere. In fact, the aforementioned taboo is the transposed transcription of another more acute impasse: what would happen to the dependents if the protectors' authority were no longer accepted? What would happen to the positive characters, Estela and Luís Garcia, whose virtues the book seeks to set forth? Given their historical-dead-end situation, respect is more necessary to the dependents than to the wealthy. Thus the taboo is the transposition of the impossibility of resistance on the part of the dependent and provides honourable grounding to a practical disgrace. Although disagreeing and spiteful – and horrified by the arbitrariness – how could the dependents stop being submissive? On what basis? These are old miseries that have lasted into our own time.

For a closer view, let's look at the unrestrained way Valéria has of dealing with others: according to her fantasies but not without affection. Her *protegida* likes Jorge? She'll end up with Luís Garcia. Luís, whom Valéria herself had given a glimmer of hope and who had got into the entire affair despite his better judgment, ends up marrying Estela. And Jorge, who had been attracted to Estela, ends up with the glories of war. A complete – and satisfactory – rearrangement that allows Valéria to reconcile family pride, maternal love and care for the dependents, at the price – for the latter – of replacing their will with hers. Later, in his mature novels, Machado will study at great length the dynamics of such relationships, more complicated and rewarding than they seem. The subalterns find various satisfactions under the shadow of their protectors, and also in identification with that arrangement, which, to our individualistic presuppositions, is inconceivable. The reader may recall Brás Cubas' servant, who liked to appear at the window of his master's villa so as to make it clear that 'he was not a *nobody's* servant'.[227] There we see a different, non-individualistic sense of freedom, for those who lack the means to practice arbitrary acts on a large scale and on their own behalf, consisting of hitching a ride on someone else's arbitrariness. Or, the famous 'let's make the best of it'. Witness the expressions of one contemporary: 'To be free is to be a minister, deputy, president, chief of police, delegate, sub-delegate, inspector; it is to be from supreme commander to sergeant and corporal in the National Guard; it is to be a relative, friend, or fellow party member of the authority, of the Judge, of the High Court Justice, of the bailiff'.[228]

That, to return to *Iaiá Garcia*, is what Machado found repugnant and what, in the name of dignity, of reason and vaguely of the Rights of Man, he sought to criticise and to end, for it bespoke the complicity of the dependent in their own dependency. Which is the reason it seldom appears in the novel, save in the figure of Antunes, the book's punching bag. The ascetic ideology of Estela and Luís Garcia is designed precisely to un-identify, to separate, the will of the *protegido* from that of the protector in order to make the former stable, master of him- or herself, safe from the caprices of the wealthy. A rational and praiseworthy intention, which, however, establishes a pattern of decorum that excludes almost completely a key aspect of the entire issue and key link in its circuitry. As a consequence the material is impoverished, something is kept quiet, and, most specifically, proportions are prejudiced, uncertain. Valéria's despotism, for example, acquires excessive prominence if the enabling premise is that of paternalist routine but is treated lightly if the criterion is respect for others. The book leaves us located between the two alternatives.

---

227   Machado de Assis, *Memórias póstumas*, ch. CLVI.
228   Machado de Assis, *Memórias póstumas*, ch. CLVI.

Here we have the anti-Realist side of Machado's Realist breakthrough, the strong side of which we shall see presently. Hereafter we shall be coming across various forms that are to be seen in the mature work, albeit here still in embryonic form and dispersed throughout the novel. The will of the rich characters implies *discontinuities* in the lives and goals of their dependents, which are in effect that will's complement. The discontinuities are products of the protector's convenience, and for that reason, in addition to social impositions undergone, are services provided, that is to say, elements of connexion, not ones of antagonism. They merit *compensation*, in terms either material or involving esteem, thereby pushing the personal discontinuity to a second plane while the real guarantor of the value of life, namely continuity of protection, remains at the forefront. The distance between the two senses is insurmountable and also, according to the convenience of the moment, very easy to overcome – an ambivalence that will be one of the comic sources of Machado's future work. The reader will recall the compensations that Valéria proposes: to Estela, one man instead of another; to Luís Garcia, a wife instead of a state of constraint; to Jorge, military glory instead of Estela. They aren't simple acts of exchange, since they wouldn't have occurred to the people involved. But neither are they instances of simple violence, since they include a moment of amends-making and even of collaboration, in addition to agreement on the part of the party involved. Substitutions and discontinuities are what translate Valéria's imposition of her will into practice, along with the effective presumption of substituting her satisfaction for a dependent's, who then either suppresses the prior injunction, or, aided by the holy oils of respect and of filial admiration for authority, dismisses it with all sincerity. On the other side of the coin, if the dependent's satisfaction is negligible when it doesn't agree with the other, it is also indispensable, for what is the value of a protector whose *protegidos* live in a state of dissatisfaction? The discontinuity in the lives of the latter group is compensated for by continuity of protection, and the satisfaction of the authority has more real importance in their lives than their own dissatisfaction. In this sense, by calculation or by obfuscation, the former is theirs as well, and there is no way to separate such intermingled things. In short, one satisfaction is the same as the other, as long as approval from on high, coin of the realm for this system, is in force. In other words, personal identity's most impregnable redoubt – namely, satisfaction experienced – is less delimited and secure than is generally believed, and it lends itself to a quid pro quo. (Consider, in contrast, that nineteenth-century Realism in Europe valued character continuity – an ideal that leads to the individualistic separation of people and, inside of them, the separation of their faculties, to an ultimate tragic end.) It is clear that a 'progressive' figure like Estela 'holds her soul above her destiny'.²²⁹ That is, she is independent in spirit even though she is an *agregada*, and does not allow the substitution of one love for another just because Valéria wants it that way: she has her inner self, and the preferences of her *protetora* are not what determine hers. Now her father, who is a 'subaltern' soul,²³⁰ lives and breathes the prestige of the wealthy, to the point of being unable to distinguish between his own will and theirs. And naturally he finds his daughter's ideas about autonomy incomprehensible. It should be observed that the book takes a breather whenever Antunes comes on stage, despite the antipathy that Machado has for him: his figure undisguisedly incarnates the cycle of the material and symbolic compensations – abject to modern eyes – that is proper to paternalistic protection. One example more of the unexpected paths of modernity. Who would think that Machado de Assis, observing our belatedness – of which there is nothing to be proud – would be exploring the sense of discontinuity and heterogeneity in the psychic process and its imbrications with social power? In *Memórias póstumas* two years later, discontinuity, compensation and substitution in the realm of that experience called 'immediate' would be systematised and transformed into a formal principle, of narrative as well as of prose. In pursuing his study of paternalistic authority, Machado locates himself beyond the bourgeois mythology of the autonomy and authenticity of the individual person and steps into the waters of such as Proust, Nietzsche, Freud and company.²³¹ Nevertheless, discontinuity is not the province of the

---

229 Machado de Assis 1959, vol. I, p. 315.
230 Machado de Assis 1959, vol. I, p. 311.
231 This affinity between relative social belatedness and advanced forms of the critique of bourgeois culture is a constant in Machado's work. Moreover, something similar is to be found in various of the better moments in Brazilian literature. With regard to Modernism, Antonio Candido calls attention to the unexpected accord between the aesthetic primitivism of the European avant-garde, which represented social and artistic rupture, and our current primitiveness (see Candido 1965, pp. 144–5). In this same sense the linguistic inventiveness of Guimarães Rosa is both a tributary of the radical constructivism of modern literature and also finds grounding in the 'different' daily speech of a region of illiterates that is pure tradition, which gives it a verisimilitude that has nothing to do with constructivism (along different coordinates, the modern dimension of Guimarães Rosa's illiterate is analysed by Bento Prado Jr. in an article published in the review *Cavalo azul*, no. 3, São Paulo, 1968). Finally, in the poetry of João Cabral [de Melo Neto], the systematised and 'serial' variation of terms is a readily apparent element of the construction, contrary to expressive emotionality and to conventional poetry. This does not keep its abstract structure from frequently finding veristic grounding in the very violent and codified reality of Northeast [Brazilian] misery, in the traditional terminology of which the contrasts and antagonisms are organised somewhat in the manner of the antitraditional poetry of our poet-engineer [i.e., João Cabral de Melo Neto]. It is natural that self-criticism of the bourgeois order be carried out in the name of those energies that it annihilated. It

dependents alone. Although differently, it appears among the masters as well, being as it is part and parcel of the definition of the arbitrary. Let's go back to the plot of *Iaiá Garcia*.

Four years later, Jorge's return opens the novel's second part. Estela and Luís Garcia are married and Valéria has died. What should the young man do? The question arises from the very construction of the narrative. After being rejected by Estela, being harmed by his mother, after becoming a hero and spending years abroad, now facing the new situation in Rio, Jorge will do very little. He visits Valéria's grave in Minas Gerais, liquidates the estate and avoids Luís Garcia's house. Thus, his life is the connecting link between the two parts, is in fact the vague line of the book's unity. But it doesn't bring with it an answer to the conflicts of the first part. The loss of tension is the same one we have previously observed, but now its effect is total, since it derives not from one episode but from the novel's entire plot.

Jorge's behaviour carries on Valéria's arbitrariness, but now in an even more erratic key. When he gets to Rio he is a mature man. He conceives several intellectual projects, which he soon abandons in the face of the 'mound of documents that he would have to go through'.[232] He wants to live a retired life, but he lives a mundane one. He decides to avoid Estela but ends up frequenting her house, where his heart beats 'a time long ago' inside him. He assiduously fashions a friendship with Luís Garcia, whose death he awaits in order to inherit the widow, whom the whole situation terribly aggrieves. While he is waiting, the young man's heart switches preference – without any experience of conflict, 'between two cups of tea' – and he marries Iaiá. As this summary shows, it is a pathetic trajectory, one in which the respectable gesture goes hand in hand with inconstancy, irresponsibility and an abject calculus, one of second-phase Machado's favourite combinations. On a simple reading, however, this moving ground does not become salient because the contrasts get lost in the plot's extension and the decorum of the prose. The material needed a final recasting for its lines and rhythms to emerge clearly. As nexuses of the novel's pattern, then, in *Iaiá Garcia* the second-phase forms appear covered over and diluted by other forms, which are merely conventional.

For our argument, what is important is that paternalism's arbitrariness is finally transformed into a formal principle, albeit one that is little developed: its

---

so happens that in countries on the periphery of capitalism such energies are still found loose on the streets, which in terms of international competition can be belatedness, but it allows for the confluences that I am trying to suggest and which may possibly not be exclusively Brazilian.

232   Machado de Assis 1959, vol. I, p. 337.

movement is the dynamic of the plot itself. We have seen that in *Resurreição* the plot was determined by a psychological dynamic, that is, by Felix's intermittent jealousy. In *A mão e a luva* it was so-to-speak schematic, linked to the choice of a husband: between two young men with opposite defects, the best was a third, exactly what suited. In *Helena* paternalism's presence had become more powerful, orienting entire episodes. Nevertheless, the plot – which in the final analysis is the supreme instantiation of form and tacit social thesis in the nineteenth-century novel – was ultra-Romantic, connected to revelations about paternity and incest. In this sense *Iaiá Garcia* concludes the process we have been studying. The figure of the son of a good family, leading an idle life consonant with the slavocratic order, austere, as befitted the model Victorian gentleman, melancholic and confused as befits this contradiction, had been encountered in the prior novels, where he figures as the result of observation of society. Now, however, with special distinction for the combination of authority and irresponsibility, his developments acquire the generalising force through which form in literature creates the semblance of reality. From the point of view of Realism, Machado was touching land – and transforming a large social rhythm into an organising element for literature – in addition to solving the impasse in his prior books, for which he had not previously found an acceptable plot-form. Even so, note that the sequence of this exposition of ours, directed especially to the relations of verisimilitude between literary form and social process, has the defect of diminishing the merit of Machado's breakthrough – by making it somewhat obvious. To understand its audacity, which is great, consider that capriciousness is, by definition, not a *project*. Now the classic form of the Realist novel can be summed up in the phrase 'great projects by a young man'. The difference is crucial. Schematically speaking, in the project what is focused on is the conscious goal of the actions, which is what governs them and also what they must achieve. By contrast, with capriciousness the foremost elements are workings of the will, which are less purposeful and more unconscious. In other words, in the project the goal is there in the aerial shot of the meaning, and its primacy is evident. While with capriciousness it is one element among others and it does not hover above and separate itself from nature: goals weare out and are perishable like all else, and if they are to remain alive it is precariously and by dint of an effort that has nothing to do with the meaning in question, or, better, has to do with more elementary forms of meaning. The ideological-formal salience of capriciousness in *Iaiá Garcia* – its most expressive moment is the rapid abandonment of an intense and years-long love – underscores aspects that bourgeois civilisation, grounded in regular work, private property, the continuity of the juridical person, marriage, the ethic of responsibility, consciously-held goals, etcetera, tries to contain and dismiss. It happens that in the presence of such aspects the lines of the novelistic panorama are altered: unity of person and coherence of action seem to be specific cases and coexist with forces that are contrary to them. Capriciousness, as the word indicates in its pejorative sense, belongs to the order of dynamics that firmness of purpose, indispensable to the rationality of individual action, must rein in. In this sense it belongs to the conflictive subsoil of bourgeois reason. To return to our argument, we can say that when he finds a possible solution for Brazilian Realism, Machado abandons the consecrated formula of European Realism – and with it the rule of conventional rationality.[233]

Bad book though it may be, *Iaiá Garcia* is located on the terrain of the great modern literature in a sense that perhaps no other Brazilian novel, except for Machado's own later works, can be said to be. By putting arbitrariness at the centre of his constructions, Machado enters the camp of discontinuity, of contingency, of the inconclusive, of the wasted, of the unredeemed, etcetera. He renounces the consolation of providential mythology as well as the diffuse optimism that is its lay product, and even its disguised literary sublimation, poetic justice. *The form that Machado develops does not make 'meaning of life' an article of faith.* Hence the gravity that often emanates from these banal stories. The question preoccupied him very explicitly: 'Intolerable is the pain that doesn't even allow the right to argue fortune. The hardest of sacrifices is the one that does not have the consolations of conscience. Jorge suffers that pain'.[234] In other words, the pain that doesn't encounter symbolic compensation – bad fortune or personal merit – hurts the most, and, above all else, forms part of a landscape that the Guardian Angel has abandoned (despite the sententious language, the reader will notice the meditated familiarity with despair, expressed in the capacity to differentiate between its forms.) Something similar in an opposite direction: Jorge frequents the house of Luís Garcia with unspeakable thoughts, but at a given moment his interest in Estela grows cold, and neither he nor anyone else would be able to say where his intentions lie. 'No shadow of worry lay over his smiling and placid countenance. One might even say that, after a long and toilsome journey, he had reached the pinnacle of human delights'.[235] Observe that this plenitude does not correspond to new facts and that, if it goes with anything, it goes with forgetting. Jorge is in his peak years, but that is not the crowning of anything. It is possible for plen-

---

233   The philosophy of the unconscious was in fashion at the time, and it is certain that it influenced Machado. It is interesting to note, however, that he incorporates it in a rationalist spirit and that it ends up figuring in a very considerable project of social analysis.
234   Machado de Assis 1959, vol. I, p. 321.
235   Machado de Assis 1959, vol. I, p. 348.

itude not to derive from merit, suffering not to receive the consolations of conscience, preestablished harmony has vanished, and with it the certainty of the integrity of meaning. The literary and intellectual leap is great. The resigned decorum notwithstanding, Machado takes on the sombre lucidity of the true atheist and extends it to examination of daily life, the mythological devices of which he takes apart. These are very considerable first steps – albeit ones literarily frustrated – in the pessimistic and dissonant direction that will be central to modern art, a direction far from exhausted yet today, as can be seen in Beckett, and that, paradoxically, is in continuity with the anti-mythological work of the Enlightenment.[236] In this line *Iaiá Garcia* is replete with observations repugnant to the conventionally well-formed heart. They are the things that Machado knows and that, in comparison to him, make other writers, even good ones, and not only Brazilian writers, seem like children. Thus, for example, the course of the narrative will let us know that between two equally estimable persons like Estela and Iaiá, antipathy may be the definitive emotion. That a good man's death may well neither conclude nor resolve anything: 'Luís Garcia's death was one more complication'.[237] That even in the middle of the lowest of acts the conscience seeks to embellish itself in its own eyes. Such is the case of Procópio Dias when, as a last attempt, he hints to Iaiá that her fiancé Jorge really loves Estela, and it might even be that he was thinking of having it both ways: 'If anything could lessen the perversity of such an act, it was that he was completely persuaded that he was being true'.[238] That the gravest of accusations can have curiosity and pleasure as their lining: 'During a relatively long pause, Iaiá didn't take her eyes off her stepmother. Those two lamps sought to examine, at the supreme moment, every nook of her conscience and every possibly sneaky thing she might have done in the past. She said nothing, in order to savour the shock produced in Estela'.[239] That the force necessary to stifle love may not be great enough to stifle jealousy: Estela doesn't give in to Jorge, but she *is* jealous of Iaiá, and she is forced to acknowledge that firmness and renunciation don't always satisfy, or bring inner peace. That social climbing starts early: at twelve years of age Iaiá figures out what the key is to Valéria's character, 'and she opens the door with no great effort'.[240] That there is great confusion between filial love and marital love –

---

236 On the social and aesthetic significance of ugliness (and of Beckett) in modern art, consult Adorno 1970. For a contrary position, Lukács 1971c.
237 Machado de Assis 1959, vol. I, p. 395.
238 Machado de Assis 1959, vol. I, p. 391.
239 Machado de Assis 1959, vol. I, p. 399.
240 Machado de Assis, vol. I, p. 330.

which today, with the spread of psychoanalysis, no longer astonishes anyone. Etcetera, etcetera. To which must also be added the systematic mismatch of motives that pervades the entire book, and the previously analysed losses of tension.

On the level of forms, this attitude is expressed in a rule, according to which in *Iaiá Garcia* no development is allowed completion. To begin with the plot, in which discontinuity is a given of the story itself, composed as it is of arbitrariness, hesitation, frustration and inconstancy. In still other moments, when it does not derive from the issue at hand, discontinuity takes on a deliberate character, sometimes to the point of becoming itself a prejudice. In the inordinate series of misunderstandings, for example, disharmony is transformed into a thesis, and we come to expect the philosophising that now and again serves to attenuate – and not enhance – the second-phase-style pessimism. Be this as it may, this practice prepares for the extreme segmentation of material, of narrative units and even of the individual sentence, that will characterise *Memórias póstumas de Brás Cubas* and the subsequent novels. So the second part of the book does not, properly speaking, carry on from the first, the rationales for the various characters do not correspond amongst themselves, the chapters are not continuous one to the next, nor are they unified in themselves, being composed of disparate episodes the characters and centres of interest of which are not the same. This movement might be called de-dramatisation, since everything is connected up but not by means of the main action, which is extremely loose, going in no particular direction. We are – minus the note of cockiness – close to the digressive dynamic of the *crônica*, which will shortly bring fame to this practice. It is the case, however, that, in thus reining in the characters and the conflicts, Machado also deprives them of their attractive spontaneity. Although, as regards the situations it introduces, *Iaiá Garcia* belongs to the sphere of the novel for young girls, its discontinuous and diffuse plot does not facilitate readerly identification or fulfil any dream whatsoever – unless it is the dream of not dreaming. And not even that, since the novel's decorum even reduces the critical impetus of the interruptions. In the second phase, in which the mediocrity of the characters will continue to be the rule, that mediocrity will be compensated for by the extraordinary humoristic freedom and mobility of the narrator's voice, grounded in the famous and confessed example of Sterne. For our argument, however, note that the discontinuity in *Iaiá Garcia* is linked to the particularity of its historical material, which is far from funny. It precedes the incorporation of the formulas of English humour. In this same sense, the methodical suppression of the novelistic dynamic is the fruit of local observation and constitutes a realist breakthrough on the part of Machado, which, however, brings him close to that formal self-criticism characteristic of avant-garde literature, in which general premises underlying the bourgeois order are laid bare. One more example of the convergence between social belatedness and advanced artistic forms.

Although the contrary is generally propagated, linear narrative is not a characteristic of the pre-modern novel. From the genre's beginnings it made use of flashbacks, flash-forwards, intercalated episodes, postponements, narrator interventions, etcetera, resources in fact inherited from epic poetry that allowed for the interweaving of individual destinies and the totality of society within a wider action.[241] In *Iaiá Garcia* such techniques are frequently used, to set forth the action, which is common enough, but also to suppress it, which is unusual. Observe the way the narrative has us approach the central conflict. In the book's initial lines Luís Garcia receives a note from Valéria asking him to drop by her house. He answers in the positive. The narrative then cuts away, and from there to the chapter's end there pass before our eyes detailed descriptions of Luís Garcia, his modest house, of the servant Raimundo and daughter Iaiá, all interspersed with anecdotes and flashbacks in which the life of this family is characterised. The action resumes with chapter II, in which Luís Garcia goes to Valéria's house. After a mutual feeling-out process, the widow comes out with her request, which dislocates the relationship that has been being outlined: Luís's presence is a contingent factor, the real conflict is between Valéria and her son, and the line we had been following out is not the main line. Luís Garcia gives in to the widow and talks to Jorge, who explains his mother's position and his own. So the conflict is again dislocated, for it is not between mother and son as we supposed but between the young man and a young woman who wants nothing to do with him – and whom we readers are meeting for the first time. Thus, when shortly thereafter Jorge gives in to Valéria's insistence and enlists as a volunteer, his decision is the result not of her will, for that is not the decisive factor, but of the indifference of Estela (who asks nothing, which nonetheless does not keep her from breathing a sigh of relief when he leaves). In other words, Jorge's decision comes in answer to the conflicts but in a broken line that does not really carry them on or bring any spontaneous impulsion to an end. More precisely, the decision answers directly to a pressure that does not determine it and only indirectly to the problem that raised it. Third chapter: the young man comes to Luís Garcia's house to say his goodbyes and wanting to make a confidant of Luís. A somewhat forced idea, since Luís had never been an ally. And in fact the functionary, who is a cold person by nature,

---

241 For a good synthesis of the question, see 'Le roman' [The Novel], in Lukács 1974. On the narrative resources of the epic poem, see the first chapter in Auerbach 1945.

is constrained by the role he has played in the piece, so his reaction is 'singularly preoccupied and harsh',[242] which hinders the confession, which in turn causes the loss of yet another kind of plenitude. Jorge asks Luís for an embrace and Luís offers his hand (a mismatch that is replicated in the following chapter when Jorge offers his hand to Antunes when the latter wants the honour of an embrace. In the emotional leave-taking, the young man confuses father and daughter and grasps the former 'strongly to his breast'.[243] That, naturally, was a mistake). On leaving Luís Garcia's house, Jorge directs himself with unsteady step to Dona Luisa Street. Half way along, he thinks about changing direction, but he goes on, finally stopping in front of the house. This is an announcement of the main action. Before we enter, a new cut: we see the history of the people who live there in a long flashback (which, in its turn, is full of misunderstandings): Antunes' character, Estela's, their relations with the Gomes family, the episode of the kiss at Tijuca, Valéria's plans to marry Jorge off to a rich relative and then her plans to send him off to Paraguay. And when we finally get to the main conflict with chapter IV, it starts off with considerations about Jorge's prior visits to the same house, about the line of behaviour he has chosen to engage in as a way to rehabilitate himself in Estela's eyes, as well as about the latter's permanent coldness that has led him to take up the military uniform. To finish the series, Antunes leaves to go buy cigars, with the obvious intention of 'helping nature along'[244] by facilitating the meeting between Estela and Jorge – to the mortification of his daughter. It is an anticlimactic context saturated with impediments, in which Jorge nonetheless makes his brief declaration, which is rejected even more briefly: 'you, sir, are a fool'. With the passing of this brief moment, the reader must note that there will be no more presentness, in the eminent sense, in the book. Jorge leaves, and the remainder of the narrative – which is almost all of it – will have the character of waiting-time, filled with events that are secondary by definition. With greater reason the last part, when Jorge 'forgets', will take place on this same plane of indifference.

Before we move on to interpretation, note that the choice and disposition of the conflicts in the book obeys similar intentions. The hardest decision in the novel, which nothing will shake, was made before it began. It is mentioned in a few lines: the *agregada* will not yield to her protectress' son. 'Never! she swore to herself'.[245] Even the scene of the forced kiss does not have dramatic plenitude, precisely because Estela's negative decision has already been made and

---

242 Machado de Assis 1959, vol. I, p. 311.
243 Machado de Assis 1959, vol. I, p. 321.
244 Machado de Assis 1959, vol. I, p. 319.
245 Machado de Assis 1959, vol. I, p. 315.

that is the context in which everything else happens. According to its own criterion the narrative takes place within a phase of minor intensities, its moment of strength being outside of it. Analogously, if we examine the story's three crucial moments, we will see that they are in themselves antidramatic. Beginning with Estela's decision, which not only precedes the novel's present time but does not actually rise to the level of an event since it was made alone within Estela's inner self and without further exteriorisation, along with being a negative decision, which further lessens the dramatic movement rather than adding to it. The scene of the kiss, in its turn, aside from not being dramatic on Estela's part for the reason we have already seen, isn't dramatic on the part of Jorge either, for he had lost his head and was immediately trying to retract what had happened. It is a culmination that is in fact a backslide. With regard to Jorge's modified feelings at the end, 'between two cups of tea', it is unconscious, and its most interesting feature is precisely the absence of conflict about it. Refusal, compulsion, unconsciousness, the three moments are non-dramatic in their essence – if what is proper to the dramatic act is the confluence of conscious intention, deep-seated impulse and objective circumstances through which the individual seeks himself and tries to affirm himself (a definition in which the relationship between dramatic form and individualism is made clear, which is why Brecht would oppose it in his epic theatre).[246] Finally, in this same direction it should be noted that never is anything essential said among the characters. Just as he doesn't speak to Luís Garcia ('the word didn't dare go out from his heart'),[247] so Jorge will not speak to his mother, to Estela or to Iaiá, among whom as well there will never be unfettered explanation. The few serious outpourings in the book are isolated: Estela suffering in her room, hair dishevelled, which transforms her into a Romantic heroine,[248] or Jorge hating his mother from the distance of Paraguay when he learns of the marriage of Estela and Luís.[249] To be sure, Iaiá's outbursts are not solitary, but neither are they possessed of gravity, because they are childish, while the lascivious confessions of Procópio Dias have the status of aberrations, which is why they are not to be taken seriously. In the scene of the stolen kiss, which of course involves two people, the expression of emotion is entirely unilateral. The same for the good-bye scene, in which Jorge takes the risk of declaring his love, even though he has already been refused. In other words, in this novel there is a veto that

---

246   On the importance of these oppositions for modern literature, see Rosenfeld 1965 and 1969.
247   Machado de Assis 1959, vol. I, p. 311.
248   Machado de Assis 1959, vol. I, p. 398.
249   Machado de Assis 1959, vol. I, p. 326.

weighs over any engaged form of communication, a veto with which correlate, in times of explanation among the characters, the invariable downturned eyes in one of the parties, who keeps silent, resists, avoids or dissimulates without engaging in confrontation. A taciturn arrangement that is itself another form of discontinuity.

Seen as a whole, this observation calls for several comments. The reader must note the consistency, the ingenuity, the variety – which are impressive. With regard to the multiplication of discontinuities, it is clear that it is in part required by the material and in part a preference of the narrator. Nothing obliges him to mislead us, to present as central a line that will turn out to be secondary, to cut off an action at its point of interest and then still undo its suspense, and so on. We can say that he assimilates the moment of arbitrary choice that is part of the matter he is treating and transforms it into a subjective rule – and therefore too into a formal element – and then inflicts it on the reader. There are, however, two things in *Iaiá Garcia* that choice and time do not affect ('it is hard to hear, daughter of mine, but there is nothing eternal in this world; nothing, nothing,'[250] exclaims Estela near the novel's end): one of those things is the unquestionable authority of the narrator. Our narrator practices arbitrary choice within perfect gravity – a pretension that is the book's principal defect. The second thing is Estela's firmness, which, however, as we shall see, the evolution of scenes will slightly qualify. The two things are linked and will disappear together: in Machado's second phase there will be no purely positive character, or dogmatic certainties such as Estela clings to. The narrator's arbitrariness will be assumed and impudently located on the principal plane, while his authority and intent to justify anything whatever become objects of derision.

To return to our examples, it is certain that, despite the variety of ambits involved, they have a dynamic in common that sums up the position of *Iaiá Garcia*. One might label it flight from the actuality of the conflict. The latter one might be understood as past, secondary, infantile, aberrant, or evasive. This is obvious on the plane of dramatic composition, and it occurs as well in the narrative movement. The reader will have noticed about interruption-turned-rule that it has contradictory effects, one the setting-up of expectations, another their undoing. When he has us leave off one line of action for the next, and then that one for a third, the narrator not only leaves unconcluded the conflicts he has set in motion, which is a disappointment, but he also devalues those conflicts. Nevertheless, their movement is also part of a *crescendo* in which

---

250   Machado de Assis 1959, vol. I, p. 402.

it seems that at every transition we are passing from accessory to principal: diminishment or interruption, but to further increase the tension. Yet the central conflict too is treated with parsimony and back-pedalling, for to linger over it in detail or elevate it would amount to being unfaithful to decorum (doubly, once by examining the arbitrariness of authority, then by making renunciation into a spectacle). That disappointment linked to the narrative's master line is clearly the greatest of them all and transforms the preceding ascendant course into a deception, in addition to establishing a model in which the movement's limit is an ideological ceiling. Moreover, on the plane of the plot this cycle, which is completed early and thus subordinates the remainder of the book to its regime of frustration, is itself ungrounded, for the moment of decision properly speaking belongs to the novel's pre-history. This established, there is nothing to keep the expectations from returning again and again on the planes of narration, of contradictory objectives and of the characters – without their ever growing voluminous. They move about through a range of diminished intensities, as though once-burned. A strange process in which everything is cut off, even the desire to reach an end: the repetition of the interruptions, and especially of the re-beginnings, underscores the movement's purposelessness, to which reason does not conform and which requires diverse treatment (the solution of comedy would be the most obvious) in which the futility of the *suspense* would be demonstrated. It is a point of view that Machado has not yet accepted. In effect, directly or by contiguity, behind the instances of dramatic dynamism there lurk aspirations toward individual realisation that, without ever being affirmed as rights, nonetheless constitute the reference that in *Iaiá Garcia* permits the dignification of the dependents and *modern* critique of paternalistic arbitrariness.[251] Machado had no interest in disqualifying them, and even less in altogether doing away with them, or in presenting the bourgeois ideology of the individual in its emphatic and prestigious (and, for us, second-degree) versions, of the ridiculousness and falsity of which he was convinced. Clearly a delicate impasse in which criticism and defence are balanced and the aesthetic demand is one of decharacterisation: reduced to a tacit state, not even representing the characters' aspirations, the unhampered expansion of individual faculties is still present as a measure of renunciation and forms a part of the book's horizon. In sum, conflicts are not declared, but neither are they suppressed; hence the general climate of con-

---

251 'The dissolution of feudal and estate society opened up the sphere of individuality to humans at the same time that it transformed it into their task'. Lukács 1971b, p. 662. We are not from the feudal world, but who wouldn't like to be a modern individual?

straint, which expresses *Iaiá Garcia's* dual loyalties, to the spheres of paternalism and bourgeois individualism – and the sacrifices that they make to each other.

More precisely, it must be observed that discontinuity is always looked at as the *frustration* of movement. Now this is the angle of vision of the dependents, who, discreetly nourished with the Rights of Man, see the results of unchecked arbitrariness through it. Their protectors shatter their aspirations, besides involving themselves in capricious activity. Hence the conclusion that nothing is ever carried to completion in this world is one step, taken on the formal plane by means of the generalisation of interruptions. It is clear, however, that from the protectors' viewpoint the discontinuity can be seen more benevolently. Where is the wrong in switching love relationships or giving in to whims? Why does arbitrariness (under – naturally – another, more sympathetic name) not have its own complete cycles, its satisfactions and even its sense? Such rhythms, which will constitute the specialty of the second Machado, have not yet found their form. Technically because the interrupted pace of the narrative does not allow it: the stress on interruption makes discontinuity and amputation of meaning into one and the same thing. Ideologically because analytical and moral strength is linked to the dependents and is inspired in the bourgeois sense of the individual. Let us therefore say that, at the level of material, discontinuity has appeared to us through two lenses, once as an imposition suffered by the dependents, then as subjective entertainment for the well-off. Right now, on the formal level the dependents' outlook is stressed and dominates. We have already commented at length on that class perspective's literary and critical dividends. It has, however, the disadvantage of being timid. The primacy of interruption transcribes in formal language the dependents' frustration (therein lies its critical component) but also the limited appreciation of the social process linked to the weakness of their position. Implicitly this makes continuity the criterion for meaning, which in a general sense is bourgeois moralism and in our particular case is the same as locating paternalism, with its dose of arbitrariness, within the realm of the unreasonable, besides hiding its cyclical unity (hence the 'limited component'). Once again, however, it is necessary to see the opportune and realistic aspect of all this, for it is clear that our wealthy had to evaluate themselves by that measure too, it being an inseparable part of their universe too, plus it testified as much to their modernity as to their unreasonableness. As regards the latter, the criterion was appropriate. Essentially, the imposition of discontinuous form and continuity as measure kept the paternalist cycle from completing its movement and its figure. It was a real movement to which sense was not lacking, but it was a sense that for the weaker party was far from glorious. In the relationship between the wealthy and their dependents, different with us than in the classic example, the totalising class is the former. Only after switching coats would Machado embrace the totality of the process.

The terms in which our description is couched – such as discontinuity, frustration, loss of tension – all indicate that the most pronounced forms in *Iaiá Garcia* are negative. The thesis is that nothing is brought to completion, especially what is of value for individual aspirations. This, with greater detachment, is also the conclusion to *Memórias póstumas*, which ends with the chapter 'On Negatives': 'I never achieved celebrity ... I never was minister, I never was caliph, I never knew marriage'.[252] Its model, half-way between subject matter and form, lies in the ideological antagonisms that are dissipated in the comings and goings of favour, with stress on the moment of dissolution, which is also the moment of discontinuity. On the other hand, it is clear that that focus elides what, in the terms of the novel itself, represents the dynamic of reality, a dynamic that is processed during and by means of innumerable frustrations. What is the form of this movement? Most precisely put, the 'no' in this book comes with a 'yes' inside it, and, given the set-up of paternalist decorum, discontinuity includes a moment of respect and submission, the formal salience of which is small while its material weight is greater. The lack of meaning does not cease having meaning for a point of view that refrains from speaking out. Thus, in addition to the first plane there is a second one, discreet but frequent in appearance, indifferent to the normativity sought in *Iaiá Garcia*, it itself being normative as well. It is less-worked-on material, in part because of decorum, in part owing to the novel's formal and classist order, in part because Machado is still trying to find the appropriate configuration. If on the first plane the realistic note lies in the severity of the disillusionment that is, paradoxically, the book's moralistic and apologetic element, on the second, equally moralistic and apologetic but in a different vein, it lies in the willingness to take up and develop what the subject matter suggests, in which older ideology mingles with truly audacious formulations.

When he gets back from Paraguay and makes his first visit to Luís Garcia's house, Jorge tells himself that he is doing so because of family duty, even if he is upset at seeing Estela. In the same way Valéria's insistence that he enlist is sanctified by mother love, even if the motive in the case was social arrogance. In its turn, Estela's marriage is sanctified by familial favours that she and Luís owe Valéria even if the widow's motivation was to consolidate the rupture between the *agregada* and her son. Etcetera, etcetera. In other words, in *Iaiá*

---

252 Machado de Assis 1959, vol. I, p. 549.

Garcia the various kinds of goal sought seem to be unacceptable unless they benefit from the mediation of family motives, understood in their widest sense, linked to paternalistic favour. And inversely, since it is contrary to decorum to doubt such motives, they cover for all sorts of real intentions, from which comes the mix of baseness and unctuousness so characteristic of this book and so dear to the humour of the later Machado. Moreover, in the entire novel hardly a step is taken that is not intertwined with the circle of family obligations. For our argument it should be noted that this ubiquity and constancy of paternalist mediation is the systematic opposite of the discontinuity of action and narration and that if on the first plane of *Iaiá Garcia* nothing is completed, that is the very way the paternalist process *is* completed aside from the book's surface form. So let us say that the book is unified by the individual's abdication and his reabsorption into the weft of his obligations, and not by his initiative, which, however, is the dimension to which the form refers. It is obvious in this regard that in their initial moment these connections always come under the tutelage of another relationship, involving a third party who represents family and decorum. Estela comes to Valéria's house as the daughter of a *protegido*, and Jorge meets her in the condition of *agregada* to his family. Luís Garcia comes into the novel as a *protegido* of the deceased High Court Justice, in whose house he sees Estela, who by that time is the *protegida* of Valéria, who will give her a dowry as well as give one to Luís's daughter. When, in short, Jorge begins to frequent Luís's house, it is as the son of the lady whom Luís owes great benefits. Even Procópio Dias is only partially an exception, for his friendship with Jorge comes from Paraguay, where the patriotic war vouchsafed general decorum. In a certain sense they are all always *children*, and none of them acts in their own interest like someone who is on his own. This arrangement is naturally contrary to the declaration of the conflicts and is one more antidramatic element in the book. In part this is the outcome of the issue and in part preference on the part of the author, who, in representing wealthy families, kills off their father-and-chief before the start of the plot (Vale in *Helena* and Justice Gomes here) in order to deal with the widow, the sister, the children, the dependents – in short, with the subordinate sphere. Adultery, women of 'easy' life, natural children, business and political life figure only on the horizon, as a legacy of the departed man: the misdeeds of unimpeded power are the aspects of paternalism that for the purposes of decorum it was better not to touch on. Thus, within the circle that Machado profiles, aspirations as well as individuals do not have an independent existence – a separation, however, that is one of the premises upon which European Realism is grounded. The paternalist tie is felt at every moment, a limitation that is formalised negatively in the interrupted progress just analysed. Still, that stress on the negative masks the regularity of the interference and its positive valuation, which are stable and constant elements of the ideology and the subject matter of *Iaiá Garcia*. The interplay between individual aspirations and family obligations, goals from the modern world and paternalist motives, is a staple of the organisation of the material, which stands in opposition to the book's dominant form and remains to be worked out. The possible relations between these terms are many, reciprocal sacrifice being but one of them. We have seen others. For example, the truncated aspirations are also services performed, for which recognition and compensation are not lacking. Why not emphasise and follow out that aspect of the process? And especially, family mediation does not function only as a constraint but also as freedom – or, better, as permission – since, being unassailable itself, it makes everything acceptable, even the inadmissible. A conjuncture in which something certainly happens, although the subject is not the one imagined in individualist ideology. These alternations are constants of the subject matter of *Iaiá Garcia*. To formalise them, all that remains is to recognise the advantages that the dependents derive from their subordination and the indecorous character of the relationships the decorum of which Machado wishes to point out.

If we think about the definition and location of the conflicts in relation to the subject matter of which they are a part, the movement is similar. The plot tied to individual inconsistency is a critical form – Jorge's intentions that are lost over time do not constitute a myth of any sort – but it does not circumscribe the novel's sphere, the limits of which are conformist, set out by the ideology of family decorum. To appreciate its literary effect, a good strategy is to look to its antithesis. The *agregado* Antunes is clerk and man of confidence to the deceased High Court Justice. He is a master of hyperbolic flattery and opportune silence, goes on electoral errands, is a confidant in amorous undertakings, aids with domestic purchases, eats at table on common days but not when there are guests, and is a filcher of cigars. When he notices that something is going on between Estela and the son of the High Court Justice, he goes out of his way to aid nature. When that hope is dashed, he takes refuge in the Chamber of Deputies lottery. He also consoles himself by frequenting jury sessions, the galleries of the aforementioned Chamber of Deputies and the Carceler benches. He dreams about greatness and important people, doesn't like his equals, and his behaviour is always subaltern. He reads repeatedly and with delight the note in which Valéria tells him to stop by her house. He is tempted to show it to a neighbour, and on the street 'he gets away from a nuisance by telling him emphatically where he's going'.[253] As one can readily see, these are numerous

---

253 Machado de Assis 1959, vol. I, pp. 311–12, 320, 328, 407.

and sundry relationships that make Antunes an interesting character, at least virtually, given that he is little more than a walk-on. The reader, however, should note that this variety in *Iaiá Garcia* is an exception. Generally speaking, care is taken to trim characters, reducing them to the profile they have in the family sphere. It is a selective criterion linked to the notions of dignity and elevation that dominate first-phase Machado as a whole and that are thematic in the *withdrawal* practised by the estimable characters, who wish to live far from the inessential, the anecdotal and the low (that is, economic life, politics, mundanity, and extra-conjugal sexuality). Elevation and conflicts worthy of literature exist only within the family circle. So Luís Garcia is a public servant, Estela will become a salaried teacher, Jorge lives a young man's life, Procópio Dias is a wheeler-dealer, the High Court Justice was a politician. The novel does not present them in those roles, however, but rather in the roles of father, daughter, fiancée, suitor, *protegida*, etcetera. The narrowness of that lens and of the resultant distribution of materials is obvious. On the plane of ideological and literary filiation we are dealing with opposition to Realism and Naturalism, to the materialistic vulgarities to which the reaction in Europe wished to oppose another, more spiritual, view of human beings. This is the dominant aspect, which it is important to highlight at the start, before we go into the nuances – for there are those as well.

In effect, in addition to the hypocritical aspect and not in contradiction to it, the rejection of 'low' determinisms contains the search for a different explanation, a search that does produce ressultas as well. So, for reasons of decorum Machado does not bring onto the primary plane or treat openly the movement of fortunes and social classes. He prefers to treat them as an element of individual imagination, which negates the objective dynamics of society but *systematises consideration of their existence and efficacy on the symbolic plane*. Consequently, despite the panoramic purpose and the historical references, *Iaiá Garcia* lacks the great rhythms of social transformation, the profile of which only the movement of property and classes can carry out. But it is also obvious that forms of a more complex causality appear: the insertion of the individual into society is an imaginary fact as much as it is a practico-material one; appetites may not coincide across the two planes and thus lend themselves to surprising combinatorics. In Europe, this aspect of things, baptised as freedom, was accomplished by blurring the definition of material interests, which comforted the political right in its disdain for the masses' elementary needs. But, for all that, the aspect remained real, and it is interesting for precisely that reason. With apologetic purpose the right discovered in the social process, and exploited, that part that had to do with symbolic satisfactions, which the materialists considered secondary but the critical importance of which has only grown through the years. (This is not the same as ideology, which refers to the objective appearances of the process.) Thence an intricate comedy of errors, central to the development of modern ideas, in which it might happen that the party of apologetics would criticise while the party of social criticism would create myths, all of which can be studied within literature in the Symbolism-Naturalism dialectic. An ambiguity that is observable in the work of major writers like Baudelaire, Dostoyevsky, and Proust, with whose horror of simplistic or strait causalities the right undeniably identifies, even though, by comparison, the knowledge of society that those writers clearly demonstrate makes the 'social' writers seem to be living in nursery school.

Everything taken in context, let's look at some examples. Jorge is a wealthy, well-turned-out young man, and the thing he has for the unusual makes him attracted to girls of modest origin – which is thoroughly novelesque. It is for that reason he is not interested in Eulália, the girlfriend his mother has earmarked for him and who, socially-speaking, would provide an appropriate match.[254] Procópio Dias too is wealthy and likes a poor girl, but his reasons are different: 'To have her would be to do her a favour'.[255] Iaiá, being from a family without means, aspires to a life among the rich, but Estela, who is much poorer, works tirelessly to stay away from them. 'I have been humble and obscure ... Marriage between us would be impossible ... because it could always be looked at as a kind of favour, and I hold my own condition in great respect'.[256] While really in love with Jorge, she nonetheless prefers marrying Luís Garcia, whom she esteems but nothing more, but who is her equal. Valéria, who is herself proud, appreciates the *agregada*'s similar sensibilities: Estela knows her place – which is why the widow brings her into the house – all the while finding Jorge's sentiments unacceptable. And Estela recognises Valéria's moral delicacy,[257] while Antunes is of the opinion that 'so well-born a young man'[258] should not be rejected. Etcetera. In sum, social difference is everywhere, but as an element of imaginary life, the accountability of which is governed by the satisfactions of self-esteem and not by political economy. Wealth, then, can be an advantage or a disadvantage, the same for poverty, and the action does not originate directly from social position. It, namely social position, never occurs in brute form either, but rather inside the imagination of difference, in which no one is obligated to identify with their own position, especially if it is an inferior

---

254   Machado de Assis 1959, vol. I, pp. 313–14, 382.
255   Machado de Assis 1959, vol. I, p. 362.
256   Machado de Assis 1959, vol. I, p. 402.
257   Machado de Assis 1959, vol. I, p. 329.
258   Machado de Assis 1959, vol. I, p. 406.

one. Nothing is more reasonable than to identify with what we lack if we find ourselves on the bottom, or to have sympathy for the gaze of those at the bottom – which gaze recognises us – if we are on top, or to amaze our friends if we are all rich and bored. Etcetera, etcetera. In other words, Machado establishes a combination between social positions as practical reality and the social field as imaginary value, a combination the rule of which is constituted of symbolic compensations. In this perspective, social inequality is not only an antagonistic factor but also one of cohesion, for its imaginary duplication puts at the disposal of the inferior imaginings of superiority, which are the consolations that he or she needs. An outlook that is obviously conservative, which, however, says little, since it has the merit of pointing out and studying the real satisfactions of inequality, which are set up against the desire to combat inequality, an intellectual find that it would be absurd to call retrograde. Observe that we are speaking of a rational frame that explains behaviours that from other points of view are irrational, and more than the wished-for spiritualisation of practical motives, we are instead witnessing the materialist systematisation of spiritual life, which is an example of the involuntary expansion of the area of the determinism to which we referred in the prior paragraph. Later Machado would integrate such reflections with the movements of favour, especially of arbitrariness, and bring the result into the centre of his literature. In *Iaiá Garcia* these are but sundry psychological observations.

From the viewpoint of composition we are dealing with an exacting principle, for the action does not derive solely from the character's immediate circumstances, which would be the clearest way of storytelling, but always also from the representation that that character makes for him- or herself of the others and of the social sphere as a whole. Especially in the case of Estela and Luís Garcia, reflection about their own positions and those of others is the basis for every act. First consequence to take note of: the problematic nature of their actions never exits the scene, which, in a literature without problems like ours, is a factor of interest. Note as well the emphasis placed on intelligence as a normal appurtenance of the people, for they orient themselves, make mistakes, but are always thinking, not passing their lives in feelings, as is common in our literature. Hence the curious effort taken to individualise mental life, which makes up a part of each character's nature. We learn, for example, that Luís Garcia began reading when he was well past childhood, without any great plan but with considerable gusto, helped by his habit of solitary reflection. Jorge – a college graduate and wealthy – lends Luís books out of his library, which practice becomes an element in the friendship between the two men. 'And because he was an excellent reader, of the sort that relates impression to reflection, when he completed a book Luís would recompose it, embed it in his brain, so to speak; although without methodical rigour, that reading would clear up some of his ideas and flesh out others that he had previously held only intuitively'.[259] Let the reader recall that Luís Garcia is not an educated man, and he will appreciate the poetry and the realistic force of this mode of characterisation (minus the edifying prose). As for Jorge, we shall see that 'he retained a great deal of what he learned; he had a ready intelligence, rapid comprehension and a very active memory. He wasn't a deep intellect: he didn't penetrate, he embraced. Specifically, his was an intellect given to theory; for him, the pragmatist was a barbarian ... He didn't have a clear, creative imagination; his was vague, tumultuous and sterile. That was his weak point'.[260] Back from Paraguay, the young man contemplates dedicating himself to the study of history, but he doesn't have the requisite patience, which is another constant in his mental makeup: 'His impatient spirit only latched onto the first elements of an idea, which, moreover, he only glimpsed'.[261] And, to close, a true master stroke: for years on end Jorge admires Estela's impeccable behaviour – which does not keep him, early on, from suspecting her of baseness, a hypothesis 'that finally ended up not finding any revulsion in his conscience'.[262] Giving quick acceptance to 'thoughts without basis or verisimilitude',[263] his own, always decent figure rejects familiarity with any and all base acts, however easily these are suspected given his comradery with Procópio Dias. One more variant of the dynamic that we are pointing out: individual characterisation by means of modalities of intelligence forms a part of the elevated tone of the novel – and of the opposition to sordid determinism. But the result is to make intelligence a part of what is determined and natural, and so to plumb areas of sordidness that even Naturalism didn't dream of.

Without belabouring the comparison, which will become acute only as of *Memórias póstumas*, there are nonetheless a few more observations that can be made. The ongoing reference to the characters' mental life makes all the material of *Iaiá Garcia* relational, never simply self-identical. Hence Machado's famous parsimony with external details, which are never absent but are never dealt with outside of their immediate, problematic nexus. A principle of narrative economy opposite to Romanticism's picturesque prose and opposite as well to the 'servile photographic reproduction of minimal and ignoble things', with which words Machado at the time reproached the Naturalism of Eça

---

259   Machado de Assis 1959, vol. I, pp. 346–7.
260   Machado de Assis 1959, vol. I, p. 307.
261   Machado de Assis 1959, vol. I, p. 337.
262   Machado de Assis 1959, vol. I, p. 397.
263   Machado de Assis 1959, vol. I, p. 397.

de Queirós[264] – a reproach that, considering the source, in the chapter to be written on scabrous detail cannot but draw a laugh. Now the primacy of the relational dimension was opposed to yet another aspect of the contemporary movement beyond the issue of the accumulation of descriptive details: it didn't leave a place for the new scientific doctrines. Indeed, if everything is relation and then reflection upon relation, where do geographical, hereditary, racial and other determinisms fit? The decade of the '70s is marked by the arrival in Brazil of modern theories, social and other, and they are also the years when Machado wrote his first novels. His scant enthusiasm for science must have seemed backward and small-minded to the other side. Even today who is there that doesn't value the renovation of Brazilian thought that took place at that time?[265] But the fact is that the first effect of the new science was the multiplication of mythologies – and these much more aggressive than the traditional prejudices they came to supplant. Which would be better, the usual colour prejudice, scientific racism, or scientific racism in the context of colour prejudice? (There is a funny study to be written about the ironies of Brazilian Naturalism, among which ironies should figure the security it provided to the insults of classism and racism. 'Who has studied him [i.e. Machado] in the light of his social milieu, the influence of his upbringing, of his psychology, of his heredity both physical and ethnic and explained the formation and normal orientation of his talent?' asks Sílvio Romero. In response, he points out that his object of study was from a poor family, mulatto, uneducated, very unprepossessing, chronically fearful and suffering from a nervous system disorder.)[266] For his part, Machado dedicates himself to the logic of given situations and people's characters. That leads to the analysis of the givens of life in relational terms, which are strictly rational. Within the limits of family respectability, to which, for convenience, Machado adhered, let us say that in spirit his novel carried on

---

264   Machado de Assis 1959, vol. III, p. 914.
265   'There was a certain group of Brazilian Romantics who didn't have the courage to toss out the old baggage and take up another new one thereby entering into that renewal of national thought through critique, and they started being sulky, dismissive, ironic, unpleasant, convoluted, mysterious and pessimistic ... Impotent, by dint of age, as far as concerned definite participation amid the great philosophical currents that divided the century – materialism, evolutionism, transformational monism and Hartmannism – they were content to confect phrases with the enigmatic air of fakirs, in the name of I don't know what hidden things that they pretended to know. In this singular group the productive Machado de Assis as head of the line all of a sudden sensed the disgust that, in a psychological moment, had taken hold of the Brazilian soul. But he sensed it only slightly' (Romero 1936, p. 76).
266   Romero 1936, pp. 18–23.

the literary rationalism of the prior century, in which he differed from his more progressive contemporaries, who adopted the flashy, and in the main irrationalistic, scientism of bourgeois decadence. Which doesn't keep those contemporaries from being great optimists, while in Machado the climate of decadence is profoundly present. On the other hand, both parties were interested in being open to co-optation, and it would be instructive to see the contrast between them from that angle.

If we examine the characters' social trajectories, we shall see as well that they do not follow the lines of primary emphasis in the novel. The critique of arbitrariness and the interruption of movement, which provide the main note on the formal and ideological planes, seem irrelevant on this score, which is one instance more of the excess of material beyond the formal confines of the book. Thus, contrarily to the impression we have of Luís Garcia as severe and misanthropic, his social trajectory is a normal and successful one. Although preferring to spend Sundays at home, he frequents Valéria's house to 'celebrate' with his daughter, who likes luxury.[267] When, after the war, Jorge visits him, the house in which Luís is living is new and bigger than the previous one.[268] The visit constitutes a courtesy, of which the functionary is aware, and when Jorge says he had not come before because he was away, the explanation 'was a new courtesy'.[269] Further on, Luís receives orders directly from the minister, who summons him to his home, there to spend several hours outlining a commission that will oblige Luís to undertake a trip without delay – indications suggesting that the bureaucrat's stature has grown.[270] When, finally, Jorge requests Iaiá's hand in marriage, the rise of the father is complete. He knows that his daughter will have 'all the social advantages, from the solidest to the most frivolous – and this obscure man, bored and sceptical, savoured the fortune that his daughter would have found amid the whirlwind of things, a fortune that he had never coveted for himself'.[271]

In the relations between Jorge and Procópio Dias, the same weakening of seemingly unbridgeable boundaries. From the literary point of view, the two figures belong to different conceptualisations: one characterised by material appetites and external appearance (the scandalous brightness of the tie, the garnet ring on his finger, the gold-topped cane), all seemingly taken from Realist caricature of the degenerate rich man. Machado is trying his hand at the

---

267   Romero 1936, pp. 76.
268   Machado de Assis 1959, vol. I, p. 330.
269   Machado de Assis 1959, vol. I, p. 342.
270   Machado de Assis 1959, vol. I, p. 397.
271   Machado de Assis 1959, vol. I, p. 351.

style he is combatting. Jorge's profile on the other hand is mainly spiritual, located above material matters. Not that these last ones didn't exist, for Jorge too is elegant and rich, and he has his appetites, but those are not the things that define him. Behind the two characterisations lie two incompatible theses about reality that cause the two figures to be presented according to different criteria. Thence a considerable dose of inconsistency in the prose – harsh with one and tolerant with the other. On the other hand, while literary logic situates them in different worlds, the fact is that Procópio Dias and Jorge walk together in *Iaiá Garcia* – which reduces the philosophical clash to a matter of descriptive opportunity. Materialism for the unscrupulous and lascivious man of business, elevated style for the family man. An absurd arrangement – but one that, on the other hand, has a certain historical and dramatic opportuneness about it, as it configures the astonishment of traditional money at new money and the comparison between paternalist and individualist ideologies. Even that comparison goes up in a puff of smoke, however, for if the outline of Procópio Dias is despicable, Machado immediately turns around and tosses out hints that Jorge, in another register, isn't so different, a very Machadian procedure: 'They seemed satisfied with one another'.[272] And in fact Jorge's reaction before Procópio – unconfident but also curious and even a bit impressed – is one of the novel's finest turns. In Paraguay, Procópio had assailed his friend for his 'lack of experience', though the latter's recommendations had turned up some bits of business for Procópio.[273] By chance they meet again in Rio, at the house in Tijuca. Procópio observes that the house has been a bit beat up, Jorge answers than it is more beat up than that, and Procópio remarks that it isn't good for the owner to say such things because it might drive down the rent. During lunch Procópio tells his friend that he, Jorge, is leading the life of a hermit and invites him to the theatre. 'Corruptor! says Jorge, smiling',[274] and then he stops doing his studies. They have dinner together, and Jorge doesn't eat because of a lack of confidence: he doesn't want to be indebted to such a person. 'Procópio Dias understands exactly but isn't bothered; he lowers his gaze and lets the moment pass, then lifts his head back up, laughing'.[275] Later on, Jorge and Procópio are at Luís Garcia's house. Procópio asks Jorge which of the two women brings him there. Jorge becomes formal and says the relations are merely family ones. Procópio doesn't believe him and confesses for his part that he is attracted to Iaiá. And he goes on: 'since you are in love with

---

272   Machado de Assis 1959, vol. I, p. 391.
273   Machado de Assis 1959, vol. I, p. 339.
274   Machado de Assis 1959, vol. I, p. 340.
275   Machado de Assis 1959, vol. I, p. 340.

the other one, where else should my heart's first inclination go? To recruit you both to my interest. Since there was a secret between the two of you and that secret had been discovered, or suspected, by me, you and she would be my best allies, and the young lady's resistance, and her father's approval, everything would come down in my favour ... Jorge stares at him for an instant without saying a word, seemingly floored by his reasoning. He had listened to him with astonishment and satisfaction. Didn't such frankness suggest that Procópio Dias didn't suspect anything?'[276] Behind the contrast in personal style, which the preceding quotations do not sufficiently reflect, lies intimacy. Without possessing the same 'penetration and superiority to see and confess the vices of human nature',[277] Jorge does not refrain from making his own, notable, calculations – for example when he looks forward to the death of Luís Garcia. As a counterweight to Procópio Dias' caricature-like grossness, which 'defiles Jorge's beloved imaginarily',[278] Machado comes up with an even more scathing stroke for Jorge's conjugal appetites. It is to have him visit his old fiancée Eulália, who is now married. 'Eulália shows him her son, a child big enough for two, fat and vigorous. Jorge manages to get hold of him, but he can't figure out how to manage the lace, the ruffles, the ribbons. Eulália, who by now possesses all motherly prowess, takes the boy out of Jorge's hands. 'You don't know how to do it', she tells him. And, after fixing the child's bonnet and giving him lots of kisses, she laughs and tells the child a story, all of this with grace and poetry, which Jorge would never have expected of her five years back. He contemplates the young mother, elegant and natural, and feels himself consumed with envy and longing'.[279] The capper comes on the last page, when Iaiá and Jorge have found 'unqualified happiness in their marriage'.[280] They run across Procópio Dias in society, just the same as he was when he had done all the heinous things to them. At the last soiree, that villain plays *voltarete* with Jorge and accompanies Iaiá to their carriage, not without casting a furtive glance toward the step, where the latter has rested her foot, which is tired from waltzing.[281] The happy ending is the 'shipwreck of illusions' to which the final sentence refers:[282] the family decorum of paternalism has been false, its opposition to mundane corruption and to the world of money equally so, and co-optation is

---

276   Machado de Assis 1959, vol. I, p. 360.
277   Machado de Assis 1959, vol. I, p. 360.
278   Machado de Assis 1959, vol. I, p. 362.
279   Machado de Assis 1959, vol. I, p. 341.
280   Machado de Assis 1959, vol. I, p. 407.
281   Machado de Assis 1959, vol. I, p. 407.
282   Machado de Assis 1959, vol. I, p. 407.

not a clean process. The trajectory is merely episodic, since it skirts the ideological and formal construction of the novel. Still, it takes up the last page of the book, which makes it into a conclusion and an image of real social dynamics.

Estela's path, however, seems to point in the direction of a different and heroic outcome: salaried employment. Towards novel's end the death of Luís Garcia causes the reorganisation of the family relationships. After years of struggle in the opposite direction, Estela sees herself in the position of mother-in-law and dependent of her beloved and unhappy rival of her stepdaughter. She decides to move to the north of São Paulo, where she will be a teacher. Her letters, containing no allusions to the past, are written in 'the purest familial style',[283] an expression that, in context, is sarcastic and thus points to the freedom that she has finally found. The question arises explicitly when, in saying goodbye to her father, she exhorts him to leave the servile life he has lived up to then.[284] Therefore, work appears as a rupture with paternalism and as a solution. Even so, qualification is necessary: not even Luís Garcia, a civil servant, escapes paternalism's toils. And that same leave-taking on Estela's part appears strictly as a solution to her dignity problem and therefore lies within the horizon of paternalism. Without counting the fact that the word 'salary' doesn't appear: with recourse to the language of the novel itself, Estela is going to 'direct an educational establishment' that a former classmate has founded. She has freed herself from family dependency and enters the universe of worthy occupations – but 'paid work' is never mentioned. The prejudice is evident, but there is also the legitimate sense that salaried work is an unacceptable institution. That same ambiguity, which in the final analysis pertains to the whole book, has strong repercussions in its last sentence. On the first anniversary of Luís Garcia's death, Iaiá and Jorge go to the cemetery to lay a wreath in remembrance. 'Another wreath was already there, bearing ribbon that had these words on it: "*To my husband*". Iaiá ardently kissed that simple dedication, just as she would have kissed her stepmother if she had appeared to her at that instant. The widow's compassion was sincere. One thing had escaped the shipwreck of illusions'.[285] The reader, irremediably liberal and influenced by the difficult and valorous decisions that Estela has made, thinks that if anything escapes the shipwreck of illusions it is because she had the strength to resist and break through. That would be a mistake.

---

283   Machado de Assis 1959, vol. I, p. 407.
284   Machado de Assis 1959, vol. I, p. 406.
285   Machado de Assis 1959, vol. I, p. 406.

Reading with greater discernment, the reader will see that paternalism has won again. And that Estela's actions give reason for hope, because they are ... pious.[286]

Antunes' evolution is different. When he fails at his last chance to marry his daughter to Jorge, he starts pursuing public illusions. He frequents the Chamber of Deputies and jury sessions, plays the lottery, converses in the square and

---

286 At various points Estela is comparable to Caroline de St. Geneix, the main character in the 1861 novel *Marquis de Villemer* [The Marquis of Villemer] by George Sand (Sand 1948). Pujol holds that there is influence there, a question about which I do not possess the reading necessary to comment since, with variation, characters of that type must exist by the score in the second-tier novels of the time. But it is the case that similarity is present and that comparison could be suggestive. Forced by poverty, the two young women keep company with rich and capricious widows. They make an impression on the male heir of the family, but they hide the feelings that he inspires in them, for both are proud. Like Estela, Carolina 'tolerates without complaint the necessities of her situation', (p. 21) and also like her she dresses austerely, as befits her lack of fortune – which, however, only heightens her beauty rather than functioning as a sign of asceticism. In her own words, which are the same as Estela's, 'I don't dream of love, I am not novelesque' (p. 22), an expression that underscores the most novelesque characteristic of the two of them: they accept social difference but don't sacrifice their hearts to it, which, paradoxically, translates into renunciation of love. Thus, on the very abstract plane on which the transposition of European situations to Brazil is possible (supported in this case by the apparent generalisation of family relations) the similarity of both arrangement and psychological temperament is a fact. Nevertheless, the local character of the cast doesn't allow the equivalence to go very far and forces a reorientation of the conflicts: instead of the illustrious marchioness we have the widow of the High Court Justice; instead of Villemer, occupied in demonstrating historically that the aristocratic titles are usurpations, we have a simple bachelor. Instead of the poor girl, but employed and sure of her rights, an *agregada* ever on the defensive. Instead of the opposition between authenticity and money, the opposition between paternalistic arbitrariness and personal dignity. Generically, instead of the idealisation of the conflicts emerging from the French Revolution, the effort to criticise and rationalise the relations between dependents and their rich protectors (a critique that in turn is not independent of the French Revolution but whose social ground is other). In general, instead of the Romantic novel, we have a novel of frustration. For similarities and differences, see the letter in which Carolina tells her sister of her new life in the house of the marchioness: 'As for me, you well know how much I despise money! Our misfortunes haven't changed me, because I don't consider as money this sacred thing, the wage that I earn honourably now – and even with a bit of pride. That is duty, the guarantee of honour. Luxury, when it is the continuation of, or recompense for, an elevated life, does not inspire in me that philosophical disdain that always hides some envy; but opulence lusted after, sought, desired and purchased at any price, through ambitious marriages, modifications of political conscience, family intrigues around inheritance, those are the things that take, with reason, the vile name of money, and on that point I am soundly of the marchioness' opinion, which doesn't pardon unequal marriages made for interest, along with the other base acts, private and public' (p. 34).

goes back to being an assiduous diner at Jorge's house, just as he had been at Jorge's father's. A description that Machado wanted to be mind-blowing but that today doesn't seem so antipathetic, especially because the dignity that Machado opposed to it, like a positive to a negative, is unconvincing. The ideology of Estela and Luís Garcia, which is also that of the book, is a civilising one rather than a critical one. As a consequence, the negative characters incarnate the aspects that that ideology wishes suppressed, and it is deadly that those seem the more real. It is in the Machiavellian alliances and cynical words of Procópio Dias that the best commentary on Jorge's respectable comportment is to be found. Likewise for Antunes's characterless self-subordination, which seems truer than the laboriously concealed self-subordination of Luís Garcia. These are the characters who in fact announce the second-phase novel. In *Iaia*, however, they appear to be exorbitant caricatures not to be taken seriously. Let us say that Machado tried to analyse paternalist arbitrariness within the dependents' perspective to the end of liberating them from it, which led him to exclude it from propriety. Later, on the contrary, he will take it up whole, just as the *agregado* Antunes does here, and instead of hiding it, he will follow it, study its dynamic and bring it to the principal plane. It is clear that this new position is comprehensible only if arbitrariness is not felt to be humiliation. It is a fact that Machado had completed his own social rise. In his mature novels, arbitrariness will be looked at with the humouristic intimacy of someone confessing himself an adept practitioner – and who therefore has nothing to fear. The viewpoint will have become a top-down one.

Bibliography

Adorno, Theodor W. 1970, *Aesthetische Theorie*, [Aesthetic Theory], Frankfurt/M, Suhrkamp.
Adorno, Theodor W. 1958, *Noten zur Literatur I* [Notes on Literature I], Frankfurt/M, Suhrkamp.
Alencar, José de 1959, *Obra completa* [Complete Works], Rio de Janeiro, Aguilar.
Alencastro, Luiz Felipe de 1985–6, *O trato dos viventes: tráfico de escravos e 'Pax Lusitana' no Atlântico do Sul, séculos XVI–XIX* [The Trade of the Living: Slave Trafficking and 'Pax Lusitana' in the South Atlantic, Sixteenth through Nineteenth Centuries], University of Paris, Nanterre.
Almeida Prado, Décio de 1972, *João Caetano* [João Caetano], São Paulo, Perspectiva.
Andrade, Oswald de 1971, *Obras completas* [Complete Works], Rio de Janeiro, Civilização Brasileira.
Anthologie des préfaces de romans français du XIXe siècle [Anthology of Prefaces to French Novels of the Nineteenth Century] 1964, org. H.S. Gershman and K.B. Whitmore, Jr., Paris, Juliard.
Auerbach, Erich 1945, *Mimesis* [Mimesis], Berne, A. Francke Verlag.
Barreto Filho, José 1947, *Introdução a Machado de Assis* [Introduction to Machado de Assis], Rio de Janeiro, Agir.
Beiguelman, Paula 1967, *Teoria e ação no pensamento abolicionista* [Theory and Action in Abolitionist Thought], *Formação política do Brasil* [Political Formation of Brazil], vol. I, São Paulo, Pioneira.
Benjamin, Walter 1969, *Charles Baudelaire*, Frankfurt/M, Suhrkamp.
Bourget, Paul 1912, *Pages de critique et de doctrine* [Pages of Critique and of Doctrine], Paris, Plon.
Brasil em perspectiva [Brazil in Perspective] 1968, org. C.G. Mota, São Paulo, Difel.
Buarque de Holanda 1956, Sérgio, *Raízes do Basil* [Roots of Brazil], Rio de Janeiro, José Olympio.
Candido, Antonio 1970, 'Dialética da malandragem' [Dialectic of Roguishness], Revista do Instituto de Estudos Brasileiros [Review of Brazilian Studies], no. 8, São Paulo.
Candido, Antonio 1993, *O discurso e a cidade* [Discourse and the City], São Paulo, Duas Cidades.
Candido, Antonio 1969, *Formação da literatura brasileira* [Formation of Brazilian Literature], 2 vols. São Paulo, Martins.
Candido, Antonio 1965, *Literatura e sociedade* [Literature and Society], São Paulo, Companhia Editora Nacional.
Candido, Antonio 1970, *Vários escritos* [Various Writings], São Paulo, Duas Cidades.

Cardoso, Fernando Henrique 1962, *Capitalismo e escravidão* [Capitalism and Slavery], São Paulo, Difel.

Carvalho Franco, Maria Sylvia de 1969, *Homens livres na ordem escravocrata* [Free Men in the Slavocratic Order], São Paulo, Instituto dos Estudos Brasileiros.

Castello, José Aderaldo 1969, *Realidade e ilusão em Machado de Assis* [Reality and Illusion in Machado de Assis], São Paulo, Companhia Editora Nacional.

Dean, Warren 1971, *A industrialização de São Paulo* [The Industrialisation of São Paulo], São Paulo, Difel.

Dumas fils, Alexandre, *Anthologie*, various editions.

Du Val Jr., T.E., *The Subject of Realism in the* Revue des Deux Mondes, Philadelphia, University of Pennsylvania Press, n.d.

Fausto, Boris 1975, org, *História geral da civilização brasileira* [General History of Brazilian Civilisation], São Paulo, Difel.

Freyre, Gilberto 1951, *José de Alencar* [José de Alencar], Rio de Janeiro, Ministério da Educação e Saúde, Os Cadernos da Cultura.

Furtado, Celso 1971, *Formação econômica do Brasil* [Economic Formation of Brazil], São Paulo, Companhia Editora Nacional.

Furtado, Celso 1974, *O mito do desenvolvimento econômico* [The Myth of Economic Development], Rio de Janeiro, Paz e Terra.

Giannotti, J.A. 1968, 'Contra Althusser,' *Revista Teoria e Prática*, São Paulo, no. 3.

Goldmann, Lucien 1964, *Pour une sociologie du roman* [Toward a Sociology of the Novel], Gallimard.

Guimarães Rosa, João, *Grande sertão: veredas* [title of English translation: *The Devil to Pay in the Backlands*], various editions in both languages.

Habermas, Jürgen 1969, *Der Strukturwandel der Oeffentlichkeit* [The Structural Transformation of the Public Sphere], Neuwied, Luchterhand.

James, Henry 1962, *The Complete Tales of Henry James*, vol. III, London, Rupert Hart-Davis.

James, Henry 1961, *The Notebooks of Henry James*, org. F.O. Matthiessen and K.B. Murdock, New York, Galaxy Books.

Lukács, György 1965a, '*Balzac und der Franzoesiche Realismus*' [Balzac and French Realism], *Werke* [Works], vol. VI, Neuwied, Luchterhand.

Lukács, György 1974, *Écrits de Moscou* [Writings from Moscow], Paris, Sociales, 1974.

Lukács, György 1971c, *Gegenwartsbedeutung des kritischen Realismus* [The Contemporary Meaning of Critical Realism], *Werke*, Neuwied, Luchterhand, vol. IV. Published in English as *Realism in Our Time; Literature and the Class Struggle*, New York, Harper & Row, multiple reprintings starting in 1967.

Lukács, György 1971a, 'Geschichte und Klassenbewusstsein' [History and Class Consciousness], *Werke*, vol. II, ch. 4, Neuwied, Luchterhand.

Lukács, György 1965b, 'Der historische Roman' [The Historical Novel], *Werke*, vol. VI, Neuwied, Luchterhand.

Lukács, György 1971b, 'Lob des Neunzehnten Jahrhunderts' [Praise of the Nineteenth Century], *Probleme des Realismus* I [Problems of Realism I], *Werke*, vol. IV, Neuwied, Luchterhand.

Lukács, György 1971d, 'Marx und das Problem des ideologischen Verfalls' [Marx and the Problem of Ideological Decay], in *Probleme des Realismus* I [Problems of Realism I], *Werke*, vol. IV, Neuwied, Luchterhand.

Machado de Assis, Joaquim Maria 1955, *Correspondência* [Correspondence], Rio de Janeiro, Jackson

Machado de Assis, Joaquim Maria 1959, *Obra completa*, [Complete Works], ed. Afrânio Coutinho, 3 vols, Rio de Janeiro, Aguilar.

New Left Review, London, 1960 to present.

Marx, Karl 1953, *Grundrisse der Kritik der politischen Oekonomie* [Fundamentals of the Criticism of Political Economy], Frankfurt/M., Europaeische Verlagsanstalt.

Marx, Karl 1972, 'Commodity Fetishism,' *Das Kapital* [*Capital*], Berlin, Dietz, 1972.

Massa, J.-M. 1971, *A juventude de Machado de Assis, 1839–1870. Ensaio de biografia intelectual* [The Youth of Machado de Assis, 1839–1870. Essay in Intellectual Biography], Rio de Janeiro, Editora Civilização Brasileira.

Mello, Affonso d'Albuquerque 1864, *A Liberdade no Brasil* [Freedom in Brazil], Pernambuco, Typographia de Manuel Figueiroa de Faria & Filho.

Merquior, José Guilherme 1972, 'Gênero e estilo das *Memorias póstumas de Brás Cubas*' [Genre and Style in the *Posthumous Memoirs of Brás Cubas*], *Colóquio/Letras*, no. 8, Lisboa, Julho [July].

Miguel-Pereira, Lúcia 1973, *Prosa de Ficção* [Prose Fiction], Rio de Janeiro, José Olympio.

Nabuco, Joaquim 1936, *Um estadista do Império* [A Statesman of the Empire], vol. I, São Paulo.

A polêmica Alencar-Nabuco [The Alencar-Nabuco Polemic] 1965, Rio de Janeiro, Tempo Brasileiro.

Proust, Marcel 1919, *Pastiches et mélanges*, Paris, NRF.

Pujol, Alfredo Gustavo 1934, *Machado de Assis*, Rio de Janeiro, José Olympio.

Reis Filho, Nestor Goulart, *Arquitetura residencial brasileira no século XIX* [Brazilian Residential Architecture in the Nineteenth Century] (manuscript).

Revue des Deux Mondes [Review of the Two Worlds], Paris, since 1829.

Romero, Sílvio 1883, *Ensaios de crítica parlamentar* [Essays of Parliamentary Criticism], Rio de Janeiro, Moreira, Maximino & Cia.

Romero, Sílvio 1936, *Machado de Assis*, Rio de Janeiro, Jose Olympio.

Rosenfeld, Anatol 1965, *O teatro épico* [Epic Theatre], São Paulo, Companhia Editora Nacional.

Rosenfeld, Anatol 1969, 'Reflexões sobre o romance moderno' [Reflections on the Modern Novel], *Texto/Contexto*, São Paulo, Perspectiva.

Sartre, J.-P. 1972, *L'idiot de la famille* [The Family Idiot], Paris, Gallimard.
Sartre, J.-P. 1948, '*Qu'est-ce-que la littérature?*' [What Is Literature?], *Situations* II, Paris, Gallimard.
Schwarz, Roberto 1977, *Ao vencedor as batatas: Forma literária e processo social nos inícios do romance brasileiro* [To the Victor the Potatoes: Literary Form and Social Process at the Beginnings of the Brazilian Novel], São Paulo, Livraria Duas Cidades.
Schwarz, Roberto 2000. *Ao vencedor as batatas*, São Paulo, Livraria Duas Cidades.
Schwarz, Roberto 2001, *Um mestre na periferia do capitalismo: Machado de Assis* [A Master on the Periphery of Capitalism: Machado de Assis], ed. and tr. John Gledson, Durham, Duke University Press.
Schwarz, Roberto 1992, *Misplaced Ideas*, ed. and tr. John Gledson, London, Verso.
Pereira de Queiroz, M.I., 'O coronelismo numa interpretação sociológica,' [Colonelism in a Sociological Interpretation], in *Fausto*, tome 3, vol. I.
Szondi, Peter 1973, *Die Theorie des buergerlichen Trauerspiels* [Theory of Bourgeois Tragic Drama], Frankfurt/M., Suhrkamp.
Torres Bandeira, A.R. de 1863, 'A liberdade do trabalho e a concorrência, seu efeito, são prejudiciais à classe operária?' [Are Free Labour and Competition, Its Effect, Prejudicial to the Working Class?], *O Futuro*, no. 9.
Viotti da Costa, E. 1968, 'Introdução ao estudo da emancipação política' [Introduction to the Study of Political Emancipation], *Brasil em perspectiva*.

Index

abolition   10–11, 13
Adorno, Theodor W.   xiii, 24, 127, 149
adultery   105, 136
Aesthetic Theory   149
'Alencar' (José Martiniano de Alencar)   xvi, 1, 17–24, 26, 29, 31–32, 34–38, 40–43, 45–48, 52–55, 59, 65, 68, 90, 149–50
   contradictions in   16–17, 19, 21, 23, 25, 27, 29, 31, 33, 35, 37, 39, 41–43, 45, 47
Auerbach, Erich   129, 149
authoritarian regimes   48

Balzac, Honoré de   17, 22–23, 26, 29, 35–36, 39, 97
   Rastignac   31
Baudelaire, Charles   109, 139, 149
Benjamin, Walter   26, 109, 149
bourgeois individualism   30, 68, 80, 134
Bourget, Paul   45, 149
Byron   17

Candido, Antonio   17, 20, 35, 46–47, 123
Catholicism   48, 71
Cervantes   101
class consciousness   53, 97, 150
clientelism   5, 42
conformity   20, 22, 38, 42, 45, 53–55, 65, 68, 102

de Assis, Machado
   Resurreição   viii, 88, 125
   A Mão e a Luva   viii, 49, 51, 56–70, 78, 84–85, 89, 92–94, 100–2, 125
   Helena   8, 51–52, 70–93, 94, 97, 100, 106, 125, 136
   Iaiá Garcia   viii, 49, 51, 78, 85, 93–149
   Memórias póstumas de Brás Cubas   viii, 39, 70, 80, 99, 121, 123, 128, 135, 141
   Quincas Borba   viii, ix, 10, 70
   Esaú e Jacó   viii, 98
   Memorial de Aires   viii
decorum   32, 52, 54, 71–72, 79, 85, 88, 99, 117, 121, 124, 133, 135–37
dependency   xii, 13, 65, 98–99, 101, 106, 108, 114, 117, 121

Elective Affinities   90
European Realism   24, 28, 53, 91, 126, 136
   French   12, 26, 53

family   28, 32, 48, 51–55, 71–73, 75–77, 79–80, 82–84, 86, 88, 101, 104–5, 115, 136, 144
freedom   3, 54, 115, 121, 137–38, 146, 151
French Revolution   147
Freud, Sigmund   53, 123
Freyre, Gilberto   42

Giannotti, J.A.   100
Goethe   90
Gogol, Nikolay   13
Goldmann, Lucien   30, 55
Gonçalves Dias, Antônio   93

Habermas, Jürgen   53
Hölderlin   34
horror   70, 76–77, 82, 85–87, 115, 139
Hugo, Victor   17

ideological life   2, 7, 11–12, 36, 39, 101
ideologies   xiii, xv–xvi, 2–3, 6, 11–12, 27, 29, 39–40, 44, 77–79, 81, 99–100, 117–18, 137, 148
   second-degree   6, 24–25, 59
   spontaneous   29
importation   16–17, 19, 21, 23, 25, 27, 29, 31, 33, 35, 37, 39, 41, 43, 45
individualism   xv, 13, 32, 48–49, 54, 63, 131
inequalities   30, 71, 78, 84, 114, 140
ingenuousness   13, 35, 48, 60, 101
inheritance   10, 28, 32, 77–79, 147
Iser, Wolfgang   xv

Kant, Immanuel   5

landowners   4, 10, 13, 25, 32, 81
landscape   8, 126
liberalism   xv, 6, 12, 14, 27, 44, 50, 65
literary form   18, 31, 41, 55, 65, 95, 125
Lukács, Gyorgi   xiii, 7, 26, 29–30, 36, 95, 97–98, 127, 129, 133

Machiavelli   30, 148
Marx, Karl, xiii–xiv   30, 100–101
Marxism   51, 97, 100, 120
master   ix, xvi, 1, 7–8, 17, 77, 115–16, 121, 124, 137
material interests   100–101, 138
materialism   50, 54, 99, 142, 144
mathematics   80
Mephistopheles   10
Minas Gerais   124
misanthropy   103, 143
misplaced ideas   x–xi, xiv, xvii, 1, 3, 5, 7, 9, 11, 13, 15
modernisation   12–13, 64
  conservative   41
modernity   xv, 8, 11, 37–38, 49–50, 65, 81, 103, 108, 118, 123, 134
money   18, 22–23, 25–26, 29–32, 36, 46–48, 51, 53–54, 73, 79, 84, 92, 101–2, 144–45, 147
monopoly   65, 118
moralism   3, 33, 83
myths   51, 109, 118, 137, 139, 150

Napoleonic Wars   96–97
narrator   26, 33, 35–37, 66–68, 99, 105, 109, 119, 132
Naturalism   11, 138, 141
Nietzsche, Friedrich   123

obedience   31, 37, 55, 78, 113–14

Paraguayan War   49, 96
paternalism   48–49, 51, 55, 61–63, 65, 67–83, 87, 91, 94–95, 97–103, 105–7, 109, 115–21, 133–37, 145–47
poetics   20, 46, 95
poverty   52, 56, 69, 71, 139, 147
prestige   3, 17, 35, 38, 47, 63, 118, 123
production   2–5, 9, 14, 64
professions   4, 32, 83
progress   1, 12–13, 24, 35, 41, 48, 51, 65, 68, 98
property   3–4, 10, 33, 63, 79–80, 84, 138

propriety   11, 32, 75, 94, 148
Proust, Marcel   26, 123, 139
provinces   9, 45, 123
psychology   12, 29, 34, 86, 89, 142

racism   142
rationalisation   48–49, 51, 53, 55, 57, 59, 61, 63, 65, 67, 69, 71, 73, 87, 107–9
realism   3, 18, 20, 23, 34, 42, 48–50, 55, 125, 138
religion   73–74, 83, 85, 88
representation   10, 19, 26, 39, 63, 87, 140
Rio   xii, xiv, 8–9, 32, 40, 46, 49, 96, 101, 105, 113, 119, 124, 144
Romanticism   21, 29, 35, 39, 57–59, 62–64, 66, 92

Sand, George   97, 147
Sartre, Jean-Paul   26, 53
Second Empire   2
slavery   xiv, 1–5, 7–9, 11, 19, 46, 48, 76, 80, 88, 98, 102, 108, 116
slavocratic order   72, 125
Smith, Adam   3
social climbers   28, 40, 61
social relations   11, 27, 30, 47, 64, 81–82, 94, 101, 106
Stendhal   29, 97
de Carvalho Franco, Maria Silvia   72
Szondi, Peter   53

taboo   78–79, 92, 120
totality   20, 35, 65, 80, 129, 135
Tropicalism   8

verisimilitude   20, 24, 42, 100, 123, 125, 141
Villar, Pierre   101

Wallerstein, Immanuel   xiv–xv
wealth   4, 22, 30, 47, 53, 62–64, 70–71, 78, 84, 101, 139
Weber, Max   31
West Africa   89

www.ingramcontent.com/pod-product-compliance
Lightning Source LLC
Chambersburg PA
CBHW071346080526
44587CB00017B/2983